GIAMBERNARDO PIRODDI

JESUS DID NOT LOVE ENEMIES

The Bloody History of the Greek Gospels
Censored by Translations

JESUS DID NOT LOVE ENEMIES
The Bloody History of the Greek Gospels Censored by Translations
by GIAMBERNARDO PIRODDI
first edition: dicembre 2024
© 2024, Edizioni Clandestine

Edizioni Clandestine
Via Fabio Filzi, 3
Cinisello B. - Milano - 20092
340.9481047
www.edizioniclandestine.it

Edizioni Clandestineis a mark of property of Gruppo Editoriale Santelli
www.grupposantelli.it

to Claudio, spark
of these efforts

to Bart Ehrman, philologist

I know that, sick or healthy, [...] I refuse every consolation and every puerile deceit, and I have the courage to support the deprivation of every hope, to aim intrepidly the desert of the life, not to hide to me any part of the human unhappiness, and accept all the consequences of a painful but true philosophy.

Giacomo Leopardi, *Dialogue of Tristan and a friend*

I have no hope. As a layman, I live in a world where the dimension of hope is unknown [...] hope is a theological virtue. When Kant states that one of the three great problems of philosophy is «what should I hope», he refers with this question to the religious problem. The virtues of the laity are other: critical rigour, methodical doubt, moderation, not overbearing, tolerance, respect for the ideas of others, worldly and civil virtues.

Norberto Bobbio

The dirtiest book of all is the sanitized book.

Walt Whitman

WARNING FOR THE READER

The translations from the Greek text of the Gospels to which reference has been made, are those of the Italian Episcopal Conference (Cei), "Nuova Riveduta" and "Nuova Diodati" Bible. The choice was made to transcribe in original language, between square brackets, only those terms which are of particular importance for the purposes of the proceedings, preceded by the Italian transcription in italics with the correct Greek accent, for example: "*metànoia* [μετάνοια]". The rest of the terms (most) has simply been represented with letters from the current alphabet, for the convenience of the reader and not to weigh down the text.

The abbreviations *Mt, Mk, Lk, Jn* – in round brackets – indicate the authors (Matthew, Mark, Luke, John). The number after the initials indicates the chapter of the works, followed by a colon and the indication of the verse: "(Mt 3:13)". A more or less long range of text is indicated by the extremes of the verses, separated by a hyphen: "(Mt 3:13-15)". When two verses distant from each other are taken into consideration, the conjunction "and" is used: "(Mt 3:13 and 15)". Verses belonging to different chapters are separated by the semicolon: "(Mt 3:13; 4:10)". Some portions of text compared are placed within tables with two or three columns and with the indication of the author and the chapters examined:

Mt 7	Lk 6
Judge not, that ye may not be judged: for by the judgment with which you judge shall ye be judged, and by the measure with which ye measure it shall be measured unto you.	He also told them a parable: Can a blind man lead another blind man? Will they not both fall into a ditch? A disciple is no more than the master; but each one, who is well prepared, will be like his master.

In the same way we proceeded with the comparisons between Cei, Nuova Riveduta and Nuova Diodati. The words on which particular attention has been paid are graphically represented in italics (in some cases also in bold):

Cei	Nuova Riveduta	Nuova Diodati
Whoever will observe and teach them will be *considered* great in the kingdom of heaven.	Whoever will observe and teach them will be *called* great in the kingdom of heaven.	He who will put them into practice and teach them will be *called* great in the kingdom of heaven.

Finally, in the general bibliography are indicated in order: surname and name of the author, year of publication, title of the literary work (in italics), publisher, place of publication.

List of abbreviations used

Matthew (Mt)
Mark (Mk)
Luke (Lk)
John (Jn)
Acts of the Apostles (Acts)
Deteuronomy (Dt)
Jeremiah (Jr)
Isaiah (Is)
Leviticus (Lv)
Exodus (Ex)

INTRODUCTION

Text and context in the canonical Gospels

What is a literary text? What characteristics should a written work have to be defined in this way?

The answer may not be immediate, or not univocal. It may be complicated, to the extent that you want to complicate it. Or, it could be simple and clear.

In the essay entitled *Avviamento all'analisi del testo letterario* («Initiation to the analysis of literary texts»), the Italian scholar Cesare Segre, expert in semiotics and philology, proposes from the first lines of his work an effective definition of the word "literature". He defines it as a form of communication, whose purpose is already implicit in the act itself of assigning a certain composition (written or oral) to an audience with unforeseeable limitations. The sender is convinced that he can be understood and wants to be understood. So, literary communication is realized like any other communication.

Just later, the author specifies to prefer, over abstract theoretical problems, some strategies of analysis and operations applicable with greater utility to a text. In other words: better a pure and simple analysis of the text, than the too daring ramblings, of whatever nature they are, built on it.

According to this definition that we have just examined, if the canonical Gospels – namely those attributed to Matthew, Mark, Luke and John – are a written composition, and if their authors were convinced that they could be understood and wished to be, they then constitute a literary text.

Therefore, the scheme that according to the semiologist Roman Jakobson regulates the interaction between the three constituent elements of each communication, is also valid in their case:

- the sender sends a message to the recipient;
- the message requires reference to a context that can be understood by the recipient, and that is verbal;
- it also requires a communication code that is wholly, or at least partially, common to the sender and recipient or, in other words, to the encoder and decoder of the message;
- it requires a contact, a psychological connection that allows them to establish and maintain communication.

Sender, message, recipient; author, text, reader. In literary communication, sender and author coincide.

The fact that the literary text is naturally a carrier of a message, derives from the evidence that the author has placed himself in a particular relationship with the recipient (or recipients). In our case, the evangelists (authors-senders) send a message to a recipient, telling stories about a man called, in ancient Greek, *Iesòus* ("Jesus" in translations). He is the one who forwards to his people the *euanghélion* [εὐαγγέλιον], «happy announcement»: a term that does not indicate the written work or the literary genre itself, but its content (the «good news»).

The message is built according to a precise communicative code and refers to a context. The text, on the other hand, is – precisely because it is *textus* ("woven") – an autonomously structured and meaningful unit. It is characterized by two fundamental requirements of cohesion and coherence: syntactic – that is, cohesion and coherence of words in their "putting themselves together" – and semantic, that is, of meanings.

The metaphor of the text as a fabric, referring to biblical texts, emphasized, since the Middle Ages, the importance of its genuineness, opposed to the risk, always lurking, of inaccurate and misleading transcriptions. Even in the case of the Gospels, the reader must know a system of signs, decipher it and understand it: it keeps together a set of coherent messages, that gravitate around a single theme (the "good news") and have (or aspire to have) a character of completeness.

If an analysis is to be made, it will be necessary to ascertain:

- if the text contains a message transmitted in a fully explicit manner or only in part;
- if the communicative code is common to sender and recipient and to what extent;
- whether the message, if the communication code is known only in part to the recipient, can be decoded through the text itself, by means of words which provide a key for access to parts of the text which are at first sight incomprehensible;
- finally, it is necessary to evaluate the conditionings – historical, social and cultural – on the configuration of the message and therefore, inexorably, on the configuration of the whole text.

Speaking of New Testament studies, Robert Eisenman – professor of Religions of the Middle East at California State University, and among the most important experts of the Qumran scrolls – in his essay *James the Brother of Jesus* wrote that in analyzing the Gospels it is necessary to discard a considerable part of the passages who are the most loved and familiar to us, for example the parables, and the sentences placed in the mouth of Jesus, many of which have entered the Western tradition: claims that are mostly directed against the people of Palestine, and therefore clearly anti-Jewish and pro-Paul.

Eisenman refers to peremptory statements that have become proverbial over the centuries, such as «the last will be the first»; «a prophet is not despised except in his homeland and in his house»; «woe to you, Corazin! Woe to you, Bethsaida! For if at Tyre and at Sidon the miracles that have been done among you had been done, they would have repented into cilice and ashes»; "the Good Samaritan", "the lost sheep" and so on; all statements, according to the scholar, more or less related to the priority of the mission to the Gentiles, and to the admission of the Gentiles into the Church.

In this work, instead, we want to highlight the fact that, in our opinion, it is the parables and the communicative code that strictly governs them to bring out the features of the so-called "historical Jesus", in opposition to the "Jesus of faith" (philopauline); and to show how the anti-Jewish Eisenman wrote about could be linked (even before the priority of the Gospel mission to the Gentiles) to the rejection that the Jews themselves had of the "good news" (Mt 23:37):

> Jerusalem, Jerusalem, you who kill the prophets and stone those sent to you, how often I have longed to gather your children together, as a hen gathers her chicks under her wings, and you were not willing.

The attempt to reconstruct the historical profile of Jesus was strongly opposed by the German theologian and biblical scholar Martin Kähler, in particular in the essay entitled *The So-Called Historical Jesus and the Historic Biblical Christ* (1892).

The messiah to be considered true would, in his opinion, be exclusively that whose transmission took place through the apostles, especially Paul of Tarsus. Consequently, to ascertain the profile of the "historical" messiah would be, at least, irrelevant. For Kähler, the historical investigation into the biography of the messiah is an unattainable mirage. We could not sift through any source, since the Gospels would not faithfully tell the life of Jesus. Every effort would be in vain, since it is groundless: the New Testament gathers testimonies of faith, and not of events that have happened. Therefore, trying to understand what historically led to the death of Jesus (without which there would be no witness of resurrection), would prove to be irrelevant.

The German scholar Rudolf Bultmann, also theologian, in the work *Jesus* (1929) with peremptory certainty stated that we can no longer know anything about the life and personality of Jesus, since the Christian sources have not interested themselves in this matter, except in a very fragmentary way and with a legendary perspective; and because there are no other sources about Jesus. The "Jesus of history" would therefore be inaccessible.

Although the existence of Christ coincides, always according to Bultmann, with an unquestionably certain fact, "what" he preached and "how" he did it would not be given so essential and rightful. So, this would amount to arguing that the "good news" (= "what"), the parables and the speeches with which the contents of the "good news" were forwarded (="how") would not be such an important subject.

What seems however not to be open to question, is the following fact: if the genesis of (literary) text took place in a precise (historical) context, the former is as worthy of study and understanding as the latter. If, in analyzing the Gospels, we were to discard, as Eisenman writes, the parables or almost all of the Gospel message that is expressed through them, this would mean studying only the context and not the text; therefore, not the message.

While, we are convinced that only the investigation of it can enable the reader to know the communication code intentionally used by the authors. Equivalences and recurrences, related to the formal aspect of the text, can be a sign of meaningful relationships of great importance. It is in fact by trying to understand what Jesus *says,* that one can better understand what Jesus *is doing.* What he says rests largely on the parables and the precise language in which they are written. If writing is, as Roland Barthes states, the truth not of the person (the author), but of language, studying and investigating the latter will be essential for a comprehensive understanding.

Eisenman later adds, in the quoted book, that regarding the content of the Gospels it is useful to consider these two aphorisms: "Poetry is truer than history" and "It is so, if you think so".

The first can be related, according to the scholar, to what happened to the documents that have come down to us. If the Gospels represent the "poetry", or the most successful literary creations due to the breadth of their influence, then their authors were poets. Let us not forget, however, that Plato – Eisenman points out – wanted to banish poets from his "ideal republic". In his opinion, it was the poets who created the myths and religious mysteries, dear, according to Eisenman, to the less critical minds.

The fact that the Gospels constitute a literary text is also the premise of this work; but in our opinion, rather than creating the myth, the authors have codified – in a language whose understanding can be dear to the most critical minds – news events, on which the myth has subsequently been grafted; which, however, would seem to be very far from those same news events.

Stories of a people, in the language of another people

The oldest manuscripts of the canonical Gospels have been written in the so-called *koinè*, "common (Greek) language", known in all the provinces of the Roman Empire. From the 4th century B.C., with the conquests of Alexander the Macedonian, it spread widely in the Hellenized Mediterranean, establishing itself as an oral and written language. Obviously, the possible familiarity of the potential reader of the Gospels with this idiom can be an advantage, allowing a clearer and deeper understanding. If you know Greek, you can get to the source of the message; otherwise, you get it from a translation, that speaks of facts about people who did not speak this language.

They are not easy to solve problems, so summarized by the New Testament philologist Bart Ehrman, when in his book entitled *Misquoting Jesus* he asks himself:

- what can it mean to say that words "are inspired by God", if most people have no access to such words, but only to more or less clumsy interpretations in a language which has nothing to do with the original text?

In this regard, the scholar borrows an effective comparison from a colleague and friend, Jeff Siker, saying that reading the New Testament in Greek is like seeing it in color, while reading it in translation is like seeing it in black and white: one grasps the meaning, but many nuances are lost. Or perhaps, we add, it loses much more than just nuances.

Metaphors aside, if the Greek text of the Gospels represents an articulated set of messages, it will have a peculiar meaning in its essential original context, but it will come to a reader who will find himself hopelessly far from the author and his thought. The addressee will assimilate it by superimposing an interpretative lens, conditioned by many other readings of the text, all of which will follow the original drafting.

As linguist Oswald Ducrot clearly states, a communicative act cannot be interpreted, unless one is aware of the context in which it is produced: not only it will be very difficult to determine the causes and consequences of its production, but also to understand the meanings, implicit and explicit.

Therefore, in our case it is necessary to take into account not only the evangelical text, but also what emerges from the comparison with extra-biblical sources (for example, the work *Antiquities of the Jews*, by the Jewish historian Flavius Josephus). The text always remains the central element, worthy of being read and studied through the double track of analysis and textual criticism: that is, those methods, rigorous as essential, used by humanists to study the Greek and Latin classics.

The fact that the biblical text is considered by Jews and Christians as "sacred", leads to the problem of interpretation, in the broad sense. If the text is considered "sacred", its reading will inevitably be conditioned by a basic hermeneutic approach that would precede, guide and condition the analysis of the text itself. If the written work is "sacred", then it will *undoubtedly* convey a certain type of content; regardless of those portions of the text passages that would seem, instead, to contradict or even disavow the certainties that guide (and therefore mortgage) reading and understanding.

The term "hermeneutic" derives from the Greek verb *hermenèuein*, which indicates any activity of interpretation, including reflection on the cultural and historical conditions, that are the basis of the elaboration of a written work. It is a category that always comes into play lawfully when you read a text. However, often there is a real risk that the work of (too free) interpretation replaces the pure and simple analysis of the text. Interpreting the text even before reading it in its literality, one risks making the text say things that do not appear in it.

The textual transmission of the Gospels

Regarding the Greek manuscripts of the New Testament, Ehrman himself pointed out that, throughout the history of the Church, the majority of Christians never had access to the original documents: which makes their divine inspiration a little controversial. Not only do we not own the originals, but we don't even have their first copies. To be more precise, we don't even have copies of copies, nor copies of copies of copies. What we have are only copies made later than the original drafting of the texts. In most cases, several centuries later. Moreover, the copies are all different from each other, not in tens, not in hundreds, but in thousands of places in the text.

The aforementioned scholar Cesare Segre has not been less enlightening in some of his considerations, that seem to have been tailored on purpose to the Gospels, when he writes that the very rich, practically infinite implications of a text – those that attract readers even for centuries and millennia – are all enclosed in the literality of graphic meanings. Hence the importance of philology, a discipline that is committed to preserving these meanings as accurately as possible. The fact that the survival of ancient texts implies inevitable failures of their transmission, must require even more effort, continuous and intense, to protect their genuineness.

Remaining in the field of New Testament literature, it is possible to say that we have written texts, which are the last stage of an oral tradition and the result of a long selection process, carried out with the techniques of textual criticism: from surviving manuscripts to the first printed edition of the Greek text, commissioned by Erasmus of Rotterdam (1516). It is what philologists call *textus receptus*, as Ehrman reminds us, that is text "received or "accepted", consequently "fixed" in a given form (among the most well-known editions, those edited by Nestle-Aland and Westcott-Hort, now available online; the official Catholic Italian translation, edited by the Italian Episcopal Conference, readable on Bibbiaedu.it; or others in extremely curated sites, such as Bible Hub or Bible Study Tools, to name just a few).

Regarding the concept of "fixed text", Ehrman did not fail to point out that the different Greek language editions of the sixteenth and seventeenth centuries were so similar that, finally, the printers could argue that it was the text accepted by all scholars and readers of the Greek New Testament. It is precisely from the words "accepted by all" that derives the expression *textus receptus* – authentic keyword of philological disciplines –, used by scholars to refer to the form of the Greek text based not on the oldest and best manuscripts, but on the text originally published by Erasmus, and handed down to printers for over three centuries. This was until later scholars began to insist that the Greek New Testament should be based on scientific principles, centered on our oldest and finest manuscripts, and not just reprinted according to custom.

The intention of the scholars, therefore, was and is – on the basis of a certain set of criteria and applying methodologies as rigorous as possible – to try to determine which is the drafting of the text that most faithfully reflects (or less unfaithfully) the will of those authors, that is, the message they intended to convey.

This is a feat of no small consequence, with equally significant repercussions, also these listed with incisive simplicity by Ehrman, when he writes that, from the beginning, Christianity was a religion of the book that exalted some texts such as authoritative Scriptures. However, it has been widely found that we do not actually have these authoritative texts.

Christianity is undoubtedly a religion founded on books, whose texts have been modified and have been preserved only in copies different from each other, sometimes for very significant aspects. The task of the textual critic is to try to find their oldest form. It is undoubtedly a crucial task because – as Ehrman points out not with gratuitous irony but simply referring to the evidence of the facts – we cannot interpret the words of the New Testament, if we do not know what they were. Knowing those words is not only important for those who consider them inspired by God, but for all those who consider the New Testament as a book that has had and still has great importance.

Anyone who is interested in history, in society, more generally in the entire culture of Western civilization, will hardly fail to take this view: because the New Testament is not only a book revered by millions of people and is the basis of the most widespread religion in the world today, but the secular and stratified dissemination of its contents has undoubtedly influenced the life of each of us. Of those who have faith, of those who have none; the life of Catholics, of atheists, of lay people.

Since the Greek text of the New Testament has long been disseminated in a now canonized and "fixed" form, and is translated into all languages, we will dwell in this work our attention on it and on its most popular translations.

Text analysis, context analysis

As the centuries passed, the knowledge of the Gospel text was inevitably, increasingly distanced from the knowledge of the original context of the events recounted by the evangelists. This is the reason why many of the New Testament verses that have become famous as locutions or proverbial and "moralizing" phrases, are nothing but extrapolated fragments, to which a universal sense has been attached, with claims of exhaustiveness: even in the excruciating detachment from the context in which they were inserted.

However, they are part of a concluding unity of meaning, within a book which – compared to the textual mass of the Old Testament – is nothing but a booklet, called "Gospel". But, however, to that mass it is indissolubly linked: not only because the "God father" of which the book speaks is or should be the same, but, above all, because of those events of undoubted chronicle nature, happened in that portion of the planet in a precise chronological interval, the people who lived in that land were witnesses. These people spoke a certain language, and the world view that the language transmitted, inevitably they had.

Although the story of those events was transmitted in the Greek language, nevertheless this does not prevent a serene reading (and not an excessively serene interpretation that disregards reading) of those writings in the original language can return us the gist of the story called "good news" or " happy announcement".

The study of the Gospels, therefore, from whatever perspective, should proceed from an analysis of the text and con-text, historically determined, in which it is placed. According to the semiologist Jurij Lotman, who used a very effective metaphor, the "real flesh" of literary work consists of a text; of its relationship with extratextual reality, with literary norms, with tradition, with the belief system. It is therefore impossible to perceive the text without the background.

Similarly, in the Gospels the text is the flesh: firmly attached to the backbone of a peculiar, unrepeatable extratextual reality. The understanding of it should take place using tools characterized by objectivity and verifiability: that is, when you say something about a text, that "something" should at least be supported by elements inside it.

Even for the works we are examining, some of the most elementary models of analysis of the literary text (specifically of the narrative text) cannot be disregarded, starting from the decomposition into fundamental units, constituent elements and different areas:

- the lexical context, in which the choice of words directs reading in one direction rather than another;
- the syntactic scope, which relates to the way words are arranged within the sentence;
- the narrative context with its temporal, spatial and prospective levels (that is, from which point of view we perceive what happens in the text).

It is necessary to identify a narrating voice (who tells what we read), characters and narrative units. In addition, a focus will necessarily be placed on:

- static situations (physical, psychological, social characteristics of the characters: in our case disciples, publicans, Pharisees, scribes, priests, etc.);
- continuous dynamics (the "processes", that is the situations in becoming and extended in the time (the announcement of the Gospel is the most natural example);
- momentary situations (baptism in the Jordan, entry into Capernaum, expulsion of merchants from the temple, capture, crucifixion, etc.).

The characters are narrative subjects with a person name (Jesus, Peter, Judas...), entertaining relationships of various order and nature, involved in individual events. From the interaction of states, actions and processes derive the most relevant situations of the Gospel story, which is not lacking in one of the most frequent elements of a narrative text: the journey. The whole outward manifestation of the "good news" is, in fact, a journey through the land of Israel to give the "good news" and to make numerous proselytes.

If the character "Jesus" is the undisputed hero of this story, he is undoubtedly a traveller and his movements build the plot of the text. The story (or "diegesis") is what we find in a certain logical and chronological order, in which we have examples of narration following the events told (story addressed to the past or *flashback*), or previous narration (future-oriented story or *flashforward*: this is the case, for example, of prophecies).

Finally, there are numerous episodes that fall under the so-called "aretalogies": facts considered supernatural, and inserted in a precise biographical and chronicle context, of which we will have to say widely later.

Source language, target language: how is the translation oriented?

In the case of the Gospels, the basic model of communication inevitably and at various levels is complicated, as well as the decoding operation by the decoder. The first and most important increase in the level of difficulty is the fact that the authors have used a language completely foreign, both to the context to which they refer in a broad sense and, inevitably, to the text: that is, to the very message they intended to convey.

Many scholars have made it clear that the New Testament writings derive, as Ehrman wrote, from earlier documents that have been lost, in all probability partly dissimilar to the Greek texts we know. These would also reveal, according to several authors, the presence of a different linguistic substratum (the examination of the Greek text and the syntactic and lexical analysis could prove a pre-existing Semitic matrix).

Therefore, the precise Jewish historical, cultural, social, religious context is made known to the reader in a foreign language. The evangelist, evidently aware, through various sources, of the events that occurred in Palestine at that time, tries to make them live again – in the most faithful way to the original matrix – in another language. An operation far from simple, since the translator is located beyond and outside the text and the context he would like to "translate": a word that comes from the Latin verb *transducere*, that is, "to transfer" content from one language to another; although some words are often characterized by a set of connotations that are difficult or very difficult to transfer.

While text and context can be communicated to the reader as close as possible to the original text, each translation is inevitably subject to a loss of information in the target language, in this case the Greek spoken and spread throughout the Mediterranean area in the period to which the compilation of the Gospels dates (I-II century AD).

If translating into another language the worldview that the Jews had, at the time in which the protagonist of the Gospels lived, had to cause undeniable problems, not least those related to the translation from Greek to the various other languages that we speak today. Problems multiply when the translator's effort is conditioned by ideological or dogmatic factors. In this case, the translation risks becoming the «rewriting» of which André Lefevere spoke. With all the risks that this kind of operation can bring with it.

The one who translates, most of the time is outside the text he would like to translate. It is therefore necessary to overcome, but without annulling, this distance through an operation that Henri Meschonic defines as «decentralization», which is preferable to simple «annexation». Decentralisation is, in fact, a textual relationship between two texts in two languages and cultures, even within the linguistic structure of the language; and this linguistic structure is a value in the text system. Annexation, on the other hand, is the annulment of this relationship, the illusion of the natural, the so-called "as if": as if a text in the source language were written in the target language, regardless of differences in culture, era, linguistic structure.

Those involved in the transfer of content from one language to another have a difficult task and a delicate mediating role, as they are responsible for the correct reception of the text by the reader. If, in the presence of two different languages, it is not possible to find identical systems of organization of linguistic signs and their meanings, the effort must be directed towards achieving, at least, the «dynamic equivalence» of which Eugene Nida, the founder of translatology as an autonomous discipline, speaks: if the Greek construct does not find exact correspondence in the construct of the language in which we are translating it, it will be necessary to find the best solution by scrupulously ensuring that the content expressed in the target language is the same expressed in the peculiar Greek construct (which is not exactly replicable).

Therefore, using the terminology coined by Gideon Toury, to a target-oriented translation (oriented to harmonize the text in the cultural and literary context of arrival), one is inclined to prefer the source-oriented, which proposes maximum adherence to the text and the context of the linguistic system of origin. This means, in a nutshell, that if in the Greek text an adjective appears which could be translated with three different adjectives in the target language, the meaning most appropriate to the context of the passage being translated will be chosen; avoiding a fourth option, perhaps more elegant in the target language but arbitrary, as not included in the list of possible meanings.

On the difficulties related to the translation of the Old and New Testaments, various scholars focused, including Nida himself who coined the term «natural equivalent»: that is, the meaning of the word must not be altered in relation to the source language. The «equivalence in difference» (the expression is by Roman Jakobson) must be pursued, in the conservation of the invariant core of the original text. It does not change in substance, although the words used may vary from one translation to another.

Having a network of meanings that must coincide with what the author wanted to communicate, it is necessary to proceed with caution, as Umberto Eco writes, to the recoding or reformulation of the text, since a satisfactory translation must return (that is to say: keep fairly unchanged) the sense of the original text, and must be faithful. The loyalty criteria may change, however:

- they must be contracted within a certain culture;
- they must be consistent within the scope of the translated text.

It is thus faithfully translated when the text is not in obvious contradiction with the context; and when the translator's interpretation does not contradict both.

I

JOHN THE BAPTIST AND JESUS

Metánoia, the keyword of the synoptic Gospels

In the texts written by Mark, Matthew and Luke, great importance is given to the events concerning John the Baptist, which make known to the reader some keywords useful for understanding the facts told in the New Testament.

The beginning of Mark's narration coincides with John's baptism and his discipleship announced, according to the evangelists, by the Old Testament prophets (Mk 1:1-4):

> As it is written in the prophet Isaiah: "Behold, I am sending my messenger ahead of you; he will prepare your way. The voice of one crying out in the wilderness: Prepare the way of the Lord, make his paths straight". Hence, John the Baptist appeared in the desert, proclaiming a baptism of conversion towards the forgiveness of sins (Cei 2008).

The "forgiveness" or "remission" of sins consists in the "good news", which belongs to (and is brought by) Jesus the Christ (*Christòs*): a Greek word that translates the Hebrew title of messiah (*mashīaḥ*, «anointed»), indicating the individual (king or high priest) subject to divine anointing. He is sent by Yahweh as king and deliverer of his people from all foreign domination. He establishes the "kingdom of heaven": *malkut shamayim* in the Hebrew language, *basilèia tòn ouranòn* [βασιλεία τῶν οὐρανῶν] in Greek. This is the expression used by Matthew, whose equivalent is the "kingdom of God" (*basilèia toù theoù*) of which the other synoptic authors speak, to designate the definitive fulfilment of the messianic expectations of the people of Israel.

The term refers to a time when Yahweh will reign forever over his people. Thus, if Jesus (the "son of God") defines himself, several times, as the king of Israel, then between the "kingdom of heaven" announced by him, and the kingdom of Israel of which he says he is the king, there must be some link of considerable importance.

As we said, according to the evangelists the herald of the messiah is John. He is the Baptist, «baptizer»: he who ritually plunges into water those who intend to approach the baptism he is proclaiming. The events that characterize his action, as well as everything related in a broad sense to the synoptic Gospels, are indissolubly linked to a compound word, *metànoia* [μετάνοια]: from the Greek verb *metanoèo* [μετανοέω], which means «I change idea, opinion, way of thinking». It, in turn, derives from the union between the verb *noèo* [νοέω], «I mean, I think, I judge», and the preposition *metà* [μετά], «beyond, after». The latter is found in compound words of very common use, as a prefix indicating:

- change ("metamorphosis");
- transposition ("metastasis");
- transfer ("metaphor": a word used to express a meaning different from what it normally expresses, which is then "transferred").

In all the cases mentioned, the transition from a starting point "A" to a finishing point "B" is always present. The Greek term *metà*, in a temporal sense, indicates posteriority (*metà* = after) and consecutivity; a change from a previous time interval to a subsequent time interval, which involves abandoning something in favor of something else; the action of turning to everything that can imply a "change of page", compared to what is already known and established.

However, changing one's mind about something, long held to be established, is not necessarily the same as grieving or repenting of the past. This concept ("repentance") is instead expressed in the Vulgate:

the Latin version of the Bible by Sofronius Eusebius Jerome (Saint Jerome, 5th century AD), adopted by the Catholic Church.

The Council of Trent (1546) decreed it the only authentic among the various Latin versions, giving the consent for the publication of an official edition (despite the fact that humanist philologists had already raised more than one doubt about quality and value of work). Translations were made from the Greek text (part of them were revisions of earlier Latin versions, conducted on the Septuagint, the Greek version of the Old Testament).

In the verses of Mark (1:4) concerning the Baptist, we read:

Fuit Ioannes in deserto baptizans et praedicans baptismum paenitentiae in remissionem peccatorum,

that is: «There was John baptizing in the desert and preaching a baptism *of penance* for the forgiveness of sins».

Here, *metànoia* («change of mind») is translated with the Latin word *paenitentia*, which derives from the noun *poena* («penalty, punishment») and from the verb *paeniteo* or *poeniteo* («I regret, I repent»). However, if you notice that in Greek the term *noèma* – again derived from *noèo* – indicates everything that is the object of intuition and abstract capacity of the mind; or even that in Linguistics is so called the minimum unity of meaning of a word, it can be easily understood how the meanings of *metànoia* can only affect (and actually affect) the intellectual and thought sphere.

Changing thinking (turning to the future) does not necessarily mean rejecting something (turning to the past). Also because of this, the translation related to *"repenting* of something" seems problematic. It in fact affects the meaning of feeling remorse; feeling pain for having committed a fault; regret for a wrong choice; sorrow. These meanings are absent from the etymology of the verb *noèo* and of the nouns derived from it.

Probably, even a not excellent novice student engaged in consulting the dictionary of the Greek language, would be aware that translating *metànoia* («change of mind, of thought») with the Latin noun *paenitentia* («repentance, regret») would be flagged as error by the teacher.

In the Greek dictionary we find the verb *metalghèo*, literally «I have pain *after*». This certainly indicates repentance, regret; the pain that comes after doing something. In Greek, the concept of "pain" is expressed by the noun *àlgos* (the same etymology of the verb we have just mentioned): a term from which other words such as "neuralgia", etc. While *metanoèo*, "I *change my mind*" about something, it is not *metalghèo* at all ("I *feel pain after* something").

Having ascertained that the translations «repent you!» and «repentance» are not reflected in the verb *noèo* and in the preposition *metà*, we ask ourselves:

- for what reason are these meanings found in the Vulgate?
- from the concept expressed by verbs such as "to think beyond", "to change thought, idea", the translator comes to meanings such as "to feel remorse, pain, regret": what is the motivation for such a large gap?
- what legitimized the translator from Greek to Latin to choose a word (*paenitentia*) and a verb (*paenitèmini*, «repent!») unrelated to the original Greek that he was called (or at least should have been) to translate faithfully?
- is it realistic to assume that he had no awareness of the authentic and literal meaning of the Greek noun and of the verb from which it derives?

Whether it was a deliberate choice or not, in both cases it seems to us that one can find, more than the correct translation of the meaning expressed in Greek, the betrayal of the real meaning of that term. Not faithful adaptation in the target language would seem to be, but forced interpretation.

In Latin other terms would translate much more faithfully the Greek noun *metànoia,* not least the word *conversio*:

conversion, upheaval, transformation, change, change of opinion, reversal.

It shares its etymology with the verb *converto* («I turn, I turn to, I direct the thought, I turn something so that a change results; I undergo a change, I convert, I change»). Specifically, the conversion is directed towards him who brings the *euanghèlion,* the "good news" (from the union of *èu,* «good», and *anghèlion,* «news»).

The translations that we find today in commerce, including that of the Italian Episcopal Conference, translate the word *metànoia* with the noun «conversion». However, a major problem in spreading the message is that, for several centuries, the meaning of "penance" has been matched to this word; with all that obviously follows, in relation to the shaping of a collective theological and doctrinal imagination, for which even today conversion is considered a synonym for "penance". Despite the word in question in the original Greek text means "change of mind" and not "atonement for guilt".

In the seventeenth century Giovanni Diodati, considered authoritative biblical scholar, translating the Gospels from Greek to Italian still attributed to the Greek term *metànoia* the meaning of "penance": a fact sufficiently illustrative of how much influence has the indelible presence of the theological imagination of which we have said.

Jerome's translation of the Greek word *metànoia* with the Latin word *poenitentia* ("penance") aroused many perplexities, centuries ago, in Lorenzo Valla: an illustrious philologist, one of the most representative figures of Italian Humanism. He gave life to a project of profound renewal, which is not reflected in other humanist scholars for breadth, incisiveness and novelty.

The main instrument of this scholar was philological hermeneutics, based on the idea of the historicity of language, which in Valla becomes the most suitable means to free texts from prejudices, falsehoods and deformations; philological hermeneutics, that is, interpretation of the text starting from *fidelity to the text.*

In 1440 he wrote the essay entitled *De falso credita et ementita Constantini donatione declamatio* ("Discourse on the donation of Constantine falsely attributed and falsified"): a treatise that, with extreme rigor, demonstrated the falsity of the edict on which the temporal power of the Church was based. According to tradition, this power derived legitimacy from a document in which the Emperor Constantine would cede to Pope Sylvester I the possession of the future Papal States. It could only be published sixty years after Valla's death in 1517. Exclusively among Protestants. The Catholic Church promptly placed it on the Index of Forbidden Books, during the Council of Trent.

Valla was also the later author of the essay *Adnotationes in Novum Testamentum*, "Annotations on the text of the New Testament" (1444, published by Erasmus in 1505).

According to the author, Jewish-Christian revelation as language and writing had historically assumed literary form; consequently, like any other literature, biblical literature (in all its languages and scriptures) fell naturally under the same laws of every other language and writing.

Valla, therefore, had the courage to say something sufficiently obvious: if the Greek text of the New Testament did not fall under the same laws as any other language and writing, anyone, translating it, could make the text say what he prefers the text to say. The scholar intended to demonstrate how Jerome's reliance on the Latin translation of the Gospels amounted, in his view, to basing theological speculation on the linguistic and semantic misunderstanding of the Holy Scriptures. Therefore, we should conclude that, according to one of the greatest humanist philologists, Jerome translating from Greek was not always reliable. However, the theological imaginary known to us rests on his translation.

Valla defines the text of the Gospels «*veritas graeca*» («Greek truth»). According to the authoritative scholar, the authenticity of the

Gospel message resides in the original Greek text. A statement, this too, sufficiently obvious: to make it, it is not strictly necessary to be a philologist of the caliber of Valla. In his opinion, the text translated into Latin by Saint Jerome (the Vulgate) had to be compared with the Greek original, to verify maximum adherence to the original text.

The scholar argued that in several points Jerome's translation does not transmit at all the *veritas* ("truth") of the Greek text: starting with the keyword on which the message of the synoptic Gospels is based, that is, *metànoia* ("change of thought, change of idea"). Jerome translates it *paenitentia*: "repentance", "penance". According to Valla instead, the meaning of *metànoia* can be made to correspond to that of the Latin words *mentis emendatio*, "correction of the mind", that is: *before* I thought one thing, *from now on* I correct myself, I "change my mind" and think another. It is different from repenting, that is to feel pain and sorrow for what has been thought up to now.

In addition, always according to the scholar, the Latin word *poenitentia* designates the concept of *tristitia commissi*, that is the sadness for a crime committed: a meaning that cannot be, in his opinion, the correct translation of the Greek word *metànoia*. Even in this case, it is not necessary to be Lorenzo Valla to say it: in all probability, even a student, not particularly experienced but sufficiently prepared with regard to the grammar of the Greek language, would be aware that he could not translate *metànoia* with "repentance".

Summarizing:

- the probably greatest philologist of the humanistic age affirmed that the keyword on which the entire Gospel message is based has been translated by Jerome with a meaning absent from the original Greek word.

So, can we trust the theologian Jerome or the philologist Lorenzo more? Probably, the theologian tends more to seek in the text the truth he wants to find. The philologist, instead, has only one goal: to seek the truth of the text, and no other.

Until the Second Vatican Council (1962-1965), a characteristic common to the biblical versions, subsequent to that of Jerome, was that they were based mostly on the Latin vulgate (406 AD): that is, based on a translation, rather than on the texts in the original language.

This should put some doubt on what would seem to be the (questionable?) scientific criteria of the translation work: which would seem to be lacking, even before in an unavoidable philological rigor, in simple common sense. Using a perhaps banal but effective example, the translator who uses translations from an original document which he may have, resembles that of a thirsty explorer who, finally finding himself in front of a gushing mountain spring of fresh water, inexplicably prefers to drink bottled water. Ignoring which source the water comes from and who packaged it.

Certainly, the spread of the Bible has had a difficult path, at least, especially in Italy. Despite the importance of the need for new translations from the original documents, the 15th and 16th century versions were followed by a long period of editorial emptiness.

If the Council of Trent did not address in particular the theme of the use of the Italian vernacular languages in the versions of the sacred text, the Index of Forbidden Books (*Index librorum proibitorum*), written in 1559 during the pontificate of Paul IV, introduced concrete limitations on the possibility of printing bibles, reading and consulting them. Even before reading and consulting, simply owning them. The regulation of all these cases was entrusted to the authority of the Holy Office of the Roman Inquisition.

A meditated pause of reflection lasting two centuries (200 years) will be necessary to ensure that a decree of Benedict XIV (1757) officially grants the faculty of using the sacred texts. However, making its use subject to the approval of the Holy See and to the vigilant control of the episcopate.

Baptism and "good news"

The Greek noun *euanghèlion* is present in the writings of Mark and Matthew. Luke prefers the verb *euanghelìzo*, «I give the good news». In John's Gospel, none of the terms is attested, though they constitute the fulcrum of Jesus' preaching in the synoptic Gospels.

Again in the Vulgate, of the Baptist – as we have seen – it is said (Mk 1:4):

praedicans baptismum paenitentiae,

that is «preaching a baptism of penance». However, the noun *metànoia* in the Greek text of the synoptic Gospels is never accompanied by a specification that makes us understand what should those who are baptized repent; unlike the frequent and explicit formula *àphesis amartiòn* [ἄφεσις ἁμαρτιῶν], «forgiveness of sins», in which the object of the amnesty is always clearly expressed with the specification «of sins». Moreover, not even the verb translated with the exhortative form «repent you» (*metanoèite*) in the Greek language is ever followed by a word that indicates what one should regret:

- is it possible that this happens simply because *metànoia* does not mean "penance"?

Subsequently, the words *praedicans baptismum paenitentiae* are followed by the formula *in remissionem peccatorum*: it is a complement, indicating the purpose of the action expressed, generally translated «in remission of sins», or «for the remission of sins».

The reader of the Vulgate should therefore understand that repentance is to be pursued in the hope of obtaining the forgiveness of sins. Sinners who came to the Jordan, to be baptized by John, would have to do penance, and then receive forgiveness from Jesus (which would seem to correspond to an "absolution" as taught by Catholic doctrine).

However, it is the precursor himself, John the Baptist, who says that after the baptism he officiated *èis metànoian* – «towards the change of mind» – it will be Jesus' task to celebrate another, the baptism «in the Holy Spirit and fire». Which would not seem identifiable with a simple acquittal for repentant offenders.

The Latin translation:

baptismum / paenitentiae / in / remissionem / peccatorum

slavishly follows the Greek original:

bàptisma / metànoias / èis / àphesin / amartiòn

The only difference is that Jerome translates the word *metànoia* with the word *paenitentia*. If we used, instead, the Latin noun that has a meaning closer to the original Greek, one would have:

baptismum / conversionis / *in / remissionem / peccatorum*

Thought must be changed and directed towards the concrete possibility of a forgiveness of sins. But we must be baptized in the Holy Spirit and fire and bear fruit, as in John's admonitions (Mt 3:7-12):

Seeing many Pharisees and Sadducees come to his baptism, he said to them: You vipers! Who made you believe you could escape the coming wrath? Therefore, make a fruit worthy of conversion, and do not think you can say within yourself: «We have Abraham for a father». Because I tell you that from these stones God can raise up sons to Abraham. Already the axe is placed at the root of the trees; therefore every tree that does not bear good fruit is cut and thrown into the fire. I baptize you in the water for conversion; but he who comes after me is stronger than me, and I am not worthy to bring him sandals; he will baptize you in the Holy Spirit and fire. He holds the shovel in his hand and will clean his yard and collect his wheat in the barn, but he will burn the straw with an inextinguishable fire (Cei 2008).

Those who will bear fruit (what kind of "fruits" this is not specified by the evangelist) will be like wheat, when safely stored after harvest. The others, those who have not borne fruit, will be like chaff: the waste of threshing, destined for the fire that does not go out.

However, despite the peremptory nature of these statements, it is not entirely clear to what purpose a second baptism should serve, and what purpose it should have in addition to that administered by John:

- if sinners are repentant of the transgressions of the Mosaic Law (which will be discussed later), what else should they do, besides returning to the observance of the norms?
- what «fruits» should they bring, in order not to suffer the eternal fire promised by Jesus?
- concerning what the Jewish people had known for centuries about the law given by Yahweh to Moses, what novelty should the action of the messiah be characterized by?

Certainly, to welcome his "good news" it is necessary to change the way of thinking and bear fruit: something that before him, obviously, did not happen.

John the Baptist, the groom's friend

The fourth Gospel (Gospel of John) speaks of the baptismal events described by the synoptic authors using the Greek term *katharismòs*, «purification» (from the verb *katharízo*, «to purge, to remove» by divine will unwanted impurity).

This purification would seem somehow be linked to baptism, if in the translations we read of a «discussion», born among the followers of the Baptist, on this theme (Jn 3:25-26):

> Now a dispute about ceremonial washings arose between a certain Jew and
> the disciples of John. Therefore, they came to John and said to him, «Rab-

bi, the one who was with you beyond the Jordan, to whom you bore witness, is baptizing, and everyone is flocking to him».

Bearing in mind what is written in the synoptic Gospels, it can be assumed that John preached a purification baptism. When then comes inexorably – as we shall see shortly – someone «stronger» than him, he must bear witness to Jesus, proclaiming a new doctrine: which does not belong to the Baptist. He must announce that it is necessary that the people who go to be baptized "change their minds"; and become followers no longer his, but of Jesus.

All this would suggest a much more than superficial rivalry between the acolytes of the precursor and those of Jesus. Consequently, between John and Jesus. The fact that the Baptist later affirms that Jesus must grow while he must decrease, would amount to admitting that he will be overcome in baptismal activity.

In this regard, the fourth Gospel contains a significant difference from the others. The Messiah baptizes here on his own (Jn 3:22-24):

> Jesus went with his disciples to the region of Judea, and there he stayed with them and baptized. And John also baptized in Aenon, near Salem, because there was much water there; and the people went to be baptized. John, in fact, had not yet been thrown into prison.

The author agrees with the synoptic evangelists that the messiah originally was not in Judea, but elsewhere (in Galilee?). There is no trace in the fourth Gospel of the precursor who, in the writings of Matthew, will baptize Jesus. It is simply said that John the Baptist bore witness to him: this seems to coincide with the admission of the "greater strength" of Jesus than the Baptist, of which the other authors speak.

The Evangelist John gets the wanted result of sweetening in words, but strengthening in the concepts, the inferiority of John. He does not describe the arrival of one «stronger», but the arrival of a bridegroom. To the Baptist, having the role of faithful friend of the bridegroom and nothing more, no marriage belongs. He only has to rejoice for the future husband (Jn 3:28-30):

> You yourselves witness to me that I said: «I am not the Christ, but I have been sent before him. Whoever possesses the bride is the groom; but the friend of the groom, who is present and listens to him, rejoices in the voice of the groom. [...] He must grow and I instead decrease».

The rude eater of locusts mentioned by the synoptic evangelists, dressed with a leather belt on his sides, who shouts «breed of vipers» to the Pharisees, here gives way to a meek "friend of the bridegroom": that is, to him who according to Mark, Matthew and Luke is, instead, a more decisive baptizer «in the Holy Spirit and fire».

In the Fourth Gospel, the Baptist worked very hard (does this mean that he has baptized much?) for a marriage. Next, comes a better candidate for the wedding. Therefore, he must become aware (despite himself?) that marriage and bride are not at all in his destiny.

One might now ask, by the way, if there is a connection between the passage of the Gospel in which the disciples of John the Baptist denounce the competition of the messiah, and that in which Jesus openly tells his followers (Jn 4:38):

> I have sent you to reap what you have not labored; others have labored, and you have taken over their toil.

Could these verses allude to the arrival on the scene of the followers of Jesus, who attract followers on whom the disciples of John had already spent much energy? According to the evangelist, despite the sudden diaspora – or unstoppable hemorrhaging? – of disciples, the precursor would even rejoice to know that the messiah successfully baptizes. However, it is a joy that is not at all evident in the synoptic Gospels.

Finally, there is, also in the text of John, the reference to the imminent punishment of which the other gospels speak. The wrath of the

Father will strike inexorably those who will not carry out the will of the Son (Jn 3,36):

> Whoever believes in the Son has eternal life; whoever does not believe in the Son will not see life, but the wrath of God rests upon him.

It should therefore be better to be baptized by Jesus and not by John. Therefore, it would seem better to obey the first rather than the second.

A strange case of baptismal competition

The fourth Gospel tells us that, on the arrival of the Messiah, the precursor John is engaged in baptizing in the village of Bethany beyond the Jordan (Jn 1:28-31):

> The next day, seeing Jesus coming toward him, he said: «Behold the lamb of God, the one who takes away the sin of the world. He is the one of whom I said: "after me comes a man who is ahead of me, because he was before me". I did not know him, but I came to baptize in the water, that he might be made manifest to Israel».

The Baptist and Jesus are in the same places. Later, the messiah will want to go to Galilee, to Cana, and then return to Judea. Meanwhile, John moved to Aenon, because there was a lot of water there. Perhaps in anticipation of receiving many baptizers.

Jesus, in total autonomy, baptized with his followers (Jn 3:22-23):

> Jesus went with his disciples to the region of Judea, and there he stayed with them and baptized. And John also baptized in Aenon, near Salem, because there was so much water, and people went to be baptized.

According to the translation already reported, the disciples of the Baptist would discuss the subject of purification with a Jew. Then they reach their teacher John, and tell him that the man who had been with him in Bethany is baptizing elsewhere. And everyone goes to him. While John's baptismal activities are deserted.

It seems quite reasonable to suppose that the discussion with the Jew was born because he was going to another baptism, and not that of the Baptist. John, who was in Aenon where «there was so much water», perhaps planned to baptize a large number of people. And above all, he planned not to do it alone. But expectations were disappointed: the influx of people was not what was expected.

Then, the followers of John who had known Jesus, are rightly assailed by more than one doubt. They go looking for him, and find what most likely expected to find. They then return to the rabbi and report:

Behold, he [Jesus] is baptizing and all come to him.

It seems the chronicle of a conspicuous loss of followers, badly tolerated by the followers of John. They suffer a blatant dismissal, that the evangelist has not made any effort to hide or sweeten. However:

- why were they so concerned if the Baptist and Jesus were acting in common purpose?
- if John was the precursor of Jesus, should they not rejoice that the great set of his proselytes should flow into that of the messiah?
- for what reason, knowing that the Pharisees are aware of the numerical growth of his followers, does Jesus leave Judea, in great haste, to return to Galilee?

The Pharisees were rigorous scholars and observants of the Mosaic Law: so,

- if the baptism, that Jesus administers, were a baptism of purification of the contrite transgressor who returns to the observance of the precepts, why should they represent an obstacle for Jesus, and vice versa why should the messiah worry them?
- does not Jesus preach, like John, the observance of the Law?

- do they not profess and teach the same doctrine?
- are there important differences, between them, in what they teach and what they do?

We do not understand the reasons why the Pharisees should be alarmed by a changeover in the search for a supposed spiritual and im-material "kingdom of heaven" (if this kingdom is something that has to do with the highest spheres of spirituality):

- moreover, why does the evangelist specify, as we shall see shortly, that it is not Jesus who baptizes, but his disciples?
- what are the reasons for this choice, which completely contra-dicts the affirmation of a leadership superior to that of John?
- why does Jesus not baptize himself as John did, but makes his disciples do it?

«One comes who is stronger than me».
Profile of Jesus according to the Baptist

We have seen how, in the fourth Gospel, John the Baptist willingly accepts, after the arrival of Jesus, his own "demotion": he is well aware that he is no longer a leader. He also refuses to assimilate his role to that of Elijah, the prophetic Old Testament authority (Jn 1:19-21):

The Jews sent him priests and Levites from Jerusalem to question him: «Who are you?». He confessed and did not deny it. He confessed: «I am not Christ». Then they asked him, «Who are you, then? Are you Elijah?». «I'm not», he said. «Are you the prophet?». «No» he replied.

The precursor then refers to the messiah (Jn 1:24-28):

Those who were sent came from the Pharisees. They questioned him and told him: «Why then do you baptize, if you are not the Christ, nor Elijah, nor the prophet?». John answered them: «I baptize in water. Among you is one whom you do not know, the one who comes after me: to him I am not worthy to untie the lace of the sandal» (Cei 2008).

These concepts are expressed by the evangelist Mark as follows (1:6-8):

John was dressed in camel hair, with a leather belt around his hips, he fed on locusts and wild honey and preached: «After me comes one who is stronger than me and to whom I am not worthy to bend down to untie the ties of his sandals. I baptized you with water, but he will baptize you with the Holy Spirit» (Cei 2008).

The action of untiing the laces of the sandal concerned the juridical norms governing Jewish marriage, with reference to the law of the levirate (from the Latin word *levir*, «brother-in-law»), which had as its objective the safeguarding of the patrimony of the family clan (Dt 25, 5-10):

When brothers live together and one of them dies without a son, the widow of the deceased shall not marry anyone outside the family; but her husband's brother shall come to her, marrying her and performing the duty of a brother-in-law. The firstborn son she bears shall continue the name of the deceased brother, that his name may not be blotted out from Israel. But if a man does not want to marry his brother's wife, she shall go up to the elders at the gate and say, "My brother-in-law refuses to perpetuate his brother's name in Israel and does not intend to perform his duty toward me". Thereupon the elders of his city shall summon him and speak to him. If he persists in saying, "I do not want to marry her," his sister-in-law, in the presence of the elders, shall go up to him and strip his sandal from his foot and spit in his face, declaring "This is how one should be treated who will not build up his brother's family". And his name shall be called in Israel, "the house of the man stripped of his sandal".

Keeping this cultural context in mind, in the verses we are examining the Baptist would be claiming that he does not have the dignity sufficient to deprive the future messiah of the right of the strongest: the man who baptizes with water certainly cannot take the place of the one who baptizes with fire. That is: the bridegroom is Jesus. The bridegroom is here. He is not dead and he has no intention of giving up his marriage. Therefore, for "the friend of the bridegroom", who is John, the problem of replacing the groom does not even arise.

The evangelist Matthew, on the other hand, does not refer to the action of "undoing the laces of the sandals", but uses a different verb, *bastàzo* [βαστάζω], «I carry a weight, I transport» (Mt 3:11):

He who comes after me is *stronger* than me and I am not worthy to bring him sandals; he will baptize you in holy Spirit and fire.

Regarding the comparative «stronger», the adjective used by the synoptics authors – *ischyròs* [ισχυρός] – does not refer to superiority in a figurative sense (authority, prestige), but to physical strength. This is confirmed in the Thayer's Greek Lexicon of the New Testament:

> Strong (originally and generally of physical strength): mighty, powerful, vehement, sure.

Therefore,
- does this mean that the messiah will use force to a greater extent than John did in his proselytizing activity?
- the "vehemence" with which the evangelist connotes the character of Jesus even before he begins to proclaim the "good news", presenting it as a feature that radically differentiates him from John, how should it be expressed?
- with more authoritarian ways of baptizing ("fire" instead of "water")?
- or is the reference to the harshness of punishment for those who will not accept the "good news", of which there is ample evidence, in the parables and outside the parables, in all the canonical Gospels?

In Mark's text, just before the Greek adjective *ischyròs*, we find the preposition *opìso* [ὀπίσω], «behind». Its immediate and denotative meaning is relative to the space occupied ("behind something or someone"); the more specific and connotative meaning is linked to the concept of time ("behind" in a temporal sense, then "after").

Generally, in the translations of this passage of Matthew, we find expressed this second concept: "the one who is coming *after* me". However, to express a chronological sequence the synoptic authors preferably use the Greek preposition *metà*, while with the preposition *opìso* they express a compliment of location ("behind" something or someone) and not a succession of chronological intervals. For example:

- «And Jesus said to them: come *behind* me, and I will make you become fishers of men» (Mk 1:17);
- «He called them. And they [...] went *behind* him» (Mk 1:20);
- « Let no one in the field go *back* to get their cloak» (Mk 13:16);
- «No one who has put his hand to the plow and then turns *back* is fit for the kingdom of God» (Lk 9:62);
- «Whoever does not carry his own cross and does not come *behind* me cannot be my disciple» (Lk 14:27).

Bearing in mind this information of a grammatical nature, we ask ourselves:

- for what reason Mark (1:7) would use the preposition *opìso* wanting to indicate a temporal succession («after»), while in the remaining cases – like the other synoptic authors – he uses it to indicate a position with respect to a place, that is, to express a compliment of location («behind»)?

It does not seem at all improbable that *opìso* can be translated here «behind» and that the meaning of Mark's sentence is: «who has more strength than me is *behind* me».

This is a concept also expressed in the fourth Gospel, which suggests that Jesus may have been originally among the followers of the Baptist. In fact, in Bethany the future messiah is with John, who is his precursor. If the Baptist precedes Jesus, it means that he stands *before* him: therefore, the son of God is *behind* him. However, Jesus will exceed him drastically in relation to the number of baptized persons and new followers. He will be "raised", while John "diminished". Until that moment, however, Jesus will be "minor", therefore *behind* the Baptist.

Next, in the text of the synoptic authors we find the Greek adjective *ikanòs* [ἱκανός]: «capable, suitable; good to» (generally translated, in official translations, with the word «worthy»).

The adjective *ikanòs* lends itself to a comparison with the Greek adjective *àxios* [ἄξιος], afferent to the concepts of dignity, value, merit, very frequent in the canonical Gospels. The scope of the meanings of the adjective *àxios* appears sufficiently marked: the dignity in all its forms (moral nobility, decorum, honour, office, rank, etc.):

- «Fruits *worthy* of conversion (Mt 3:8)»;
- «The worker is *worthy* of his salary» (Mt 10:10);
- «In whatever city or village you enter, ask who is there *worthy*» (Mt 10:11);
- «If that house is *worthy* of it, let your peace descend upon it» (Mt 10:13);
- «He who does not take his cross and follows me is not *worthy* of me» (Mt 10:37);
- «He *deserves* that you make him this grace» (Lk 7:4);
- «Things *worthy* of beating» (Lk 12:48).

One can easily ascertain how, from the point of view of the meaning of the word, the adjectives "worthy" and "deserving" are interchangeable. A person who is not worthy is obviously not deserving of something. By translating the adjective *ikanòs* into this passage of the synoptic Gospels, generally the various translations emphasize John's lack of dignity. However, we ask ourselves: does the obvious, consequent belittling of the Baptist coincide with the information that the same authors provide about him?

Profile of John the Baptist according to the synoptic Gospels

According to the Evangelist Luke, John the Baptist is the son of a priest of the temple of Jerusalem, Zechariah, who has as his wife a descendant of Aaron (priestly lineage), called Elizabeth:

- they were «righteous before God» and «they were blamelessly observing all the laws and prescriptions of the Lord » (Lk 1:6);
- in Elizabeth Yahweh «manifested his great mercy» (Lk 1:58);
- «many will rejoice» (Lk 1:14) at the birth of John, who came into the world through divine intervention, from parents who «had no children, because Elizabeth was barren and both were ahead of their time» (Lk 1:7);
- he will be «great before the Lord» (Lk 1:15);
- he «will not drink intoxicating drinks» (Lk 1:15);
- he will fast and live in the strictest observance of the Mosaic Law;
- «he will be filled with the Holy Spirit from the womb of his mother» (Lk 1:15) and «called prophet of the Most High» (Lk 1:76).
- he will go «before the Lord to prepare his way» (Lk 1:76) and will give «to his people the knowledge of salvation» (Lk 1:77);
- «he will walk before the Lord with the spirit and power of Elijah, to lead the hearts of the fathers towards the sons and rebels to the wisdom of the righteous and to prepare a well-disposed people for the Lord» (Lk 1:17);
- «as it is written in the book of the oracles of the prophet Isaiah» (Lk 3:4) he will be the «voice of one who cries in the desert: prepare the way of the Lord, straighten his paths»;
- he a is a «righteous and holy man» (Mk 6:20) and his fame will reach Herod, also reached by his harsh accusations;
- he is defined by Jesus as the greatest «among those who are born of women» (Mt 11:11) and identified by him in the new Elijah: «"Elijah has already come and they have not recognized

him; indeed, they have made him what they wanted" [...] the disciples understood that *he spoke to them of John the Baptist*» (Mt 17:12-13).

However, despite the exceptional, unquestionable merits, the baptizer would declare that he was not worthy even to bow to Jesus to bring him sandals. Therefore:

- how then could he be worthy to be the precursor of Jesus?
- if the messiah is aware of such unworthiness, why will he (the *stronger* one) ask, in the Gospel of Matthew, to be baptized by John (the *weaker* one)?
- does he really need it, or does he want it for other reasons?

In the Gospel of Matthew (3:13-15), we read:

> Then Jesus came from Galilee to John at the Jordan to be baptized by him. John tried to prevent him, saying, «I need to be baptized by you, and yet you are coming to me?». Jesus said to him in reply: «Allow it now, for thus it is fitting to fulfill all righteousness». Then he allowed him.

In the official Catholic translation by the Italian Episcopal Conference, we read "Giovanni voleva impedirglielo", that is "John *wanted to prevent him*". This translation would make the reader think that John only *intended to do* something, but he did not. The Greek verb *diakolýo* literally means «I prevent», therefore:

a) John *wanted to prevent him* (according to Cei translation);
b) John *prevented him* (literal translation of the Greek verb *diakolýo*).

In the first example, John would like to prevent something (but then he does not). In the second, the Baptist prevents or – keeping in mind the so-called "conative" value of the Greek verb in the imperfect tense – he actively attempts to prevent Jesus from doing something (that is, he prevents him from receiving baptism by his hand). The evangelist does not write that John had the authority to forbid something, he wanted to exercise such authority but did not exercise it; but, the author writes that he had authority and exercised it. And this happens despite the fact that the messiah, the one who came "behind" John, was "stronger", "more vehement" or "more powerful" than him.

Everything we have just seen contrasts with the "declaration of unworthiness" put in the mouth of the Baptist by the evangelists:

- if he knows that Jesus is "stronger", why does he oppose him?
- can he disobey him?

The resistance of John is expressed with the following question:

I need to be baptized by you, and yet you are coming to me?

Since the authors write that the Messiah's is a baptism of conversion, the sentences we write now below should be equivalent in meaning: "Am I the one who needs to be baptized by you, and you come to me?", that is: "I need *to be converted to you*, and you come to me?".

If John baptizes for the conversion of men to Jesus while acknowledging that he himself needs to be converted to the messiah, this would mean that he baptizes not being baptized. That is, he would lead others to conversion, without converting himself. He recognizes the greater strength of Jesus, however, inexplicably, he does not receive baptism "in the Holy Spirit and fire".

None of the canonical Gospels mentions a baptism administered by Jesus the Christ to John the Baptist. The one who "prepared the way" to the messiah seems to abandon it, once the messiah has arrived. Or at least, the path is interrupted. Abruptly, and not by the will of the Baptist.

Precisely because his baptism is "less strong" than that of Jesus, he should have asked for a "stronger" baptism: the baptism "in the Holy Spirit and fire". In this way, the admission of his own "unworthiness" towards the messiah would be certified; and he, who until that moment had prepared the way to the Lord, from then on would walk in the way of the Lord, together with the Lord. But nothing of this happens in the chronicles reported by the evangelists. Probably, because this never happened.

As to the fact that John's baptism – before he assumed the role of precursor – was of a different nature from that of conversion to the doctrine of Jesus which consisted in the forgiveness of sins, the Jewish historian Flavius Josephus did not disagree with the Gospels.

He further specifies what the synoptic authors wrote:

> John was a righteous man and exhorted the Jews to live virtuously, to justice towards their neighbour and to piety towards God. As for baptism, in his way of seeing it was acceptable not to forgive sins, but to purify the body after the soul had been purified through the practice of justice (*Antiquities of the Jews*, 18, 116-119).

The Baptist practiced a purification baptism (as reported by the evangelist John with the Greek noun *katharismòs*). Jesus, instead, baptized for the remission of sins. According to Flavius, the precursor was not willing to condone sins. According to all the canonical Gospels, only Jesus had this intention. According to the synoptic Gospels (but not to the fourth Gospel), the Baptist directed many individuals towards the forgiveness of sins desired by the Messiah. But to practice it was only and exclusively the latter.

Suitability and dignity

Greater clarity on the relationship between John and Jesus could come from the awareness that in the examined passages of the synoptic Gospels does not appear the adjective *àxios*, but the adjective *ikanòs* («suitable, capable, good for»).

If those authors always use *àxios* when they intend to talk about dignity or merit, why do they use *ikanós* in the passage in which they talk about the "thong of sandals"?

The two words do not seem exactly synonymous, that is, they do not seem to have equivalent meaning. Acknowledging that we have no dignity to do something, is not the same as admitting that we do not have the capacity or the suitability to do it. In the first case, it is stated that someone does not have enough merit for something; in the second, it is stated that someone is not capable or suitable to accomplish something. You may be capable but without sufficient merit; or you may have merits, but not be suitable.

The construction of Mark's phrase, which through the metaphor of the "shoe ties" exasperates the concept related to the imminent supremacy of Jesus in spite of John, finds correspondence in the structure of phrases such as "I am not suitable to", "good for" (that is, responding to the purpose of what you are intended).

John the Baptist declares that he is not "fit" to stoop to untie Jesus' shoes. As a result, he refuses to carry out the will of the messiah, who wants to be baptized by him. John does not want to lower himself to the future messiah, precisely because he has a long list of merits, and for his exceptional lineage. In extreme but perhaps appropriate synthesis, he who was born, by the intervention of Yahweh, from a father priest of the temple of Jerusalem and a mother descended from Aaron, has some understandable difficulty in bringing sandals to a man he does not even know; or at least so it is written in the fourth Gospel (Jn 1:31):

> I did not know him, but I came to baptize in water, so that he might be manifested to Israel.

It would seem that the use of the comparative, reported by the Baptist to Jesus, in the synoptic Gospels ("the one *more vehement* than me") evidences in a very evocative way (though significant) a not yet well defined quality of the messiah; on which John, in spite of his remarkable prerogatives, he cannot rely: "I come before (for my merits) the one who is coming, but he is *stronger* than me". The superior "strength" is the distinctive feature of Jesus: essential and characterizing, so much so that, because of this greater vehemence, Jesus obliges John to baptize him.

In the parable that follows, the adjective «worthy» translates the plural form of the Greek adjective *àxios* (Mt 22:1-8):

> The kingdom of heaven is like a king who made a wedding feast for his son. He sent his servants to call the wedding guests, but they would not come. Again he sent other servants to say: [...] "Come to the wedding". But they did not care [...] then others took his servants, insulted them and killed them. Then the king was outraged and, sending his troops, killed those murderers and set their city on fire. Then he told his servants: "The wedding feast is ready, but the guests were not *worthy*".

Guests were *suitable* to attend the banquet. Otherwise, they would not be invited. Evidently, they were in possession of the suitability requirements provided by the landlord: a king, in our case. However, while suitable, they are not *worthy* to attend the banquet at all. They had all the requirements to do so and have, consciously and assuming full responsibility, declined the invitation. This voluntary choice makes them *unworthy*.

On the basis of these examples it could be said that when John says «I am not *ikanós*», he does not mean that he is «unworthy», but that he is not "suitable", not "good to" lower himself to untie the tie of the shoes of Jesus: who is stronger than him, but still *behind* him.

Only the fourth evangelist (Jn 1:27) defines the precursor as "unworthy", using the adjective *áxios*. Thus:

- according to the synoptic authors, the Baptist claims that he is not *fit* to do certain things for a person;
- according to the evangelist John, the precursor is claiming that he cannot even compare himself to Jesus, with whom he can only establish an inferiority relationship.

One might now ask whether the fourth evangelist uses the adjective "worthy" (*àxios*) as a synonym for "fit" (*ikanòs*). In our opinion, it is precisely the fact that the author tries to obtain a variation, a distance not only formal but also conceptual from the synoptic Gospels, to persuade us that he was aware that *àxios* is not exactly a synonym of *ikanós*.

Knowing well that the Baptist is not at all the suitable person to lower to untie the laces of sandals, the evangelist John does not report:

- neither the adjective *ikanós;*
- nor the Greek verb *kýpto* [κύπτω], «I lower myself»,

both instead present in Mark. In this way, both John's unsuitability and the need to bend down (and therefore submit) to Jesus, disappear completely from the text.

According to the fourth Gospel, John is unworthy. Although born by divine intervention from a descendant of Aaron and considered by Jesus himself «more than a prophet», he is unworthy even to untie the tie of the shoes of the messiah. While in the synoptic Gospels the Baptist states "I am not fit, I am not good at lowering myself to him", in the fourth Gospel he says "I am unworthy of him".

There seems to be a difference between the two statements. The evangelist John shows that he well understands that if the Baptist said "I am not fit to lower myself to Jesus", he could not then say that "Jesus must grow, while I diminish": saying you don't want to stoop to someone would be in stark contrast to leaving him your leadership. The author understands this fact and acts accordingly, by drafting his text (Jn 1:27):

> The one who comes behind me, to whom *I am not worthy* [ἄξιος] to untie
> the tie of the sandal.

According to the fourth Gospel, of him who comes behind the Baptist, the Baptist is not worthy. It is omitted entirely what, instead, all three synoptic authors report referring to the one behind the precursor. Such a person is «stronger» (*ischyróteros*): the comparative form of a

Greek adjective that, as seen, designates physical strength, impetuosity, vehemence. So,

- why does John slavishly resume the synoptic Gospels, but omitting the comparative «more vehement, stronger»?
- Mark, Matthew and Luke do they use the adjective *ikanòs* («suitable, capable, good for») to emphasize that the Baptist is not really the kind of person suitable to accept and suffer that greater impetuosity of Jesus, which inevitably leads John to lower himself to the messiah?

Failing, in the fourth Gospel, the "greater strength" of the messiah, as a result of this the Baptist must no longer declare that he is not *fit* to submit to such impetuosity, and therefore to lower himself to it. Instead, the declaration of the Baptist's "unfitness", in the synoptic Gospels, obviously is followed by the refusal to do something: that is, to baptize Jesus.

Although then, according to Matthew, the precursor lets himself be persuaded, he will not receive baptism in the Holy Spirit. He will continue to purify people in water, on its own. Despite his important prerogatives, he could not count on the "strength" of Jesus: who, thanks to the water baptism granted by the precursor, would be formally legitimized to be his successor.

The implications of this handover become clear to the evangelist John (Jn 1:15), in a verse that seems a free paraphrase of what is reported by the synoptic authors, but with more details. Here the Baptist specifies, to avoid misunderstandings, that the future successor, the one who is *behind* him and is about to take his place, «*èmprosthèn mou ghègonen*» [ἔμπροσθέν μου γέγονεν]; translating literally, «has become ahead of me»:

> John gives him testimony and proclaims: «It was of him that I said: he who comes after me is ahead of me, because he was before me» (Cei 2008).

Also in this case we could translate the preposition *opìso* («he who comes *opìso* me») with the word «behind», since even in the fourth

Gospel to express temporal succession is generally used the preposition *metà*. The Evangelist John emphasizes, with softened terms, what the synoptic evangelists mean when they speak of the "greater strength" of Jesus: he passed on to John because he is *pròtos* [πρῶτος], a Greek adjective («first»): the one who comes first. Then, more important, remarkable. Therefore in an advantageous position. Jesus passed on to John: it is a sudden change, which marks the fervent baptismal activity of the messiah, to the detriment of the languishing one of the Baptist.

One could say that the author is describing a overtaking. The gap between something that happens now and is already changing is highlighted, due to a sudden change of situation:

Behind me comes he who has [already] become ahead of me.

Using a more free translation, but always respectful of the literal meaning of the text, we could say: «He who is behind me has now passed ahead of me».

The interval of time that separates Jesus who was before *behind* John, from Jesus who has now passed on to him, is minimal. However, the action relating to the "overtaking" of Jesus at the expense of John is not clearly expressed in the Cei translation which dates back to 2008:

He who comes after me is ahead of me.

The reader will understand that the messiah has always been ahead of the Baptist. On the contrary, in the Cei version that dates back to 1974, the concept of Jesus' "overtaking" of John was fully transmitted:

He who comes... *has passed on* to me.

So, for what reason in the translation Cei 2008 is dampened in a decisive way the reference to the "overtaking", that is instead so evident in the version Cei 1974?

The Evangelist John maintains the conceptual structure of the synoptic Gospels, introducing some adjustments. He agrees with Mark, Matthew and Luke that someone is coming "behind" the precursor. However, he expresses a different opinion on the characteristics of this man. The advantage that Jesus, according to synoptic authors, gains over John thanks to his greater vehemence, in the fourth Gospel is purified of any reference to "strength". The reason for the primacy of the messiah, for the evangelist John, can only be his importance, power, prestige. Therefore, if Jesus is hierarchically above the Baptist from the beginning, there is no need for the messiah to exert any force on him.

But then, why would Jesus make himself "open the way" and be announced by a man who is so less important than him?

Probably, the Evangelist John strives to soften the contrast, difficult to hide, between the Baptist and Jesus, outlining the figure not of a predecessor to whom his successor owes much, but of a servant. A servant to whom the master owes nothing. A servant who does not resist his master.

The Baptist of the synoptic Gospels, on the other hand, strongly opposes the water baptism of the messiah. When, in the fourth Gospel, John must justify himself to his disciples who are incredulous that the reins of baptismal activity have been taken by Jesus and his followers, he will say (Jn 3:27):

> No one can take anything if it has not been given to him from heaven.

What in Mark, Matthew and Luke is the fruit of the greater vehemence of the messiah, in the Gospel of John it is heaven to confer it. However, the exhortation of Jesus to John that Matthew – as we are about to see – reports («let it be for now»), is nothing more than a peremptory order. A question addressed to the Baptist, so that he does not oppose any resistance.

Evidently, in the opinion of the evangelist Matthew, the handover between Jesus and the Baptist does not come at all from heaven. The baptism of the messiah by his precursor appears as an indispensable thing: as we are about to read, it is something «convenient»:

- and why should baptism be associated with the concept of "convenience"?
- why does John the Baptist absurdly want to prevent Jesus something that is convenient, that is opportune?

Generally, in the translations of the text of Matthew (3:15) we read:

Jesus said to him in reply: «Let it be for now, for it is fitting that we fulfill all righteousness».

The Greek text clearly reports the first-person plural pronoun *emìn* [ἡμῖν]: «for us, to us». Therefore, the correct translation is precisely: «It is convenient *for us* to fulfill all righteousness».

However, this precise meaning is not transmitted, for example, in the translation by the Italian Episcopal Conference: «Lascia fare per ora, poiché conviene che così adempiamo ogni giustizia», that is:

Let it be for now, since it is convenient that we thus fulfill all righteousness.

The same thing occurs in the Nuova Riveduta version:

Let it be so now, for it is fitting that we thus fulfill all righteousness.

The meaning of the phrase in the Greek language is not simply "it is necessary, it is a good thing, it is convenient", but «it is convenient *to us*». It suits both of us: Jesus and John. Not others.

According to the evangelist, there is a definite advantage that the "fulfillment of righteousness" should bring to both:

- what advantage?
- why in the Cei or Nuova Riveduta version do we ascertain the obvious omission of the first person plural pronoun?
- is it likely that it escaped the translator of the above mentioned editions?
- and if it were a voluntary omission, what could be the reasons? What are the justifications?

Now, focusing our attention more on the meaning of the phrase, we ask ourselves:
- why should "the fulfilment of righteousness" represent something specifically beneficial for the messiah and for John?

Finally, here are the most important questions:
- if John's baptism is put by Jesus himself in relation to the "fulfillment of righteousness", does this mean that John wants, by obstructing him, to prevent such fulfillment?
- how is it possible that the precursor has such a will, which is diametrically opposed to that of the messiah (so much so as to prevent his realization)?

John, as we know, is the "righteous" par excellence. However, the evangelist tells us that he opposes the fulfillment of all righteousness:
- would John therefore prefer the continuation, to a certain extent, of the absence of righteousness, that is, the non-observance of the Mosaic Law?
- or, more likely, does Jesus attribute a very different meaning to the word "fulfillment" than the Baptist?

The proclamation of transgressions

To the words "cleansing", "ritual purification" and "washing" – which translate the Greek term *katharismòs* used by the evangelist John – correspond in the Latin Vulgate the words *purgatio* (cleansing), *purificatio* and *emundatio* (purification). This textual response leads us, once again, to ask ourselves why the Greek word *metànoia* ("change of mind") should be translated with the Latin word *paenitentia* ("repentance"), since the three terms mentioned above, all indicating purification, would indicate without any possibility of misunderstanding the essential condition for a conscious and desired penance. The etymology of those words has nothing to do, as is easily verifiable, with the "change of mind" that characterizes baptism in the three synoptic Gospels: which do not speak of purification and/or repentance.

It is the Baptist himself who puts the accent, during the arrival of Jesus, not on the necessity of atonement, but on that of "bearing fruit". By saying "he who is behind me is stronger than me", John would communicate to the baptizing aspirants that they must, through the baptism of *metànoia* ("change of mind"), have as a reference point not him, but Jesus.

There is no need to atone for sins, if they are forgiven. Atonement, in fact, is not remission. In the first case (atonement) the debt is not simply written off (or "remitted"): the debtor must do something to get it remitted. In the second case (remission), the debt is forgiven by the unilateral decision of the one who has the faculty of condoning it. Regardless of the actions of the debtor.

Since the violations of the many commandments of the Mosaic Law were sanctioned, and punished in some cases even with death, forgiveness necessarily implies, as can be ascertained from numerous speeches and parables of Jesus, the withdrawal and therefore the absence of the sanction.

Conversely, atonement implies the presence of a sanction or punishment. Sins are expiated if they correspond to a reparatory action (just think, in the Old Testament, the many sacrifices pleasing to Yahweh); and if there is the acceptance and enduring of a penalty that is imposed. The sins are forgiven when they are cancelled, together with the punishment that would result.

Having clarified this, one can easily deduce how "good", for sinners – that is, the transgressors of the Mosaic Law – the "news" of an imminent remission of sins could be. To them, to the transgressors, is addressed the "good news". But on condition that they "bear fruit", being baptized "in the Holy Spirit and fire". And not in water.

Regarding the work and action of the Baptist, the evangelist Mark writes (1:4-5):

> The whole Judean countryside and all the people of Jerusalem went out to him. *Confessing* their sins, they were baptized by him in the Jordan River (Cei 2008).

The verb "confessing" translates the Greek participle *exomologoùmenoi* [ἐξομολογούμενοι]: more literally, «proclaiming». This participle can also be translated with a gerund: «proclaiming; admitting; confessing solemnly».

The Greek verb *omologhèo*, in this case reinforced by the preposition "ex" (*ex-omologhèo*), is not attributable to meanings similar to the concepts of "contrition" or "repentance"; it follows the meanings of the Hebrew verb *yadà* («I know; I recognize; I admit»).

In the New Testament Dictionary, edited by Xavier Léon-Dufour, we read:

> "To speak (*lègo*) in a similar way, in agreement (*hòmos*); to agree to, to commit to, to recognize, to proclaim openly". Term of profane juridical language, with the value of attestation by affirmation and negation, this word strengthens a public statement.

So,

- why did the evangelists choose a term belonging to the profane juridical lexicon?
- does this mean that the context to which they refer was not a "religious" context, in the sense that today we could attribute to this word?

The same dictionary, for the purpose of establishing a comparison with the Greek verb *exomologhèo*, provides in detail the meanings of the Hebrew verb *yadà*:

> To know, to learn to know; to perceive, to discover, to discern; to distinguish; to recognize, to admit; to consider, to come to know; to know carnally; to know how, to be skilled in something; to be perceived; to be educated; to be cause of knowledge.

All these verbs that we have reported are firmly anchored to the concept of "knowledge". Bearing this in mind, it should therefore be concluded that, when the synoptic Gospels report that the crowds around the Jordan publicly acknowledged their transgressions, they meant that all those people knew well that they had committed them; and made the others aware of this. The Baptist before all. They certainly revealed their faults, confessed them. But in public, solemnly. And not in secret, ashamed of it.

The verb *exomologhèo* indicates a confession, but not as we could understand it nowadays, by virtue of secular cultural heritage. The evangelists undoubtedly speak of a unanimous admission of guilt. Even some nouns and verbs, that we use in everyday common speech, derive from the Greek verb *omologhèo*: "homologue", "to homologate"; "homologation", that is, assessment, validation; official recognition, by a competent authority, of the conformity of an act or fact with the rules governing it.

All this has much in common with what is narrated in the Gospels. The competent authority, in this case John the Baptist, officially ascertains and testifies, through the public proclamation of the faults, that the people who go to be baptized are violators of the Mosaic Law.

The verb "to homologate" means properly:

- to recognize as homologous what is corresponding and conforming to something;
- to approve, to attribute effectiveness, more generically to ratify, to validate something;
- to recognize as valid after having verified the regularity.

The many people, who have come to the banks of the Jordan, confirm their transgressions, or officially acknowledge to themselves and to others that they have committed them. They ratify them in front of the Baptist. To John, who preaches in public, respond individuals who, likewise publicly, proclaim that they are transgressors of the Law: that is, sinners. So, they claim to be the only set of individuals whose transgressions can be condoned. If they were not transgressors, no transgression could be forgiven them.

The limited scope of the meanings of the Greek verb *omologhèo* (a strongly connotative verb: otherwise it would not be defined as "belonging to the juridical lexicon") remains so even in the words of the modern languages derived from it. This verb is not related, as we have already said, to the meanings of contrition or repentance: otherwise, the "confession of sins" could have as a synonym the "homologation of sins"; the "act of contrition" could be called "act of homologation". This verb is so connoted that it cannot be bent towards interpretations excluded by its own etymology.

In the Gospel of Matthew (14:6-7), the tetrarch Herod is celebrating his birthday, rejoicing in the dances of Herodias' daughter:

> When it was Herod's birthday, the daughter of Herodias danced in public and so pleased Herod that he *promised* her with an oath to give her what she had asked for (Cei 2008).

The translation «he promised» it doesn't seem entirely adhering to the Greek verb that is translated here: once again *omologhèo*. Promising something does not necessarily mean declaring it in public; while the verb *omologhèo* has, as we have seen, this last meaning. Herod is thus ratifying his intention in the presence of others.

In the Acts of the Apostles (23:8) we read:

> The Sadducees in fact affirm that there is no resurrection, neither angels nor spirits; the Pharisees instead *profess* all these things.

«Profess» translates the verb *omologhèo*: they declare therefore publicly to believe in resurrection, angels, spirits.

Remaining within the context of the synoptic Gospels, we provide a further important example (Mt 11:25; Lk 10:21):

> I give glory to you, Father, Lord of heaven and earth (Cei 2008).

"I give glory" is the translation of the verb *exomologhèo*: I "declare publicly" your glory. It is very clear the meaning that the Thayer's Greek Lexicon does not fail to specify:

> To confess, to profess, to acknowledge openly and joyfully, to one's honour: to celebrate, give praise to, to profess that one will do, to promise, to agree, to engage something.

In the passage of Matthew and Luke is easily detectable the emphasis of which the dictionary speaks («openly and with joy»).

We ask ourselves:

- can a verb, that is strongly connotated by the semantic area related to "joy", be linked at the same time to the semantic area related to contrition, pain, repentance?
- just as dictionaries point out that the "public declaration of guilt" can be joyful, why do they not indicate it could also be characterized by pain or contrition?

Finally, Luke (22:6) uses the verb *exomologhèo* to say that Judas "publicly declared" to consent to the surrender of Jesus:

> He *agreed* and was looking for the propitious occasion to deliver him to them secretly from the crowd.

In all the cases, the Greek verb mentioned is used to indicate the statement of something that you have done, are doing or will do ("I promise"). In this regard, it seems appropriate to focus attention on the use that the verb "to proclaim" can have, if combined with the word "innocence", using an example. A man unjustly accused of some crime will most likely publicly shout "I'm innocent!". He proclaims his innocence in relation to the guilt attributed to him.

The synoptic Gospels describe the exact reversal of this situation. In our example, an innocent man proudly and shamelessly declares his innocence to many individuals; in the case of the baptism at the Jordan, so many individuals without doubt guilty – they themselves are accusing themselves – proclaim in unison and without shame to be transgressors of the Law. In front of a man who takes note of their guilt, becomes aware of it and plunges them into the waters of the Jordan.

The information transmitted by the evangelists does not provide any further information. No clearer mention is made of the reasons and purposes for this public proclamation, which took place at a precise moment, and involved a large number of people. Trying to verify whether in the text of Matthew (more detailed than the Gospel of Mark in relation to the baptism of John) you can find clear references, as well as to the already established proclamation, to a sincere contrition of sinners, there is no trace of it. Instead, it would seem that the author (Mt 3:5-6) wanted to clarify the character of a real event, constituted by the arrival of such a large number of people in the presence of the Baptist. And the inhabitants of Jerusalem, and all Judea, and all the region by the river Jordan, were coming to him in great numbers. Not only, therefore, individuals from the holy city.

This information has its undoubted importance, if one keeps in mind that the crowds of the subdued populations, whatever their composition and nature, worried not little the Roman rulers.

In this case, the crowds consisted of people who had crimes and faults to declare publicly. They were sinners, or transgressors of a law: the Mosaic Law, which consists of 613 rules (divided into positive and negative rules, orders and prohibitions). The range of gravity of the infractions could therefore be extraordinarily wide (from theft to adultery, murder, violation of absolute rest prescribed on the Sabbath day, etc.).

Also according to the evangelist Matthew (3, 6), the people who come to the Baptist are baptized in the Jordan river publicly proclaiming their transgressions. What is already known, is found also here: whoever admits the sins is admitted to baptism. It is not written that those who repent are baptized, but that the one who certifies aloud that he is a transgressor of the Law, is baptized "in the direction of the change of mind" addressed to the "good news".

The author uses the same participle used by Mark (*exomologoùmenoi*, «proclaiming in public»). It cannot be understood whether those who aspired to baptism were in the majority or only men (male individuals), or whether there were also women and children. Since it is sufficiently unlikely that children would be able to recognize their own eventual transgressions of the Law, it would seem more reasonable to assume that men and possibly women, all adults, would gather on the banks of the Jordan.

The only certainty concerns the absence of concrete references to a baptism having as its exclusive condition contrition and repentance. Yet, for editors sufficiently attentive to the news, the rush of crowds of individuals, who beat their breasts because of their faults and invoke divine forgiveness, should have been a very attractive story to portray and pass on. On the contrary, what concerns the baptism administered by John is reported by the evangelists in an extremely dry and narrow manner.

So,

- did the evangelists not consider it important to pause and describe in detail a rite of collective atonement and purification?
- or, more simply, do they not tell that kind of ritual at all?

On one thing they certainly agree: only those who solemnly admit that they have transgressed the Law are baptized; in front of an individual who, although charismatic, has no power to condone the sins: that is, to put them back, in the name and on behalf of Yahweh.

The role of John provides exclusively for the ratification of a successful conversion or "change of mind"; the passage to a "novelty (*anghèlion*) good *(èu)*", whose paternity belongs to Jesus. Not to the Baptist. If the messiah represents the novelty to which the mind turns, John represents what is old. And what must give way to what is new.

Therefore, even more so we wonder why hundreds of people had to collectively atone for their sins, by confessing them publicly to John:

- was the Baptist alone the authority recognized to preside over such a rite?
- could not the supposed "cleansing of sins" be done in the places of origin of the people who were to be baptized?
- those who have sins to confess flock to the Baptist: does this fact mean that the observants of the Law do not need neither the water baptism of John nor the subsequent baptism of Jesus in the Holy Spirit and fire?
- finally: assuming that all the righteous (that is, the observants instead of sinners) had gone to John's baptism, would they also have been called to "change their minds"?
- and to what should they be converted, if they were already righteous according to the Law?

There seems to be no doubt that the Baptist was a strict observant. It is difficult, then, that John had faults to proclaim in public:

- is it perhaps for this reason that he will not ask Jesus to be baptized "in the Holy Spirit and fire"?

- the Baptist is faithful to the Law: yet, the evangelist Matthew makes John say that he would need the baptism of Jesus ("I am the one who needs to be baptized by you"). So, according to this logic, for John is there something even more perfect than the rigid observance of the Law?

Whatever the answer, from the synoptic Gospels we ascertain that John is not baptized by Jesus, who would have all the prerogatives to do so, having the Baptist himself recognized the messiah as the one who is "stronger" than him.

However, it remains not entirely clear why so many went to the Baptist to proclaim their transgressions, far from the cities of origin: evidently, such revelations were opportune to have no disclosure, except among the transgressors gathered in the desert. Recalling the famous Gospel episode of the stoning of the adulteress, the transgressors probably considered it more appropriate to proclaim their sins in places far from the cities of Judea and Jerusalem itself.

In the text, there is no news about where the crowds went after the "public proclamation": which was not a solitary confession made quietly, as a very well sedimented imaginary – cultural in a broad sense – may have made us imagine until now.

The amnesty of transgressions (or "the good news")

We have seen so far as in the synoptic Gospels the so-called *àphesis amartiòn* [ἄφεσις ἀμαρτιῶν], the "forgiveness of sins", coincides with the *euanghèlion* (the "good news"): that is the scope of action of Jesus, and not of John the Baptist. If this had not been the case, the evangelists would, in all probability, have written that both, John and Jesus, had forgiven sins. While, to condone transgressions (literally, to "let them go") is intended Jesus. It would seem precisely for this reason that the messiah requires a "change of mind" (from what John originally did), turned towards him.

At the baptism of John are admitted those who have violations of the Law and faults to proclaim: but for what reason, in order to "change the way of thinking", it is necessary to have faults to be exposed in public?

John would appear to have to verify the requisites for the baptism of conversion to Jesus: that would seem very different, in form and substance. The Baptist baptizes in *water*. Jesus in the Holy Spirit and *fire*. The word "fire", placed in strong antithesis with respect to the word "water", suggests a clear change of substance between the action of John and that, unavoidable, of the messiah.

The Baptist only acts as a *passepartout*. He opens the doors to transgressors who proclaim sins: but does John do it on his own initiative or because someone else told him to do it?

He has no duty to judge the work of anyone. He who is imminent (Jesus) will judge with severity those who bear no fruit, sending them to the inextinguishable fire. This would seem to be the reason – contrary to what one might expect if one considered John the precursor of a joyful announcement of love, peace, forgiveness – why the Baptist on the contrary uses a harsh vocabulary; severe; threatening. A terminology that undoubtedly evokes, through the image of fire not extinguished, terrible and certainly punishment more than infinite mercy.

In the Gospel of Matthew is reported an event that concerns the observants of the Law who go to his baptism, in our case Pharisees and Sadducees: representatives of the major doctrinal currents of that time; scholars, intellectuals, experts of the Scriptures, and therefore knowers of the Law in every detail. Observant as strictly as possible.

This does not mean that they were "without sin". However, the aforementioned 613 rules of the Law, the Pharisees taught to observe them. And not to violate them. For this reason alone, they were in a very different position than the transgressors who emphatically proclaimed guilt in public.

In spite of all the differences that might exist between the public life of the Pharisees and Sadducees, and the heremitic-ascetic way of life of the Baptist, John had much more to share with them than with the habitual transgressors of the Law. For John the Law and its scrupulous observance defended and taught (as his lineage shows).

Therefore, we might expect that the Baptist, who is engaged, from dawn to dusk, to plunge into water transgressors of that code of norms of which he is a strict observant, after having sighted illustrious exponents of the religious, doctrinal and legal establishment of that time, finally rejoice in his heart. Are, in fact, just come to his presence individuals who know the Law and hand it down. They don't despise it, blatantly violating it.

But none of this happens. On the contrary, something radically different occurs (Mt 3:7-10):

> Seeing many Pharisees and Sadducees come to his baptism, he said to them: «You vipers. Who made you believe you could escape the coming wrath? Therefore, make a fruit worthy of conversion, and do not think you can say within yourself: we have Abraham as father. Because I tell you that from these stones God can raise up sons to Abraham. Already the axe is placed at the root of the trees; therefore every tree that does not give good fruit is cut and thrown into the fire» (Cei 2008).

Luke (3:7) tells us partially different things:

> To the crowds who went to be baptized by him, John said: «Breed of vipers, who made you believe you could escape the imminent wrath?».

John's harsh words here are addressed not only to the Pharisees and Sadducees, but entirely to the crowds who go to be baptized by him. Unlike Mark and Matthew, the participle *exomologoùmenoi* is not present in Luke's text. In his Gospel, the crowds do not seem to have transgressions to proclaim publicly: just like the Pharisees and Sadducees in the Gospel of Matthew.

This marks a radical difference from the baptism on the banks of the Jordan told by the other synoptic authors: the words «breed of vipers, who made you believe you could escape the imminent wrath?», in the Gospel of Luke are addressed *to all those who are baptized*, without distinction.

In Matthew's text, John does not make any accusation or reproach to the crowds who proclaim guilt. The harsh accusations are reserved only for those who have no transgressions to declare, and the text of Luke confirms this: in it appear crowds who, just like the Pharisees of whom Matthew tells, do not declare transgressions. To them is reserved the same treatment of the Pharisees: «Breed of vipers».

Therefore, if in the Gospel of Matthew (3:11) Pharisees and Sadducees are baptized "under condition", that is, only on the condition that they produce "fruits of conversion", we should deduce that in the Gospel of Luke the crowds are also baptized "under condition": waiting for them to hurry up to bring fruits of conversion.

All that we have found forces us to ask ourselves:

- whether there is a relationship between declared sins and immediate baptism;
- whether, on the other hand, there is a relationship between:
  1. the absence of guilt to be declared;
  2. the lack of "fruits of conversion";
  3. the baptism, which is administered but "under condition".

If the Pharisees and Sadducees, after being almost overwhelmed by the fury of John, declared that they had committed transgressions of the Law, would they be better received by the precursor?

The Evangelist Matthew (23:33) informs us of Jesus' invective against them. He uses the same words of the Baptist:

> Serpents, brood of vipers, how can you escape from the condemnation of Gehenna?

However, is it Jesus who uses a hard vocabulary because he heard it from John, or is John doing it because he heard it from the one to whom he is "paving the way?" Moreover, it is legitimate to ask ourselves what exactly are the "fruits of the change of mind" requested by John on behalf of the messiah: are we to understand that transgressors are not treated as badly as the Pharisees because they arrive at baptism "bearing fruit" by shamelessly proclaiming the sins committed?

Since sinners from Judea, Jerusalem, and the vicinity of the Jordan travel considerable distances to come to the Baptist (and with no little discomfort), we can reasonably assume that they do so to proclaim transgressions to more burdensome precepts than, for example, «you will not muzzle the ox during threshing» or «you will not eat meat and milk cooked together». So, what kind of transgressions do they proclaim?

Contrary to what we might expect, transgressors are not reprimanded in any way. They are welcomed. And immediately baptized. Conversely, the observants of the Law are first welcomed with very harsh words, and then admitted to baptism but on an exclusive condition: they must hurry to "bear fruit".

So, why then does the Baptist not address the same exhortation to all those who have declared themselves transgressors of the Law?

Assuming for a moment – and absurdly – that the translation of the Greek word *metànoia* is that of the Vulgate ("penance" or "repentance"), and that the synoptic Gospels intend to transmit to us precisely this meaning, we ask ourselves: what better occasion than baptism to urge such a number of transgressors to bear "fruits of repentance"?

Instead, always according to the translation of the Vulgate, to "repent" of transgressions should paradoxically be the zealous observants of the Law: that is, Sadducees and Pharisees. The Baptist first stigmatizes them harshly, and then would urge only them to repent. Meanwhile, numerous individuals, around him, are blatantly proclaiming that they are transgressors of the Mosaic Law:

- should we then take seriously the assumption that the word *metànoia* ("change of thought") doesn't really mean "penance"?
- does John intend to urge observants to "change the way they

73

think" and, like transgressors, to bring "fruits of change of mind" (that is, to have something to proclaim)?

- "Bearing fruit" is it perhaps the abstract metaphor that hides the concrete invitation to have faults to be admitted publicly?

John and Herod between Gospel text and historical context

If the profile of the Baptist coincided with what has always been outlined and has been handed down to us – a peaceful preacher who exhorts us to the purification of sins and the observance of the Law –, it would seem at first difficult to explain why he should worry the governor Herod. For the Roman tetrarch, the "repentance" of a large number of transgressors should be not only good, but definitely desirable thing:

- what nuisance can create, for the governor, a man who invites people to purification from transgressions, to spiritual perfection and to detachment from the vanities of earthly life?
- if he is proselytizing and recruiting new potential followers destined to live in prayer and asceticism in the desert, what should Herod fear?
- if he feared the disturbances that the violent anti-Roman opponents (the so-called zealots) could stir up in Jerusalem, precisely the fact that, from there, a large number of people went to the desert to listen to a preacher of peace, should this not be an unmissable advantage, or in other words a real fortune for the tetrarch?

Conversely, in the Gospels (Mk 6:20) it is written with great clarity, as we shall see shortly, that Herod *fears* John. The fact that the tireless preaching of the Baptist did not concern exclusively ascetic contents, seems to be shown by the Evangelist Luke (3:10-14):

The crowds asked him: «What should we do?». He answered them: «Who has two tunics shall give to those who have none, and who has food shall do likewise». Some tax collectors also came to be baptized and asked him: «Master, what shall we do?». And he said to them, «Do not ask anything more than what has been fixed for you». Some soldiers also asked him: «And we, what shall we do?». He answered them: «Do not abuse or extort anything from anyone; be content with your wages».

If the crowds had gone to the Baptist to repent and make public amends for their sins, they should have already known well the few actions with which to remedy their conduct: to repent with all their heart, purify themselves with water, return to embrace the precepts of the Law, promising for the future the strictest observance of the norms. In this passage, instead, the author describes the Jews who came to the Baptist as completely unaware of what they are going to do. Unaware of the most elementary of notions for a Jew: the Law is observed, any sins are atoned.

In Luke's account, the crowds seem to need simple and timely operating instructions:

The crowds questioned him: «What should we do?»

One would expect, at this point, that John would address his reproaches to a crowd that should already know how to behave: beating their chests and repenting. On the contrary, instead of saying «breed of vipers!», he gives only very narrow instructions:

Who has two tunics shall give to those who have none, and who has food shall do likewise.

We now wonder if this verse has any relation to the following, in which it is Jesus who speaks:

He called the Twelve to himself and sent them two by two, and gave them power over the unclean spirits. And he ordered them not to take for the journey anything but a stick: neither bread, nor bag, nor money in the belt; but to wear sandals and not to wear two tunics (Mk 6:7-9).

Obtain neither gold nor silver nor money in your belts, nor travel bags, nor two tunics, nor sandals, nor a stick, for the worker is entitled to his nourishment (Mt 10:9-10);

Take nothing for the journey, neither stick, nor bag, nor bread, nor money, and do not bring two tunics (Lk 9:3);

To those who pluck your cloak, do not refuse even your tunic (Lk 6:29).

John, who perhaps is aware of the planning of Jesus, says:

Who has two tunics shall give to those who have none.

We know from the synoptic Gospels that Jesus sends his disciples two by two to the villages, prescribing that they absolutely do not take tunics with them. From this, one could deduce that the future followers of the messiah are precisely, by his explicit will, people who will need a tunic. They must receive it from the inhabitants of the places where they go to "evangelize": that is, where they bring the "*euanghèlion*".

In Luke (3:11) the Baptist says:

Who has two tunics shall give to those who have none, and who has food shall do likewise.

One cannot fail to detect significant assonances (and it would seem non-random) with the following verses:

And he ordered them not to take anything for the journey but a stick: neither bread, nor bag, nor money in the belt (Mk 6:8);

Obtain neither gold nor silver nor money [...] nor travel bag, nor two tunics [...] those who work have the right to their nourishment (Mt 10:9-10);

Take nothing for the journey, neither stick, nor bag, nor bread (Lk 9:3).

The consonance with the prescriptions of the Baptist is not little. It can also be inferred that, when the messiah speaks of hungry and naked persons, he does not refer to a derelict and suffering humanity in general, but specifically to his disciples. He sends them two by two, without tunic or food, in the villages. It will be from the inhabitants of those villages that his followers will have to be fed and clothed (Mt 25:34-40):

> Come, blessed of my Father [...] I was hungry and you gave me food, I was thirsty and you gave me a drink, I was a stranger and you welcomed me, naked and you dressed me, sick and you visited me, I was in prison and you came to see me [...] Truly I say to you: all that you have done to only one of my littler brothers, you have done to me (Cei 2008).

On the basis of these elements (the associations between the nouns "tunic-food" and the adjectives "naked-hungry"), it is clear enough that when Jesus, in the Gospel of Matthew, says «all that you have done to one of these brothers of mine you have done to me», he is referring to his followers (as will be clearer later).

Tax collectors and Roman soldiers at John's baptism

We have already seen how the Baptist, during his baptismal activity, does not warn the publicans of "the imminent wrath": yet, they are the moneylenders and loan sharks of his own Jewish countrymen. However, he simply advises them to continue to be collectors, without exaggerating with the collection of money.

In the territories of the Roman Empire, taxes – both land taxes and per capita taxes – were levied by officials, who officially performed that specific task. A public auction was necessary to obtain authorisation for the collection of imported and exported goods. The right to collect went to the highest bidders, who derived from this a gain that exceeded the sum paid. The Evangelist Luke seems to refer to this when he says:

> Tax collectors also came to be baptized and asked him: «Master, what should we do?». And he told them: «Demand nothing more than what has been fixed on you».

The publicans also subcontracted the right to collect taxes. The subcontractors, in turn, could have subcontractors who collected personally (Lk 19,1-2):

> And here is a man named Zacchaeus, chief publican and rich.

The man named Matthew, whom Jesus invites to be his disciple, is a person in charge of collecting taxes (Mt 9:3):

> He saw a man, sitting at the tax counter, called Matthew, and told him: «Follow me». And he got up and followed him.

Mark (2:13-15) is more detailed:

> All the crowd came to him and he taught them. As he passed by, he saw Levi, the son of Alpheus, sitting at the tax office, and said, «Follow me». He got up and followed him. While Jesus was at table in his house, many tax collectors and sinners set themselves at table together with Jesus and his disciples; in fact, there were many who followed him.

One can deduce from this that there were not a few Jews who did the trade of publicans. We could say, euphemistically, that the people did not love them, because they often demanded more than their due (Lk 19:7-8):

> Seeing this, everyone murmured: «He went to stay with a sinner». But Zacchaeus, rising, said to the Lord: «Behold, Lord, I give half of my goods to the poor; and if I have defrauded someone, I return four times so».

The Jews avoided in every way to be in the company of publicans, considering them sinners:

> Seeing this, the Pharisees said to his disciples: «Why does your master eat with tax collectors and sinners?» (Mt 9:11);

> The Son of Man, who eats and drinks, came and they said: «Behold, a eater and a drunkard, a friend of publicans and sinners» (Mt 11:19);

> Indeed, I say to you: tax collectors and prostitutes pass you on to the kingdom of God (Mt 21:31).

Last but not least, the publicans were despised because they were at the mercy of the foreign dominating power, Rome, and in close contact with the Gentiles, who were considered unclean with respect to the Mosaic Law. Moreover, John the Baptist gave at least a singular treatment to the Roman soldiers who were stationed in Judea:

> «What should we do?». He answered them: «Do not abuse and do not extort anything from anyone; be satisfied with your wages».

With those to whom he has a great influence (the crowds), John seems to bluntly use the "hard knocks". On the contrary, with those who have direct contact with the Roman power, it seems that he prefers to remain (at least externally) in good relations.

If one still wants to investigate the reasons why the activity of the Baptist worried Herod, it would be necessary to recall how John, a supposed peaceful preacher who would have nothing to do with the tax collectors and transgressors of the Mosaic Law, gave instead them precise instructions upon timely request. And again: the Baptist, the last person who should have had contact with the Roman soldiers – that is, men of Herod who occupied the territories of Israel militarily – instead gave them precise orders, always at their request. The fact that very well-armed men demanded and awaited instructions, of whatever nature, from a Jew before whom crowds of people went to proclaim their transgressions, would seem sufficient at least to understand the reasons for the "perplexities" that Herod had, and of which Mark speaks.

«*Herod feared John*»: *an inexplicable reversal of roles*

In the Gospel of Mark (6:20), about the tetrarch of Galilee we literally read:

ὁ γὰρ Ἡρῴδης ἐφοβεῖτο τὸν Ἰωάνην,

that is: «In fact Herod feared John».

Among the translations of this passage, the Italian version of the Nuova Riveduta edition stands out, which translates the imperfect tense *efobéito* («feared») with the words «he *was in awe*».

From this translation it would follow that Herod Antipas, powerful tetrarch of Galilee and Perea, who had an entire army and lived in a fortified and impregnable palace, "was in awe" towards a vegetarian mystic, who practiced asceticism in desert solitude.

A translation of this content, before inevitably having to reckon with the historical context (the son of Herod the Great "in awe" of a peaceful Jew fasting), must do so with the text.

The Greek verb *fobèo* leaves little room for choice or indecision about its meaning. The etymology is the same as the noun *fòbos* («fear, terror»). Dictionaries indicate that «to be afraid, to fear, to be frightened» is the most appropriate translation. The meaning of «being in awe» of someone does not appear: in all probability because, just as «changing one's mind» is not «repenting», in the same way «fear» is not «subjection». Herod feared John. He was afraid of him,

> knowing him to be a righteous and holy man, and kept him in custody. When he heard him speak he was very much perplexed, yet he liked to listen to him.

The reader who has no contact with the Greek text, will get the following idea: John is a righteous and holy man. So, Herod can only fear him.

However, if it is true that a tetrarch should have enemies far more dangerous than a fasting ascetic, it would be natural to ask: precisely because John's fame was of justice and holiness, why should one fear him?

According to the Cei translation, «Herod... *watched over* him; listening to him he was very perplexed, however he listened willingly».

So, we ask ourselves: since Herod himself had chained John and put him in isolation in the fortress of Machaerus, what further vigilance could that man, who was also righteous and holy, need?

Always according to the translation quoted, the tetrarch has talks (in prison) with the Baptist, as a result of which he remains very perplexed. Nevertheless, he willingly listens to John.

All this makes the reader imagine a continuation, in prison, of the preaching activity of the Baptist; of which, however, paradoxically, only Herod can benefit. Herod, the one who, among other things, had imprisoned John. However, this fact does not seem to have affected the relations between the two. Indeed, the tetrarch entertains himself with the ascetic. Despite his words (on what subjects it is not specified by the evangelist) arouse great perplexity in him, he is nevertheless happy to hear him speak. He even listens to him with pleasure.

A picture like this is generated in the reader's imagination by the above translation. However, the Greek text would seem to express different concepts.

Herod was afraid of John, knowing, evidently from his informants, that he was considered "righteous" and "holy" according to Jewish law; being an observant, he was held in high regard by the crowds who followed him. This could not but worry Herod, as it was the ideal terrain to foment hatred against the Roman occupiers. To them, Yahweh's name meant nothing. Less still represented something his precepts (Herod and Herodias, adulterers with respect to that Mosaic Law which the Romans certainly did not recognize, were the confirmation of what we have just said).

In our opinion, it is precisely as a consequence of the fact that John was considered, by the crowds of the Jordan, as a saint and a prophet, that Herod *synetérei* [συνετήρει] John: literally «preserved, guarded, spared» John. That is, he preferred not to put him immediately to death, as Herodias would have wanted according to the Gospel story.

A tetrarch like Herod, if he had only wanted to satisfy the whim of a woman, would also have had then to justify, before the high spheres of Roman power, the riots, highly probable, put in place because of the death of the Baptist by many of his followers. Tumults very difficult to manage, triggered by the death of the «prophet of the Most High» (as John is defined by the Evangelist Luke).

Therefore, the translation (as in the Cei version) of *synetérei* with the verb «to watch over», which would make the reader understand that Herod watched over an unarmed Baptist, already put by the same tetrarch in chains and in isolation in the fortress of Machaerus, seems to us, as well as unreliable from a logical point of view, without foundation from a textual point of view. «To preserve, to guard» someone does not correspond to "watching over someone" or "controlling someone".

In Thayer's Greek Lexicon, relative to the Greek verb *syntereo* we find written:

> To preserve (a thing from perishing or being lost); to guard one, keep him safe.

Immediately afterwards, Thayer cites as an example Mark himself (6:20), that is to say the passage we are analyzing.

In the Gospel of Matthew (9:17) we read:

> People do not put new wine into old wineskins. Otherwise the skins burst, the wine spills out, and the skins are ruined. Rather, they pour new wine into fresh wineskins, and both are *preserved*.

«Preserved» is precisely the translation of *syntéreo*: it is a meaning that has nothing to do with "being supervised" or "controlled".

Again, Luke (2:19) writes:

And Mary *kept* all these things, reflecting on them in her heart.

With the verb "kept" is, once again, translated the Greek verb *syntéreo*. Synonyms of the verb "to keep" are "to defend", "to protect, to safeguard"; but not the verb "to watch", which has instead as equivalent "to be very careful to", "to check", "to look after", "to attend to", "to follow carefully". They are all verbs that do not imply the precise meaning of *preserving* something or someone from something or someone else. However, in the Cei translation of Mark's passage (6:20) we inexplicably find a completely different meaning ("to watch").

Herod's uncertainty and perplexity grew probably because the portrait of John as «righteous and holy man» began to be enriched with other nuances. This is why the tetrarch, on whom huge responsibilities weighed (like boulders), was moved to ask himself some doubts about the nature of the discipleship of the Baptist. Therefore, rather than taking pleasure in listening to the Baptist speak, he listened willingly to him in order to have a picture of his activity as clear as possible.

If we finally – and absurdly – decide to consider the translation «Herod watched over him» as correct, we ask ourselves:

- could the Baptist, though in chains, become the protagonist of acts, of whatever nature, on which Herod should have watched?
- was it possible for him to have contact with the outside world, to issue directives to the disciples outside the prison?

John, precisely because he was «righteous and holy», was not supposed to be able to exchange information in a clandestine way – and therefore very risky – with his followers. Then, we wonder for what reason Matthew (11:2-3) clearly writes:

> John, who was in prison, having heard of the works of Christ, sent through his disciples to tell him: «Are you the one who must come, or must we wait for another?».

Does this mean that the alleged "vigilance" of the powerful tetrarch could be avoided by some appropriate means?

In this case, it would be necessary to consider the hypothesis that John, from the prison, could rely on preferential treatment by some Roman soldiers. Although it can legitimately make the reader smile that a man arrested by Herod could have contacts and entrances among the soldiers of Herod himself, the evangelist Luke (3:14) reports that, when John baptized, «some soldiers also questioned him: "And what should we do?"».

So, first of all, we ask ourselves:
- what did Herod hear in prison from John?
- what did he want (or hope) John would tell him?
- what did he want to know?
- did John speak spontaneously, or did Herod question him?
- why was he «greatly perplexed» when he heard the Baptist?
- were not good news for Herod what the prophet reported?
- did Herod listen to the news that John gave him so that they might not become even worse news for the tetrarch?
- did Herod willingly listen to John because, as is almost always the case with the feared prisoners, the Baptist was able to reveal the most important news about the many reasons that led him to imprisonment?

The questions about the multiple reasons why a man who is an expression of the power of Rome, carefully chosen to rule the region most dangerous to the empire, should fear a eater of locusts and wild honey, can only arise as spontaneous as many. It may well be that Herod feared the crowds that the Baptist recalled. Although, if they really – as has always been handed down to us – were urged by him to contrition, it is difficult to imagine what Herod should have feared.

We must be content with what the historian Josephus and the evangelists wrote. They have given us some brief and concise information on which, while it is true that clear things are not interpreted, it is not necessary to exercise wise hermeneutic arts. One of these reports seems of some relevance: Herod Antipas has arrested John the Baptist. However peaceful and pacifist the baptizer might be, he was «thrown into prison» (Jn 3:24).

The Evangelist Matthew (14:3-5), although in his Gospel the ultimate cause of John's arrest is attributed to the Baptist's accusations against Herod for taking his sister-in-law Herodias as his wife, portrays a governor who is anything but inclined, even though he desired it, the idea of putting the Baptist to death:

θέλων αὐτὸν ἀποκτεῖναι ἐφοβήθη τὸν ὄχλον ὅτι ὡς προφήτην αὐτὸν εἶχον

Translating literally from Greek, in the text we find the following:

Wishing to kill him he *feared* the crowd, since as a prophet they had him in consideration.

So, a powerful tetrarch would then be put in a position to fear crowds of Jews (we must suppose that they were unarmed, if they really were repentant sinners), who proclaim their guilt to the Baptist, whom they regard as a prophet.

The historian Josephus Flavius, in his work intitled *Antiquities of the Jews* (XVIII, 118-119), writes:

Around John a multitude gathered and was enthusiastic to hear him speak. Herod feared that such an oratorical force might provoke a revolt, since the crowd seemed willing to follow all the advice of this man. He preferred to insure his own person before riots against him occurred, rather than repent too late [...] once a sedition had taken place. Because of these suspicions of Herod, John was sent to Machaerus.

If the authors of the synoptic Gospels (which neither historians nor chroniclers could be exactly defined) have provided some pieces of the puzzle concerning the Baptist, the historian Josephus adds some fragments which are as essential as the eyes, nose and lips to recognize a face.

Herod feared that John's undoubted oratory skills might «provoke a revolt»:

- but if such strength was expended by the Baptist in order to make men repent of their sins, for what reason should it ever have aroused a will to revolt against Herod?
- subversive action would have necessitated the use of weapons and bloodshed. How could contrite and purified sinners by baptism think to take up arms to make a violent action against the Romans?

Flavius specifies how the fear of a revolt stirred by John was linked to the fact that «the crowd seemed willing to follow all the advice of this man»:

- what kind of «advice»?
- did the Baptist only intend to persuade the crowd, with mild advice, to change their ways of life, or, since the historian writes «to follow *all the advice* of this man», did he bestow on other "advice" which were beyond simple invitations to repentance?

The author's chronicle continues with a portrait of Herod, which says a lot about the fears and anxieties that besieged his soul. It may seem incongruous with the sedimented imagery of the Baptist, but it is clear, if we read the Greek text of the Gospels and the writings of Flavius, that the tetrarch must have had more than one reason to fear an innocent voice crying out in the desert. Probably, because the voices were more than one. And they were not preparing the way for the Lord in a completely peaceful way:

Because of these suspicions of Herod, John was sent to Machaerus.

This is essentially equivalent to saying that the Baptist was arrested by the Roman authorities for suspected – as for the historian evidently documented – subversive activity.

The Baptist betrayed (that is, delivered under arrest)

About the incarceration of John, the synoptic Gospels say that he was «delivered» to authority. The Greek verb used by Mark (1:14), in the passive form, is *paradìdomi* [παραδίδωμι], «I deliver» (something or someone to someone else):

After John *has been delivered.*

The Greek text does not therefore say that John was «arrested, captured»; although generally in the translations, with regard to the verse we are examining, we find that the Baptist was *arrested*. In the Gospel of Mark, instead, it is written very clearly that John was «delivered». It would not seem an irrelevant difference. To say that the Baptist was delivered by an individual "X" to Herod – who thanks to this delivery can then capture John – is very different from saying that the baptizer was simply "arrested" by Herod. In the latter case, no delivery is necessary. In the first case, instead, a person "X" delivers John – most likely without his knowledge and therefore by surprise – to the tetrarch.

Concerning the fact that the Greek verb *paradìdomi* must be translated «to be delivered», the synoptic Gospels themselves comfort us. It is, in fact, neither more nor less than the same word used to describe the action done by Judas Iscariot against Jesus. The Christ «is delivered», by a disciple, to the Roman authorities. They only later arrest him.

Identical, from the point of view of the terminology used by the evangelists, is the case of John the Baptist. He is first *delivered* (by someone to Herod); then *arrested* (by Herod or whoever for him). It would seem sufficiently clear that being handed over to someone is not the same as being chained by someone. Further proof of this is paradoxically contained in the same Gospel of Mark (14:17-18):

> When evening came, he came with the Twelve [...] said: [...] «One of you, the one who eats with me, will *betray* me».

That is, he will «deliver» (this is the meaning of the Latin verb *tràdere* that we find in the Vulgate) Jesus to the authorities. They will arrest him only thanks to the commitment of the one who wanted to give him to them. This passage of the synoptic Gospels is the clear textual proof that the Baptist was «delivered» by someone, before being arrested.

Later, once again in the Gospel of Mark (14:21), we read:

> Woe to that man, by whom the Son of Man is *betrayed.*

If you translate the Greek verb *paradìdomi* in the way it is translated, in the same Gospel of Mark, when he refers to the Baptist («he was *arrested*»), the verses would sound like this:

> Woe to that man, by whom the Son of Man is *arrested.*

As a result, Jesus in this case is *arrested* by Judas. But according to the synoptic Gospels, he is arrested by others. Judas merely *delivers* him. Therefore, if Jesus is delivered, then so is John the Baptist: the verb used is exactly the same. "To deliver" and "to arrest" signifies two actions which are essentially the opposite of each other. In the first case something is given; in the second, something is taken:

a)   John was delivered (to Herod);

b)   John was arrested (by Herod).

In example A, you put the Baptist in someone's hands; in example B, you proceed independently to capture. As in the case of Jesus with Judas, there is someone who facilitates or makes possible the arrest of the Baptist.

Expired time or good opportunity?

According to Mark's account, as soon as John is delivered, Jesus from Judea – where he is and, according to Matthew, received baptism from John – goes to Galilee to proclaim the "good news", saying (1:15):

> The time is fulfilled and the kingdom of God is near; be converted and believe in the "good news" (Cei 2008).

However, this translation can lend itself, in the mind of the reader, to different and not unique interpretations:
- time is up?
- time has come?
- time is completed?

Conversely, the Greek text contains very clear and unambiguous terms.

One may now wonder what the reader – preferably the less experienced and aware of the historical and political context in which the characters operate – should understand:
- after the delivery and subsequent arrest of John, is the messiah officially proclaiming that the time of preaching of the precursor has expired because now begins the "good news" of Jesus?
- is it therefore necessary to "change the way of thinking" and be faithful to the "good news" that the messiah is bringing?
- with the eclipse of the Baptist does a mysterious divine plan begin to take place, concerning the imminent advent of an other-worldly kingdom?

The multiple interpretative hypotheses, on the other hand, clash with the univocal clarity of Mark's Greek text. In this passage of his Gospel does not appear the word "time", as we can understand it in the common language of every day. The Greek word indicating the concept of chronological time is also known to non-experts, as a good number of words is composed of its union with other nouns: it is *chrónos* [χρόνος], from which come the words *chronology, chronicle, chronicler, chronometer*, and so on enumerating.

The sentence "the time is fulfilled" will inevitably generate, in the mind of the reader, the belief that the author is talking about a chronological succession of moments, that concerned the Baptist and that has now come to a conclusion; to the end; to completion.

However, this can only contradict what the evangelist reported in the previous verse, that is: if John was delivered under arrest, and the phrase "the time is fulfilled" is to refer to him, the time of John was not fulfilled spontaneously. Someone, handing him over to Herod, has made the time of the Baptist complete. We would be led to exclude that John, if we have not forgotten the very harsh words with which he lashed out against the tetrarch, had surrendered on his own.

But it is for another precise reason that the "time" of John cannot be over: in the Greek text, of the noun *chrònos* (time understood as chronological succession) there is no trace. The subject of the sentence is instead the word *kairòs* [καιρὸς]: «the opportune moment», preceded by the verb *peplèrotai*: «has come to fullness». The word *kairós* does not indicate chronological sequence. Quantitative time is expressed, in Greek, by the noun *chrónos*; qualitative time by *kairós*. The latter indicates par excellence, according to the dictionary:

> the appropriate; the opportunity; the right moment; the propitious, suitable, convenient moment; the good opportunity; the favourable circumstance.

Until it became, in the Greek culture in the broad sense, the personification (and even deification) of the "opportune moment". So, if the concept conveyed by the word *kairós* could be personified, even to embody the "opportune moment" par excellence, it would seem difficult to translate it (in a misleading way) simply "time". One thing is the time that comes to an end for someone. Another thing is the "opportune moment" or "propitious occasion" that comes to someone. Also in this case, as in some previous ones, the original text says A. The most popular translations, inexplicably, say B.

Having ascertained that:

- the meaning of the word *kairós* refers to an opportune moment (finally come), or to a propitious occasion (which is grasped);
- the verbal form *peplèrotai* comes from the Greek verb *pleròo* which means «I fill, I make reach the top, I bring to completion»;

let us now see what the translation of the passage looks like, remaining as faithful as possible to the Greek text:

> After John was *delivered* [*betrayed*], Jesus went to Galilee, proclaiming the "good news" of God, and saying: «*The opportune moment* has come to fullness and the kingdom of God is approaching. *Change your mind* and believe [my] good news".

One cannot fail to note that the «opportune moment» immediately follows the temporal phrase «after John was delivered». The author is relating the capture of the Baptist with the presentation of a «opportune moment» for someone. With the delivery of John, undoubtedly comes a propitious opportunity. In the event that such things were not in close relationship, it would have sufficed for the author not to write the phrase «after John was delivered», and simply report that Jesus went to Galilee, proclaiming the "good news" of God and saying "the opportune moment has reached fullness". Instead, the structure of the sentence establishes a link between the capture of John and the arrival of an unspecified opportune moment or propitious occasion:

- propitious for whom?
- by whom was the Baptist arrested?
- who "delivered-betrayed" him?
- why did the Roman authorities seek him?
- why did he live in desert areas?
- for what reason does the evangelist immediately make follow the concept of "opportune moment" to the news of his arrest?

It must also be noted that in none of the synoptic Gospels there is mention of a possible great sorrow of Jesus for the arrest of the one who was, according to what the messiah himself says in Matthew quoting the prophet Isaiah, his precursor. So we ask ourselves:

- what was the relationship between John and Jesus? Did they trust each other blindly?
- how is it that, in translations, what clearly indicates the "opportune moment" – therefore the quality of a precise time of which we speak – has been translated with reference to the concept of "quantitative time", thus leading the reader to understand that it is a "time ended" chronologically, while the phrase instead suggests the opposite? That is, the advent of a qualitatively opportune moment that opens a new situation, at the expense of an old one that closes, in our case, in a very violent way?
- the evangelist Mark does not say at all that the propitious occasion was fortuitously presented, but specifies that it has come to «fullness»: does this mean that at other times the "occasion" had approached but had not materialized? Or that opportunity had been long awaited, and now it has finally come?
- why is the «opportune moment» related by the evangelist to Jesus' public proclamation of the "good news"?
- why should the kingdom of God be closer after John's surrender? Did the Baptist slow down the coming of the kingdom, in any way?
- if John had not been somehow the cause of slowing down

and hindering Jesus' action, why in the fourth Gospel do his disciples complain that he is not baptizing with John but on his own, with his own ways and in different places and distant from those of John?

- why, as soon as the "opportune moment" of which Jesus speaks occurs, should a "change of mind" immediately take place in those who listen to his "good news"?
- is this something completely new when compared with the teachings that John gave to his disciples?
- if John was baptizing with conviction in order to make the "change of mind" possible in the direction of Jesus and to his advantage, why did the messiah, after the surrender of John (that is, when he stopped baptizing), say that the opportune moment has come to its fullness?
- was John's baptism not "appropriate" enough for Jesus?
- when the Baptist had not yet been delivered, did he work together and in agreement with Jesus?
- if so, why does the fourth Gospel report that one made more disciples than the other, and that John's followers were annoyed and alarmed? Did Jesus himself prefer to proclaim the "good news" on his own?
- does the fact that the precursor prepares the way for the messiah necessarily mean that John loves Jesus fraternally and vice versa?
- did the Baptist share the messiah's plan and act in full accordance with his directives, or did he do so only because Jesus was, as he himself claimed, "stronger" than he was?
- did John fully recognize Jesus' greater authority? If so, why does Matthew report that he wanted to prevent Jesus from receiving baptism by his hand?
- if John had not been arrested, would he have brought the "good news" in harmony with Jesus or, having acknowledged his superiority, would he have retired after resigning himself?

- if John had not been arrested, would he have continued to pros-elytize? On his own behalf or on behalf of Jesus?
- why does the fourth Gospel paint us a submissive Baptist, who must "diminish" compared to the continuous growth of Jesus, while Matthew clearly writes that John wanted to oppose the messiah, preventing him that act of very strong legitimacy, that is, the baptism administered by his precursor?

It is not obvious that there should be a plausible answer to every question. What, however, seems clear without too much effort reading the text, is that the Jesus told by Mark seems to turn the very sad event of the delivery of his precursor in a "right moment" to go away from Judea – John's scope of action – and announce, this time alone and in Galilee (his homeland), the "good news".

In this regard, we ask ourselves if the passage of Mark is somehow related to the fourth Gospel: it is written here that, when Jesus heard that the Pharisees had learned how he made many more disciples than John, he immediately left Judea to go to Galilee.

We ask ourselves:

- are Mark and the Evangelist John talking about the same chron-ological interval?
- when the author refers to the conspicuous success of Jesus in terms of discipleship with respect to the Baptist, was John about to be handed over?
- does Jesus succeed in achieving a very great result in terms of the number of proselytes because John, alerted that his possi-ble surrender and subsequent arrest represent an imminent and very concrete risk, has by his choice slowed down his activity, momentarily eclipsing himself?
- does Jesus hasten away from Judea because, by making many more followers than John, he is at an exponentially greater risk of the same fate?
- could it have been the Pharisees themselves, notoriously unwill-

ing to oppose the Roman power, who had advocated the delivery of John, who called them "brood of vipers"?

- did the messiah have good reason to fear that the Pharisees, having ascertained his frenetic baptismal activity, would work to ensure that this news spread rapidly in the palaces of the Roman power, and among the high priests of the temple in Jerusalem?

- if to Jesus it was not necessary to avoid a possible pharisaic hostility, why then does the fourth Gospel so blatantly relate his departure from Judea to the fact that the Pharisees had learned that he was far more successful than John in proselytism?

Mc 1:14	Gv 4:1-3
After John was *delivered*, Jesus went to Galilee, proclaiming the "good news" of God, and said: «*The opportune moment* has come to fullness and the kingdom of God is near; *change your mind* and believe in the good news».	When the Lord heard that the Pharisees had heard: Jesus makes more disciples and baptizes more than John – although it was not Jesus himself who baptized, but his disciples –, *he left Judea and went back to Galilee.*

The Jesus told by Mark, who from Judea goes to Galilee saying "the opportune moment has come" after the delivery of John, is he perhaps the same Jesus of whom the fourth Gospel speaks, where a few verses before the departure of the messiah to Galilee it is written that the Baptist had not yet been thrown into prison?

Among the doubts and uncertainties, a certain news in the synoptic Greek text seems to be: the "good news" of the Gospel of Jesus officially begins when his precursor finishes "preparing the way" for him: since he is handed over to Herod. A delivery that the messiah strangely defines "opportune moment".

II

JESUS AND THE DISCIPLES: "LITTLE ONES" FOR THE KINGDOM OF HEAVEN

The semantic area of "smallness" in the synoptic Gospels

Examining the most evident formal peculiarities of the synoptic text, we cannot help but point out that both the programmatic discourses of Jesus concerning the "kingdom of heaven", and the parables in which these contents are in various ways declined, are strongly characterized by the punctual use of words belonging to a precise and structured lexical and semantic area: the one related to "littleness", mainly expressed by the adjectives "small-little", "least", "young", "last", "poor".

Having identified this area, we soon realize that the meaning of the words that revolve around it must be considered by analyzing the entire structure in which they are inserted; the network of relations of mutual significance, in their articulated coexistence. If we want to understand the unique sign, we must broaden our gaze to the field of signs in its entirety.

The terms of our investigation concern the following adjectives:

- *mikròs* [μικρός]: "small", "little";
- *tapeinòs* [ταπεινός]: "small" (compared to stature); more connotatively, referring to moral qualities, "miserable", "poor".
- *nèos* [νέος]: "young" ("small" relative to age);
- *èschatos* [ἔσχατος]: "last" (very small, relative to order or hierarchical position).

While each term has its own nuances of meaning, the common denominator between them seems evident: it is the concept of "smallness", that constitutes the core of a semantic area in which these words, within the Gospel text, are not isolated or thrown at random, but vice versa they acquire pregnancy and peculiar sense if inserted in such group. This happens not because of particular etymological affinities: more simply, the words all have to do with the concept of "smallness" or "littleness", variously declined: "small-little" *vs* "large-great"; "new-young" *vs* "old"; "child" *vs* "adult".

The lexical field is further enriched by expanding to comparatives and superlatives:

- *elàchistos* [ἐλάχιστος]: "very small", "minimal", "least" (superlative);
- *mikròteros* [μικρότερος]: "smaller" (comparative);
- *neòteros* [νεώτερος]: "younger" (comparative).

What we have just seen further reinforces the importance that the Gospel text confers on words belonging to this semantic area, as is very clear from the following passages:

- Among those born of a woman, no one *greater* than John the Baptist has arisen; but the one *smaller* in the kingdom of heaven is *greater* than him (Mt 11:11);
- At that moment the disciples approached Jesus saying: «Who is therefore *greater* in the kingdom of heaven?». And he called to himself a child, and put him in the midst of them, and said: «Verily, I say unto you, if ye shall not be converted, and become like children, ye shall not enter into the kingdom of heaven. Therefore whoever will become as *small* as this child is the one *greater* in the kingdom of heaven (Mt 18:1-4);
- For who among all of you is *smaller*, he is *great* (Lk 9:48);
- Who among you is *greater*, he shall become like the *younger* and who governs as the one who serves. For who is *greater*, who is at the table or who serves? Is he not who is at the table? Yet I am among you as one who serves (Lk 22:26-27).

The first three examples show the opposition between *mikròs* («small») and *mègas* [μέγας], «great, large, big». In the last example, the concept of "smallness" is still recurrent, but with different modes of expression: "great" *vs* "young", instead of "old" *vs* "young".

All the verses, in addition to having in common the concept of "smallness", have the same syntactic structure:

- one *smaller*... is *greater* than him (Mt 11:11);
- whoever will become *as small as* this child is the one *greater* (Mt 18:1-4);
- who among all of you is *smaller*, he is *great* (Lk 9:48);
- there is none *greater* than John, but one *smaller* [...] is *greater* (Lk 7:28);
- who among you is *greater*, shall become like the *younger* (Lk 22:26-27).

The concept expressed is always the same. Who is already or becomes "small", he is or will become "greater" than him who now, like John, is defined "great". A dark sense, in inverse proportion to the clarity of the syntactic structure.

The presence of the comparative *neòteros* («younger»), in the last example, allows to add another piece to the analysis: the permanence of the same structuring of the sentence («those of you who are *greater* hall become like the *younger*») suggests that Luke speaks of the things Mark and Matthew speak of. He expresses those concepts («smallness» *vs* "greatness", *mikròs* vs *mègas*), but using the adjective «young». The disciples wonder who among them is «greater»: "great", it would seem to understand, for hierarchy and prestige. Jesus answers that those who want to be *greater* among them must become *younger*:

- but according to what criterion, within a group, should be hierarchically "greater" the one who is "younger"?
- how do you become "younger"?

The adjective *nèos* ("young") is used by Luke neither more nor less as a synonym for *mikròs* ("small"). We go on asking ourselves why, in order to be "greater" than John, it is necessary to become "smaller"; and why he, who in the kingdom of heaven is "smaller" than the Baptist, is already, for this very reason, "greater" than him. But even before these things, we simply ask ourselves:

- what does it mean to be "great"?
- what does it mean to be "small"?

If to the set we have examined (that of the qualifying adjectives) we make the relative semantic area correspond, we soon realize that it does not satisfy the legitimate demand for logic by the reader. That is: if we match the Greek adjective *mikròs* with its meaning ("small"), we do not understand what is or should be the meaning of the verses quoted:

- "small" for what?
- in what sense?

Certainly – we would be led to believe – not in terms of height, physical build or age. So,

- with regard to an unspecified hierarchy present in the kingdom of heaven?
- but what hierarchy can it be and what can it be based on?

The adjective "mikròs" in the Gospels

In the dictionary of the ancient Greek language, under the word *mikròs* we find the following meanings:

- small in size (relative to people or things);
- small in quantity (translatable as "little");
- small in quality (of little importance, slight, of little value);
- small in time (short, little).

For logical consistency we would be led to exclude, in relation to John the Baptist, the meaning of "small in size": it can hardly be the smaller stature, or the thinner body of the followers of Jesus to decree their greater importance in the kingdom of heaven.

We could proceed with the second option ("small" relative to quantity). However, the hypothesis that Jesus meant that his disciples, being small in number, would be by reason of this greater than John and therefore more important than him, seems unlikely. We know that the disciples of the messiah were not few: the evangelists also report of crowds following him.

Then, we come to the third option: "small" in terms of quality, and therefore of little importance or, if referred to the social class, not of high rank. We would then have the following:

1. he who is less important, in the kingdom, than John is greater than him;
2. he who is less influential in the kingdom, is greater than John;
3. he who is of lower rank in the kingdom, is greater than John.

According to option 3, being greater than John would refer exclusively to social status.

According to options 1 and 2, those in the kingdom who have less importance (in the hierarchical sense) than John, are greater than him; that is, they surpass him in importance.

We would be persuaded to exclude option 3. If it were true, it would mean that it would be enough not to belong to upper classes to be greater than John; and that therefore all the crowds who followed Jesus, for the mere fact of being composed in all or almost of poor and marginalized, occupied in the kingdom announced a position higher than that of the Baptist. Moreover, although the lineage of the Baptist was of all respect, according to the Gospels he dwelt in the desert, with life far from comfortable.

Options 1 and 2 (relating to the presumed irrelevance or "littleness" of the disciples of Jesus as a value irrevocable to being greater than John) pose more than a doubt, in that:

1. either John was not the deliberately poor preacher in the desert of which the Gospels speak to us;
2. or he was, but he held one or more qualities – not clearly expressed but summarized in the adjective "great" – that placed

him in clear, irreconcilable antithesis with respect to the disciples of Jesus (who were instead "small"). Therefore, inevitably, with respect to Jesus.

The same opposition (Jesus "little" *vs* John "great") is repeated in Matthew (18:1-4):

> The disciples approached Jesus saying: «Who then is *greater* in the kingdom of heaven?» [...] «Whosoever shall be as small as this child, he is the *greater* one in the kingdom of heaven».

The above question arises: *mikròs* means "small", there is no doubt. But "to become small as a child", exactly, what does it mean?

It is precisely this famous similarity that makes even clearer, if it is not already enough, the fact that the adjective *mikròs* is used, by the protagonist of the Gospels, to indicate a precise and peculiar meaning that *he only attributes* to this term; a meaning out of the area of meanings found in the dictionary. *Mikròs* is translated "small" because it cannot be made otherwise. Any other translation would not be a translation, but a free interpretation of the translator. For this reason, the passages quoted are usually explained, in the comments present in the various editions of the New Testament, as invitations of Jesus to the disciples, to reach an alleged "innocence" or "purity": exclusive characteristics of children, and essential qualities upon entry into the kingdom.

However, these readings are not supported by elements within the text. Neither a supposed innocence or childlike immaculateness, nor a purity in the broadest sense are present in the adjective *mikròs*: which simply means "small", and not "innocent", "immaculate", "naïve" or "pure".

So, we ask ourselves:

- if the disciples of Jesus must strive to become more innocent and candid than those of John, and more candid than John himself to be "greater", then was the Baptist not entirely innocent and candid?

- was he – who had been chosen by Yahweh as a precursor, conceived in the Holy Spirit, zealous and rigorous observant of the divine Law – not sufficiently innocent and pure?
- instead, were the followers of Jesus – including Peter who will cut off the ear of the high priest's servant, or the ambiguous Judas Iscariot – potentially more innocent than the Baptist?

Scandalizing the "little ones", hindering the disciples

Let us now proceed to the analysis of another well-known Gospel passage, in which the adjective *mikròs* appears (Mt 18:6):

Who will scandalize only one of these *little ones* who believe in me, it is convenient to him that a millstone is hung around his neck and is thrown into the depths of the sea.

Assuming once again that the evangelist actually used the adjective *mikròs* to express the quality of innocence or purity, let's try to insert it in the translation, instead of the word "little":

Who will scandalize only one of these *innocents* who believe in me, it is convenient to him that a millstone hangs around his neck and is thrown into the depths of the sea.

The most common interpretation – or perhaps the most simplistic trivialization? – would suggest to understand that Jesus is greatly angry against those who "scandalize" children. However, in the Greek text there is not the word "children", but the usual adjective *mikròs*, in the plural form ("little ones"). We know that "little" is the favourite adjective reserved by Jesus for his followers: all of whom had long since passed childhood. Jesus is not talking about children, but about adults. Of children, in the literal sense of the term, here there is not even the shadow; although the most extensive interpretations have even seen in this verse a universally valid and clearly manifest condemnation of pedophilia.

A particular consideration deserves the Greek word *skàndalon* [σκάνδαλον], from which derives the verb that is translated here «to scandalize»: the same with which Jesus identifies the action of the disciple Peter, when he wants to oppose the foretold death of his master. The messiah intimate him (Mt 16:23)

> Go behind me, satan. You *are a scandal* to me.

That is, «you are an obstacle to me»: *skàndalon* means «obstacle, stumble». The verb *skandalìzein,* therefore, means first of all «to hinder», and not "to scandalize" as we commonly understand it, where the verb is loaded with denotative valences foreign to the original Greek ("to offend the conscience, modesty and moral sentiment of others with words or actions contrary to an ethical or religious norm"; "to disturb susceptibility, to shock, to baffle").

The translation «you scandalize me» risks being misleading and does not exactly convey the meaning of the original Greek word *skàndalon*. Knowing this, we will have:

> Who *will be an obstacle to* only one of these little ones who believe in me, it is convenient to him that a millstone hangs around his neck and is thrown deep into the sea.

Now, we ask ourselves:
- if the only task of the disciples was to become "innocent and pure like children", thanks to a rigid discipline of self perfecting, who could or should have hindered them?
- if they were hindered, then they supposedly had to do something or act in some way, and not simply try "to be innocent as children": so, what did the disciples of Jesus do to make it necessary for someone to hinder them?

Those who did not believe in Jesus were not "small-little ones" (not *mikròi*). Therefore, it must be assumed, those who were not "small-little" could only be an obstacle to the "little" disciples of Jesus. So, if John was "great", he did not have the qualities to be "small":

- then, were he and his "great" disciples an obstacle to the "small" followers of Jesus?
- for what reason would those who obstruct the disciples of Jesus be better to die drowned with a millstone firmly tied to the neck?
- to whom does Jesus refer in this invective?

In the same way is Matthew (18:10):

Watch not to despise only one of these *little ones*.

Also in this case we ask:

- if the adjective "little" was referring to spiritual qualities, who and why should despise them?
- the Baptist also had disciples: why is it that only for the "little ones" of Jesus there is talk of the concrete risks of being despised and hindered?
- what were they doing different from the disciples of John the "great"?

Always addressing his own, Jesus in the Gospel of Mark (9:41) affirms:

For whoever will give you to drink a glass of water in my name because you are of Christ, verily I say to you, he will not lose his reward.

His followers seem to take non-metaphorical risks:

- what does the need of the disciples to drink have to do with a supposed "purity of heart"?
- what does being despised or hindered have to do with a supposed innocence?

- how is it that such physically concrete terms appear in the text, when it is speaking of things pertaining to the highest (we suppose) forms of spirituality?

There seems little chance that there are, in this passage of the text, abstruse symbolism. Instead, it emerges from it that the followers of Jesus may find themselves without water with them. Probably, because they do not live in their homes but – as the Gospels themselves inform – they turn from village to village. This continuous wandering, at once, is not pleasing to those who could host them (Mt 10,14-15):

> If someone does not welcome you and will not listen to your words, get out of that house or that city and shake the dust from your feet [...] on the day of judgment the country of Sodom and Gomorrah will have a more bearable fate than that city.

Those who do not host the followers of the messiah, and possibly do not quench their thirst or feed them, are considered opponents, as it seems to be, with a certain symmetrical evidence, always in the text of Matthew, in chapter 25:

> Then he will say to those on the left: «Away, far from me, cursed, in the eternal fire [...] I was hungry and you did not give me to eat, I was thirsty and you did not give me to drink, I was a stranger and you did not welcome me, naked and you did not dress me, sick and in prison and you have not visited me [...] all that you have not done to one of these littler ones, you have not done to me (Cei 2008).

The same author (11:25) also writes:

> Jesus said: «I give you praise, Father, Lord of heaven and earth, because you have hidden these things from the wise and learned, and you have revealed them *to the little ones.*

With renewed, powerful clarity emerges, from elements within the text, the apparent disadvantage of those who are "small" only in the name. Instead, they are given the greatest advantage: knowing the mysteries of the kingdom. A prerogative reserved for the "little ones" disciples, of which John presumably should not be considered worthy: John, the "precursor" of Jesus, who, however, does not adhere to his planning. If he had adhered, he would have become "small" and a follower of Jesus. But about this, the Gospels do not give news. Probably, because it never happened.

Conversely, it is said bluntly that who becomes "small-little" surpasses John; who instead remains "great", therefore inferior, in this inverted logic, to the disciples of the messiah. "Small-little ones" is the nickname, strongly distinctive, that Jesus imposes on them, because they have agreed to become "like children". They know things of the kingdom that all others do not know (Mt 13:10-11):

> The disciples approached him and told him: «Why do you speak to them in parables?». He answered them: «For to you it is given to know the mysteries of the kingdom of heaven, but to them it is not given».

"Little" disciples, but wiser than wise men

Supposing once again that the equation "small" = "pure as children" is correct, however it is not clear to us why adults, become "small-little", should know things originally destined for wise and learned people:

- if the disciples tried to return to a childish innocence, what knowledge should they be aiming for or what knowledge should they be receiving?
- why would they know things that were deliberately veiled or hidden from a large number of people?

Always on the basis of the most frequent interpretations, we should say that wise, learned and crowds were not part of the mysteries of the kingdom, because they did not have a "pure" heart enough. They were therefore not able to accept teachings directed not to intellectual understanding, but to the "spiritual" one: the only one able to grasp any supernatural or metaphysical reality, in the broadest sense of the term. However,

- if crowds anyway did not have the "spiritual" characteristics to receive the message, what was the need to veil?
- wise and learned men did not have a "pure heart" like the "little ones": they were thus cut off from knowledge. Yet, Jesus says that certain things were deliberately hidden from them. If it were a matter of knowledge that is beyond rational understanding, why does the messiah conclude many parables with the exhortation «who has ears to hear, may he understand»?

In all probability, learned men and crowds could be absolutely capable of understanding something of the "mysteries of the kingdom". To these, however, it was permissible to access only the "small" followers of Jesus. If there was a risk that such things would be understood by others, then it should not be about content concerning the "spirit", but about intellect and rational understanding. Jesus hoped that those few able to decrypt his language would do so and become "little" (that is: officially his disciples), like the Twelve faithful followers.

The examples listed seem sufficient, therefore, to pose more than a few doubts about the correctness of the equation "small" = "innocent". It is arbitrary, while our intention is:

- to try to understand what the synoptic evangelists mean when they use the adjective *mikròs;*
- to understand it not on the basis of abstract conjectures, but on the basis of textual evidence.

It is necessary to assess whether there are passages in the text (and not outside it), in which the author himself makes clear what the words "small", "little", "very small" or "least", "great" mean in the peculiar language that the editors attribute to Jesus.

The mustard seed, or the parable of John and Jesus

We now read a parable, in which the programmatic contents of Matthew 11 ("in the kingdom of heaven the one who is *smaller* than John is *greater* than him") converge in a precise manner, and have a formal reworking (Mk 4:30):

> What can we compare the kingdom of God to [...]? It is like a mustard seed which, when sown on the ground, is *smaller* than all the seeds which are on the ground; but when sown, grows and becomes *bigger* than all the plants in the garden and makes branches so large that the birds of the sky can nest in its shadow.

The formal and content relationship between the parable of Mark and Matthew 11 seems evident:

> Among those who are born of women, there is not one *greater* than John the Baptist; however, the *smaller* one in the kingdom of heaven is *greater* than him.

Both in Mark (parable) and in Matthew (programmatic discourse), the conceptual pivot around which the message revolves is represented by the use of comparative adjectives: «smaller» and «greater». In both is strongly emphasized a starting condition, characterized by disadvantage. Among those born of women, no one is *greater* than John (position of advantage); but he who in the kingdom is *smaller* (apparent disadvantage), is *greater* than him (superior advantage than that which John currently has).

The mustard seed is *smaller* than all seeds (initial disadvantage). Then, it grows and becomes larger than any other plant. It is a superior advantage to that of the other seeds, which were at the beginning larger, but did not bear fruit as much as that grain which seemed destined to not bear fruit.

If we decode the parabolic language, we will have that the Baptist is an undisputed leader. However, who, in the logic of the kingdom inaugurated by Jesus, becomes "smaller" than John, he will become "greater" than the leader now recognized by all: since the kingdom of heaven is a "good news" that coincides with the proclamation of the *euanghèlion*. Whose unique actuator is Jesus. Not John, who must leave the scene.

A clear contrast can be ascertained: on the one hand the "great" John. On the other, the "small" Jesus.

We ask ourselves: when the messiah says that in the kingdom (of which he will be king) the one who is "smaller" than John will become greater than him, is he referring also to himself?

It is not yet clear what need John should ever have to be "overcome", he who is simply making, for a short time, the precursor of Jesus. Nor is it yet clear why, if the Baptist is destined to eclipse, Jesus instead speaks of him as someone who must, together with what he represents, be overcome.

Small seed, discarded stone

The parable of the mustard seed contains some meanings also expressed in Luke and Matthew, where these concepts appear, so to speak, changed of dress. However, some unmistakable elements remain on the conceptual skeleton: the comparative "smaller" and "greater".

In Mark, behind the concepts of "smallness" (smallness of the seed) and inadequacy expressed by the adjective "*mikròs*-small", is the always fixed conceptual pivot of the story: the seed must be "small" to become "large" and overcome all the plants in the garden.

We also find these meanings in a quotation from the Old Testament, that Jesus refers to himself (Mt 21:42; Mk 12:10; Lk 20:17):

The stone discarded by the builders has become a cornerstone.

Behind the union of noun and adjective ("*discarded* stone" *vs* "cornerstone") is hidden the usual concept: what was previously "small", becomes "large". The stone discarded by the builders, considered initially unsuitable, too "small" or crumbly to be put to the foundation of the building, just like the "small" seed that no farmer would ever sow, has instead become a cornerstone: a boulder, placed at a right angle at the meeting point between two walls.

From the seed that is *smaller*, is born the tree that is *larger*. From the stone discarded, a mighty building. An inverted logic, that contradicts another more or less famous statement of Jesus (Mt 7:16-20; Lk 6:43-45):

> Is it possible to collect grapes from thorns, or figs from brambles? Thus, every good tree bears good fruit, but the bad tree bears bad fruit. A good tree cannot make bad fruit, nor a bad tree make good fruit.

This is what the messiah says to the disciples, with rhetorical questions and elementary and compelling logic. However, it is the same person, Jesus, who affirms the opposite:

- the "small" seed becomes a "bigger" plant than all the others;
- the discarded stone becomes a cornerstone.

This is equivalent to saying that figs will ripen on the brambles; that the eagle can be born from the mouse; or that a small mouse will be able to give birth to a large mountain.

All this does not say at all that Jesus was inconsistent, or that he fell into contradiction. Instead, it suggests with increasing insistence what the text confirms at every step: the adjective "small" refers to qualities that are beyond the denotative (that is, literal) meaning of the term. "Small" qualities that, if put to use, will produce "great" results: better than all those results that others, eventually, could have produced before the messiah. The "little ones" will be greater than those who are now great. Those who are last, will be first. Those who are now first, will become last. Those who are "younger", will be "greater".

If the text provides us with certain elements of understanding, there would be no need to interpret anything. Therefore, before imagining, or assuming without textual confirmation, what the words enclosed in quotation marks could perhaps mean, we should ask ourselves if a search in the Gospels (in the Greek language) was first conducted, to verify if the meaning of those adjectives revolving around the concept of "smallness" is already explained *inside the text*; in one or two precise passages. This is useful to ascertain if it is Jesus himself – the one who inaugurated the use of that precise language – to clearly tell us the meaning he attributes to those recurring adjectives; thus relieving us from the burdensome and risky task of arbitrarily interpreting.

We should therefore consider the hypothesis that a set of words relating to a very precise semantic area (the "smallness") is used to transmit, on the basis of a communication code assigned to those words by the user, information and more complex messages which go beyond that semantic area, while keeping intact the shape of the word known ("small", "least", "last", "young"...).

So, the adjective *mikròs* ("small, little") and the superlative *elàchistos* ("least"), will have to refer to meanings that do not concern neither the stature, nor the dimensions, nor the age of the disciples; nor will they be improbable affectionate nicknames ("my dear little disciples"). In the same way, the adjective "great" will refer to a semantic area that does not concern the size or age of the Baptist, but a quality that John had. A very different quality from what Jesus wanted his disciples to have.

The conceptual scheme "small *vs* large" is repeated with programmatic obstinacy, and attributed not only to people but to things (Mt 7:13-14):

> Enter through the narrow door, because wide is the door and spacious the way that leads to perdition, and many are those who enter it. How narrow is the door and cramped the way that leads to life, and few are those who find it.

He who invites his followers to become "small" in order to be "great", is the same one that invites them to enter the kingdom not through the "wide" (or "great") door, but through the "narrow" (or "small") door. It seems difficult to doubt that the adjectives "cramped" and "narrow", referred to the door and to the way, indicate nothing else than the preference that Jesus accorded respectively to the concept of "smallness" and "littleness": and this is clearly shown here in the text.

The door into which the messiah suggests to enter is *stenè* [στενή], «narrow»; *tethlimmène* [τεθλιμμένη], «crushed». However, despite having such disadvantageous qualities, it alone leads to life (*zoè* [ζωή]). But those who enter are few.

If we wanted to find a semantic area to which these words could belong, this area would be, once again, that of "smallness", variously declined; and this concept would be the common denominator of all these words. Narrow entrance, narrow street. Few find them. If they find them, it is because they have sought them. They have expended energy to gain entry. They didn't enter through the narrow door by accident.

Conversely, the other option consists of a door *platèia* [πλατεῖα], «wide»; a street *eurýchoros* [εὐρύχωρος], «large», in which many (*pollòi* [πολλοί]: "large-great" in terms of number) simply enter. They did not search with obstinacy. It was evidently easier to pass through the "great" gate. It was not necessary to become "smaller". The door is big and wide, but unfortunately leads to the *apòleia* [ἀπώλεια]: «perdition», «ruin».

At this point, we believe that even a neophyte in the field of textual analysis would begin to think that all the passages of the Gospels in which the binomial opposition "small-large" / "narrow-wide" and so on appear, are firmly linked to each other.

One foot and one eye are better than two

The following verses of Matthew (18:8-9) give no less thought than those already seen:

> If your hand or your foot is cause of scandal to you, cut it and throw it away from you. It is better for you to enter into life maimed or lame, rather than with two hands or two feet being thrown into eternal fire. And if your eye gives you cause for scandal, gouge out your eye and throw it away from you. It is better for you to enter life with one eye, rather than with two eyes being thrown into the Gehenna of fire.

This passage, often considered inconvenient because of the extreme severity with which Jesus – who should be docile and meek – turns to those who listen to him, is counted and with a certain hastiness inserted in the set of those more "dark" and "mysterious".

Keeping in mind the image of the messiah that has always been given to the collective imagination, the unfathomable "darkness" of these words would be constituted by the seemingly inexplicable presence of very violent contents: the invitation to cut off, of own initiative, important and essential parts of the human body that could hinder the «entry into life». Otherwise, you will end up in the Gehenna of fire (the messiah here mentions the depression outside the walls of Jerusalem, where the waste of the population was constantly burning).

The reader may wonder what this passage has in common with the previous one about the "narrow gate". Not a little:

- the same syntactic and conceptual structure;
- the presence of words relating once again to the concept of "smallness".

It is preferable to amputate a limb (upper or lower), if it is an obstacle («scandal») to enter life. It is better to be maimed or lame, but safe to enter life, than to be thrown into the inextinguishable fire.

Extratextual flights or hermeneutical funambolisms are not necessary. But, it is sufficient to find the twinning between this passage and that relating to the "narrow door". It is good to have the same characteristics that are useful to enter the "narrow door", or to pass through the "narrow way", in order to "enter life": just the use of the latter expression, in both passages, tells us that they are linked.

Both in the case of the "narrow door" and in the case of the "maimed" or "lame" individual, obstacles appear to the so-called "entry into life": that is, to everything that falls within the semantic area of what is "small". The field of action of the "little ones" is always hindered (Mt 18:6-9):

> Whoever scandalizes even one of these *little ones* who believe in me, it were better for him that a millstone were hanged about his neck, and that he were drowned in the depth of the sea. Woe to the world for the scandals. It is inevitable that scandals happen, but woe to the man for whom the scandal happens. If your hand or your foot is occasion of scandal, cut it off and throw it away from you.

For those who are already "small" like the disciples of Jesus, it will be inevitable to find obstacles. Whoever has two hands and two feet, and is therefore "big-great" and has not yet become "small-little", must be willing to eliminate the obstacle at the root. Even if it is represented by something very precious and indispensable. The obstacles can be traced back to the semantic area of what is "great". To go through the "narrow door", one cannot be "great": this is not an adjective or a qualification that can be used to "enter life". Proof of this is that the "great door" and the "wide way" lead to perdition; the "narrow door" (and therefore the "small" opening) leads to salvation. You have to be "small". We must become "small". We must not increase, but decrease. We must not enlarge, but shrink.

Other passages, which have become proverbial (Lk 14:11 and 18:14), confirm the solidity of these concepts. Therefore, not only those who become *small* will be *great*, but also "those who raise themselves will be lowered" or, in a more literary and elegant form, "those who exalt themselves will be humiliated, those who humiliate themselves will be exalted".

The forms change, the meaning remains granitically unchanged (Lk 14:1-11):

> One Sabbath he went to the house of one of the leaders of the Pharisees for lunch and they were watching him. [...] He told the guests a parable, noting how they chose the first places: «When you are invited to a wedding by someone, do not put yourself in the first place, so that there is no other guest more worthy of you, and he who invited you and him comes to tell you: "Give him the place". Then you will be ashamed to occupy the last place. Instead, when you are invited, go and put yourself in the last place, so that when the person who has invited you comes, he says: "Friend, come further". Then you will have honor of it in front of all the diners. Because whoever is exalted will be humiliated, and who is humiliated will be exalted».

It would seem a trivialization to believe that here the protagonist of the Gospels is giving advice on how to behave properly, while sitting at the table during a wedding banquet. The story is preceded by the words «he told the guests a parable». Therefore, these are deliberately veiled contents, that refer to something much more precise to which the parable intends to refer. Jesus seems to allude to an important situation that he knows well, similar to a wedding feast, where there is an invited person who is in first place. Among others, there is one considered more worthy of him. The landlord wanted both present.

However, he orders that the guest who is in first place get up and leave the place to the other, more worthy. This "last" thus takes the place of the "first". The "first" guest is shamefully downgraded. Whoever was *first* became *last*, who was *great* now is *small*, who was above now is below. The apparent disadvantage of sitting in last place turns into an unexpected advantage: the wedding organizer promotes the guest who had chosen the "lesser" ("smaller") position.

The lowering, the humiliation, the act of becoming "small" is not spontaneous and gratuitous. It is aimed only at obtaining something.

Subsidence is not a purpose. It is the only means to achieve a precise and well-defined purpose. If the purpose (to be "great") did not exist, the means (to become "small") would have no reason to be.

Certainly, the theme of the "banquet" also concerns other parables. If we consider the interpretation, often present in the commentaries to the text, that the banquet is a metaphor for the "kingdom of heaven", we should remember that:

- John the Baptist came chronologically *before* Jesus;
- both were remarkable guests, invited by Yahweh, of the "wedding";
- it then happens, unexpectedly, that the landlord, in order to fulfill the secular promises made to his people, prefers Jesus (the second or "last" invited) to John (the "first").
- the Baptist, although he had many disciples who followed him, thus becomes the *predecessor* of Jesus;
- the latter assumes a more important role (son of God) than the reduced John (prophet of the Son).

The apparent disadvantage of becoming "small", choosing the last place or passing through the narrow door, turns into advantage: the landlord will choose to promote (that is, to make "great") the candidate for the kingdom who had wanted to become "small" (Mt 11:11):

> Among those who are born of woman there is no one *greater* than John the Baptist; but the one who is *smaller* in the kingdom of heaven is *greater* than him.

Again in Matthew (19:23-24) we read:

> Hardly a rich person will enter the kingdom of heaven. I repeat: it is easier for a camel to pass through the eye of a needle, than for a rich person to enter the kingdom of God.

Even in the case of this famous saying, the bizarre of the comparison refers to the absolute impossibility, for the rich who does not want to strip his possessions, of entering the kingdom. The verse acquires fullness of meaning if one is aware of the dialectic that rigidly governs the code through which the Gospel message is transmitted.

The "eye of the needle" is just another variant of the "narrow door": you can pass through it only if you become "small". What is "great", "rich", "abundant" (as opposed to what is "small" and "poor") does not pass. A camel cannot cross the eye of the needle, because of the "big-great" humps. He should at least lose one (like the man a limb) to have a minimum chance of passing through the narrow eye (which is still a "door"). However, it is absurdly more likely that the "great" camel becomes "small", rather than a rich – or a "great" relative to accumulated goods – can enter the kingdom of heaven.

If the kingdom of heaven were indeed, as we have always been taught, a "spiritual" reality, one might wonder why it must be strictly necessary to sell all one's belongings to enter the "narrow" door. There would seem to be no doubt that Jesus was alluding to tangible possessions (Mt 10:21-22):

> Jesus said to him: «If you want to be perfect, go, sell what you have, give it to the poor and you will have a treasure in heaven; and come. Follow me». Hearing this word, the young man went away, sad; in fact he possessed many riches.

The metaphor of the camel and the needle is aimed at expressing a maximum impossibility: the impossibility, for the rich, to enter the kingdom, remaining rich.

On the camel and the eye of the needle, then, several hypotheses were made. It is a combination that can hardly be fully understood outside the conceptual dialectic between "large-great" and "small-little". If, instead, the combination "camel-eye" is considered within this dialectic and as the umpteenth product of the communicative code that supports it, then that combination is fully justified in the perspective of this ubiquitous dialectic.

In the past, it was thought that the evangelist may have mixed up, translating from an original Aramaic source, the word *gamta* («hawser») with *gamla* («camel», in Greek *kàmelon*). In that case, he would have made a translation error (because *gamta* and *gamla* differ by only one letter).

However, although the hawser can be considered an image very close to a group of former fishermen more than a camel, from the point of view of meaning nothing changes. Always something impossible is involved. A large mooring cable is however infinitely large for the eye of a needle. We should also ask ourselves if Matthew makes the same mistake in another passage (Mt 23:24):

> Blind guides, who filter the midge and swallow the camel.

In a very harsh apostrophe addressed to the Pharisees, Jesus not only uses again the image of the camel to signify the abundance of dimensions, but always does so in stark opposition to a term of confrontation (a midge) that recalls the exact opposite: the *smallness* of dimensions. "Big camel" *vs* "small needle and midge". Precisely the presence, in another passage (Mt 23:24), of the word "camel" used in the same way ("small" *vs* "great") is an eloquent signal that the author really wanted to speak of a camel.

With the pair "midge-camel", instead, the relationship is reversed: it is not what is "big-great" to have difficulty going through the "small", but the "small" (midge), filtered, cannot pass through the opening where the "big" (camel) enters.

In the episode of the "camel-eye of the needle", Jesus is addressing his "little" disciples. As such, they are destined to pass through the "narrow gate" of the kingdom. Who is "great", like the camel, will certainly not pass. Unless he voluntarily becomes "small".

In the episode of the "midge-camel" couple, instead, the messiah speaks to the Pharisees: who certainly are not "small". Bitter opponents of Jesus and his followers, these scholars of the Law "swallow camels". Their door is therefore not "narrow". It is "wide". The narrow one can be crossed exclusively by midges. The big one only by camels. This is the reason why the midge is *filtered* by the Pharisees: the "small" is not allowed to go where only the "big-great" pass.

Setting a proportion, we will have:

$$\text{camel} : \textit{great} = \text{midge} : \textit{small}$$

The camel is related to the "great" as the midge is related to the "small". With the adjective "small-little" Jesus always unequivocally designates his disciples. Therefore, camels are related to the "great" like midges are related to the followers of the messiah. Camels and midges are in sharp and incurable antithesis; "large" and "small" equally. We know that the "little ones" are opposed to the Pharisees and their disciples. Therefore we will have:

$$\text{midges} : \textit{disciples of Jesus} = \text{camels} : \textit{Pharisees}$$

Midges are related to the followers of the messiah, like camels to the Pharisees. Small midges, big camels. Both are related to something and refer to something else.

Only in the perspective of using precise language is justified the programmatic use of terms belonging to such a specific lexical area (the zoological one: camels, midges, but also pigs, sparrows, snakes, vipers, and so on). A rich repertoire to which the protagonist of the Gospels draws, by bending it towards purposes that go beyond the mere occasional exclamation of an incidental phrase, as it could seem the sentence «blind guides, who filter the midge and swallow the camel». Which is, instead, the textual spy of the mathematician result that in the text produces the use of a communicative code with iron rules, known only to the one who is pronouncing those words.

It is precisely the short circuit triggered by the pair "midge-camel" (everyone would ask the meaning of this curious statement) to make it clear that at the base of all these oppositions ("great-small") there must be a systematic logic, that must be sought *within the text*, and not outside it.

If we were to consider "midges" and "camels" outside the confrontation between "small" and "great", they would only be the protagonists of a hyperbolic expression with which Jesus would refer to Jewish usage – in accordance with the norms written in the book of Leviticus – to filter drinks in order to avoid swallowing midges (Lv 11:1-2 and 20-25):

> The Lord [Yahweh] spoke to Moses and Aaron and said to them: «Speak to the Israelites saying: [...] All winged creatures that crawl upon four legs will be considered to be an abomination for you. Yet from among the insects that walk upon all fours, you may eat those that have two legs above their feet to jump upon the earth. Therefore, you may eat the following: all kinds of locusts, every kind of bald locust, every kind of grasshopper, and every kind of cricket. But every other flying insect that has four feet will be considered to be an abomination. By these you shall become unclean, whoever touches their carcasses shall be unclean until the evening and whoever carries their carcasses must wash his clothes and shall be unclean until the evening [...]».

It was also necessary to refrain from consuming meat of large animals such as camels (Lv 11:1-8):

> The Lord spoke to Moses and to Aaron and said to them: «Speak to the Israelites saying: [...] You may eat any animal that has a cloven hoof and that eats its cud. From among those animals that chew their cud and have cloven hoofs, you shall not eat the following: camels, for it chews its cud but does not have a divided hoof, so it will be considered to be unclean; the rock badger, for it chews its cud but does not have a divided hoof, so it will be considered to be unclean; the hare, for it chews its cud but does not have a divided hoof, so it will be considered to be unclean; the pig, for its hoof is divided and is cloven hoofed, but it does not chew its cud, so it will be considered to be unclean. You shall not eat their meat nor shall you touch their carcasses. They will be considered to be unclean».

Regarding the behaviour of Jesus before eating, in Luke (11:37-38) we read:

> A Pharisee invited him to lunch. He went and sat down at table. The Pharisee saw and was surprised that he had not made the ablutions before lunch.

Jesus neglects the hygienic norms concerning meals. This can only arouse wonder in an observant of the Law. Before sitting at the table, the Pharisees wash themselves to the elbow. The messiah prefers not to adapt (Mt 15:1-2):

> Some Pharisees and scribes, coming from Jerusalem, approached Jesus and told him: «Why do your disciples transgress the tradition of the ancients? In fact, when they take food they do not wash their hands».

If we do not take into account the "small-great" dialectic, with which Jesus strongly characterizes his language, we should think that he is leaving out the pedantic observance of the norm concerning the midges: the Pharisees, therefore, would strive not to ingest them (they *filter* them), but would violate the ban on eating camel meat (they *swallow* it). However, this would conflict with the profile of the orthodox Pharisee. It is difficult to think that precisely this category of people, severely pointed out by Jesus because of the literal observance of every precept, is trying to comply with the law concerning midges but is violating the much easier-to-observe camel ban. The laws of Leviticus are very clear: they all revolve, indifferently, around the theme of impurity. Impure are midges. Impure camels. Both abominable (Lv 11:46-47):

> This is the law [...] to distinguish what is impure from what is pure, the animal that you can eat from what you should not eat.

If for the Pharisees a midge was unclean, so was the camel. They could not ignore it, since they were zealous about the rules: it seems difficult to think that the Pharisees eat impure animals (that is: in abomination to Yahweh). It is easier to assume that Jesus uses the terms "midge" and "camel" in a particular language.

As for purity and impurity, Mark (7:15-19) seems to clarify Jesus' position better:

> «There is nothing outside man that, by entering him, can make him unclean. But it is the things that come out of man that make him impure» [...] His disciples questioned him on the parable. [...] «Do you not understand that everything that enters man from the outside cannot make him impure, because it does not enter his heart but his belly and goes into the sewer?». Thus he made all foods pure.

Therefore, the one who did not take into account in any way the rules on the purity of food transmitted by Yahweh (his Father), however made pure all food but, at the same time, accused the Pharisees of violating one of those norms (swallowing camels). Instead, it would seem more reasonable to conclude that it was Jesus who had no problem swallowing camel meat; while it is difficult to believe that the Pharisees did it lightly, being strict observant.

In Leviticus (11:24-25) we read:

> The Lord said: [...] «For the following animals you will become unclean: whoever touches their carcasses will be unclean until the evening».

The statement «for the following animals you will become unclean» undoubtedly corresponds to the concept expressed by the words below:

> What enters man from the outside can make him unclean.

Jesus, instead, says the exact opposite:

> Whatever enters man from the outside *cannot make him unclean.*

Therefore, we should logically deduce that the messiah was repealing at once numerous norms transmitted by Yahweh (his Father) to Moses.

«Woe to you who close the kingdom before men»

The fact that the verses concerning camels and midges in all probability do not refer to the entry of dead animals into the oral cavities, but to the affiliation of disciples to opposite doctrinal currents, can be inferred also from the preceding verses (Mt 23:13):

> Woe to you, scribes and hypocritical Pharisees, who close the kingdom of heaven before the people; in fact you do not enter, and do not let in even those who want to enter.

«You who close»: in the Greek text we find the verb *klèio* [κλείω], which links to the noun *klèis*, used by Matthew (16:13-20) about the assignment given to Peter, universally known:

> «Who do people say the Son of Man is?». They answered: «Some say John the Baptist, others say Elijah, others say Jeremiah or some of the prophets». He said to them: «But who do you say I am?». Simon Peter replied: «You are the Christ, the Son of the living God». And Jesus said to him: "Blessed are you, Simon [...] neither flesh nor blood have revealed it to you, but my Father [...] you are Peter and on this stone I will build my assembly and the gates of hell will not prevail over it. I will give you the keys to the kingdom of heaven» [...] Then he ordered the disciples not to tell anyone that he was the Christ.

Scribes and Pharisees close the doors of the kingdom. Peter opens them. The former prevent access («do not let in even those who want to enter»); the second is responsible for giving access.

The fact that the discourse about the keys revolves around the usual, irreconcilable clash with the Pharisees, is suggested by the phrase «the gates of hell will not prevail». The key of Peter opens the door of the kingdom: therefore, it is undoubtedly a "narrow" door. The "wide" door-gate leads to perdition. So:

narrow gate : kingdom of heaven = *wide gate* : hell (Gehenna)

The narrow gate is related to the kingdom of heaven as the wide gate is related to hell. The evangelist is talking about something that is diametrically opposed to "life" or "eternal life" (*zoén aiónion* [ζωὴν αἰώνιον]), guaranteed in the kingdom. The Greek word translated «hell» is *ádou*, "Hades", in Hebrew *Gheénna* (the "Gehenna" of which we have said).

We know that through the "narrow door" only midges can pass, while camels must opt for the "wide door". Therefore, we can change the place that is crossed (narrow or wide door) with the subjects that could cross it (midges or camels). We will have:

midges : kingdom of heaven = *camels* : hell

Midges are related to the kingdom of heaven like camels to hell. The conceptual constants of the language of Jesus are like granites: they do not move an inch. What pertains to the semantic sphere of "smallness" is related to the kingdom of heaven as that which pertains to "greatness" is related to hell. Since we know that the qualification of "little ones" is attributed by Jesus exclusively to his disciples, we will have:

Small-little: kingdom of heaven = *great* : hell

The "little ones" are related to the kingdom like the "great ones" to hell. If the "little ones" are the followers of Jesus, the "great ones", who will burn, will be the Pharisees. The precise confirmation of this, timely, is in the text (Mt 23:33), in the quoted invective:

> Snakes, breed of vipers, how can you escape the condemnation of Gehenna?

The Pharisees will not be able to escape hell. Their "wide" doors lead inexorably to that place. However, they will not prevail over the "narrow" doors of which the "little" Peter holds the keys, despite the fact that Matthew himself (16:21) states:

> From then, Jesus began to explain to his disciples that he had to go to Jerusalem and suffer a lot from the elders, the chief priests and the scribes, and be killed and resurrected on the third day.

If, on the one hand, the "wide" doors of scribes and Pharisees will not prevail over the "narrow" doors of the followers of the messiah, on the other, for a certain period of time, the "wide-great" Pharisees will dramatically prevail over him. At least, during arrest, condemnation and crucifixion of the master of the "little ones".

The custodians of the Law must in every way hinder the disciples of Jesus. One more disciple for the kingdom of heaven would mean one less for them (Mt 23:15):

> Woe to you, scribes and hypocritical Pharisees, who travel the sea and the earth to make one proselyte and, when he has become so, you make him worthy of Gehenna twice more than you.

For Jesus, the Pharisees are "sons of Gehenna". Every new follower they manage to bring into their "wide way" is a "son of Gehenna" twice more. Or, if you prefer, he is a blind man led by another blind man, who will end up in a ditch, like his guide.

Peter, instead, is a disciple of the messiah. He is "small". He has the keys of the "narrow door" and can let in other "small ones". He does not think of the "great" scribes and Pharisees. He knows well that being able to convert a Pharisee to the kingdom would be like passing a camel through the eye of a needle. This is why he focuses his efforts on the "little ones", or on those who want to become like them. Any other attempt would be wasted time (Mt 15:12-14):

> Then the disciples approached him to tell him: «Do you know that the Pharisees, to hear this word, were scandalized?». And he answered: «Every plant, which has not been planted by my heavenly Father, will be uprooted. Leave them alone. They are blind and blind guides. And when one blind man leads another blind man, both will fall into a ditch».

The messiah does not point the finger at the fact that the Pharisees try to procure new disciples: this is part of the normal dialectic between two opposite movements. Rather, he does not tolerate them putting the proverbial tares among his potential followers (Mt 13:24-30):

> The kingdom of heaven is like a man who has sown good seed in his field. But, while everyone was asleep, his enemy came, he sowed weeds [...]. When the stalk grew and bore fruit, the weeds also appeared. [...] «Lord, you have not sown good seed in your field? Where does the weeds come from?». And he answered them: «An enemy has done this». And the servants said to him: «Do you want us to go and collect it?». «No – he replied – so that it does not happen that, gathering the weeds, with it you also uproot the wheat. Let one and the other grow together until the harvest [...] I will tell the reapers: first collect the weeds and tie them in bundles to burn; the grain instead put it back in my barn».

Jesus well knows that the Pharisees do not intend to enter by the "narrow" door. But woe to them, because they try to suffocate, like the weeds, the purposes of those who would do it.

In the light of these considerations, the message conveyed by the imaginative language of a bestiary would seem clear: camels, if they wish, can also swallow their camels. The midges, on the other hand, have to swallow midges. The quadrupeds can take care of their quadrupeds, that is, the blind can also guide the blind. The important thing is that who swallows camels does not put obstacles to who swallows midges. The midges do not interfere in the affairs of those who swallow camels (like the Pharisees):

Leave them. They are blind and guides of the blind.

Therefore, the "great ones" (scribes and Pharisees) can also recruit other "great ones", but they should not try to prevent the "little ones" from taking on other "little ones". The "narrow path" must not be blocked to those who want to enter. This simple concept, made difficult to understand by the parabolic language that has in itself the programmatic intent of veiling the meanings, is reiterated by another proverbial pair of opposites, "the mote and the beam" (Lk 6:41-42; Mt 7:3-5):

Matthew	Luke
Judge not, lest ye be judged; for by the judgment with which ye judge ye shall be judged ye, and by the measure with which ye measure it shall be measured unto you. Why do you look at the mote in your brother's eye, and you don't see the beam in your eye? Or how will you tell your brother: "Let me remove the mote from your eye", while in your eye there is the beam? Hypocrite. First remove the beam from your eye and then you will see well to remove the mote from your brother's eye.	Can a blind man lead another blind man? Won't they both fall into a ditch? A disciple is no more than the master; but each one, who is well prepared, will be like his master. Why do you look at the mote in your brother's eye and not notice the beam in your eye? How can you say to your brother: "Brother, let me remove the mote that is in your eye", while you yourself do not see the beam that is in your eye? Hypocrite. First remove the beam from your eye and then you will see well to remove the mote from your brother's eye.

What is "great" is represented by the camel and the beam. What is "small" by the midge and the mote. One can easily ascertain the close relationship by exchanging the terms:

Blind guides, who filter *the midge* and swallow *the camel*.

↕

Blind guides, who filter *the mote* and swallow *the beam*.

As the one who swallows camels does not resist the temptation to filter midges, so who has "big" eyes so much to host a beam would still want to prevent the mote from entering the "small" eyes. Yet, those accustomed to having beams in their eyes (or camels in their mouths), would already have to deal with such "large" measures, rather than thinking about the "small" measures that others have (motes in the eye or midges in the mouth). Only in one case who has the "big" beam could put a word on the "small" motes of others:

> Remove first the beam from your eye and then you will see well to remove the mote from the eye of your brother.

If the eye is used to "great" things, it will perceive as normal only what is of the same measure. In the same way, those who usually swallow camels will be scandalized by those who swallow midges, and will think to tell them: «Stop swallowing midges!». Beams will be normality, motes the "small" exception confirming the "big-great" rule. Only by first extracting the beam from the eye, renouncing the "big" measure, it is possible to have a say on "small" sizes (motes).

All this is consistent with what is stated in the discourses concerning the kingdom of heaven, to enter into which it is necessary to become "small". If the wood is extracted from the eye, the sight is recovered. Who is accustomed to sifting according to the "camel-beam" measure (that is, who refuses the "small" measure), will be screened with the same criterion: he will be refused. Those who judge according to the "midge-mote" measure (therefore those who do not hinder the "small ones"), will not be refused.

If we remove the beam from the eye, it will inevitably become "smaller". It will have the right vision, not deformed by the "big" beam, but calibrated to the "small" measure. Who judges according to the pair "camel-beam", will be judged according to "greatness". And what is "great" leads to hell.

Who measures with the "big" meter, will be measured with the "big" meter. Big with big. Small with small. There is no chance of dialogue between these measures. The beam cannot judge the mote, unless the judging eye, so far dilated by the beam, shrinks adequately and becomes able to «see clearly» (*anablépo* [ἀναβλέπω]: a verb repeatedly used in several episodes of "healing of the blind", as we will see).

The Pharisees were certainly not only blind, but also guides of the blind. Individuals with beam, who spawned in turn and in large numbers disciples with beam. However, although very remote, there was, also for them, the possibility to remove the wood and see finally clear.

The mote is a scandal to those who have the beam in their eye. As long as you see with a "great-big" eye, the mote in the eye of others will always be an obstacle. To those who do not see in this way, instead, the mote does not bother. "Great" and "small" are antithetical values, like the disciples of John towards those of Jesus: old wineskins (John) that cannot contain new wine (Jesus).

Camel and needle are opposite, but if the camel manages to shrink, the opposition ceases. The "big" has stopped being big, changing to "small".

Now, the camel will not be shocked if a midge passes through the eye. Indeed, also the camel, at the end, will cross it: because has become "small" like the insect previously despised, and now no longer. Likewise, the man who has freed the eye from a beam will certainly not regret a mote. Nor will he wish to remove it from another's eye.

The fact that even behind the combination "beam-mote" there is the duel between the Pharisees and Jesus, is also suggested by the way in which Jesus apostrophes the imaginary interlocutor equipped with a beam (Mt 7:5):

> *Hypocrite.* Remove first the beam from your eye and then you will see well to remove the mote from the eye of your brother.

"Hypocrite" is a word that the messiah prefers to define scribes and Pharisees, and of which Matthew (23:23-29) offers a sufficiently exhaustive sampling:

- Woe to you, scribes and *hypocritical* Pharisees, who pay the tithe on mint, dill and cumin, and transgress the most serious prescriptions of the Law [...]
- *hypocrites*, who clean the outside of the glass and the plate, but inside are full of greed and intemperance [...]
- *hypocrites*, who look like whitewashed sepulchres [...]
- *hypocrites*, who raise up the sepulchres to the prophets and adorn the tombs of the righteous [...]

All this leads to believe that the hypocrite with the beam, intent to remove the mote, corresponds no more or less to the Pharisee who swallows the camel and filters the midge. Nor would the relationship between "the inside of the glass" or of plate and "the outside" seem different. Inside there is the "great" dirt; outside the "small-little" dirt.

As to remove the mote you must first remove the beam, before cleaning the outside of the glass you must clean the inside. First the inside, then the outside. First the beam, then the mote. First the camel, then the midge. First the "big", then the "small". The "small" exists because there is the "great". The "great" hinders the "small", and vice versa. One cannot pretend to remove the "small" before the "great". The "small" is there in opposition to the "big-great" (the dirt "outside" would not be there without the one "inside"). If the "great" one disappears, the "small one" has no more reason to be. If you take off the "great" dirt, also the "small" one goes away (Mt 23:26):

> Blind Pharisee, first clean the glass inside, so that the outside also becomes clean.

Pharisees and their followers are the opposite of Jesus and his followers. Never would the messiah have defined the "little ones" in the same way with which he labeled the Pharisees. He reproached them for exhibiting "great" beams and camels that they could not bear (Mt 23:4):

> They bind heavy and difficult burdens and place them on people's shoulders, but they do not want to move them even with a finger.

This verse, if it is not yet sufficiently evident, brings us back once again to the semantic area of "greatness". In Jesus' opinion, the Pharisees do not really want to carry those burdens at all, but strive to do so (after all, it could not be otherwise: to be observant of a set of 613 rules it will take a lot of effort).

At the end of the routes among the couples "camel-eye", "camel-midge", "mote-beam", we become even more aware that the comparisons made by Jesus don't express maxims detached from the context in which the messiah worked, universally shared in all areas of human action and at all times. On the contrary, similarities and metaphors communicate precise teachings, arising from equally precise (and unrepeatable) social, doctrinal, historical contexts to which they are linked; and without which we would not have had "large-great" camels and beams, nor "small" midges and motes.

If there were not a precise dialectic to anchor these hyperbolic comparisons to a peculiar context, and they were only examples of virtues to be exalted (innocence) and vices to be abhorred (hypocrisy), there would be no difference between what Jesus said and what was asserted by countless men, more or less wise, of every time, in every corner of the world.

The protagonist of the Gospels, trying in every way to inculcate in disciples and crowds his teaching, behaves in a manner not unlike that of a fabulist who invents a thousand different stories, to always reiterate an identical moral: if you do not want to end up eaten by the wolf (perdition or Gehenna), it is better not to pass in the woods but take another road: maybe more "narrow" and tiring to travel, but that guarantees salvation ("eternal life").

As Gotthold Lessing wrote in his essays about the fairy tale, this literary genre does not aim to involve the recipient by touching the deep chords of feelings. Instead, its objective is to solicit the intellectual faculties («who has ears to hear, may he understand»), wanting to convince the reader of what is an objective and recognizable truth. In the same way acts who, instead of fairy tales, conceives stories interwoven with similarities or parables: the intent is always to convey something that coincides with the proverbial "moral of the story".

In addition to this, the static framework of the parables of Jesus has in common with the fable the predominance of roles over characters. Proof of this are the same titles with which these parables were disclosed ("the sower", "the weeds", "the two sons", "the bad winemakers", "the prodigal son", "the lost sheep", "the two debtors", "the servant and the master", "the workers of the vineyard", "the Pharisee and the publican", etc.). They are all characters who have no value in and of themselves. It matters what their actions connotes. It is not essential "who they are". It is essential "what they do".

"Greatness" of John, "smallness" of Jesus

From the fierce contention between "great ones" and "small ones", of which the Gospel story is drenched, it would seem logical to deduce that the "great" John, despite being the precursor of the messiah, strangely had as a qualification (recognized by Jesus himself) what the son of God himself abhorred: being "great". The Baptist had opposite merits to the ideal disciple of the messiah (who was to be absolutely "small" and pass through the "narrow" door). We now imagine, absurdly, that John had never been killed by Herod, as written in the Gospels. Given the "great *vs* small" opposition, we ask ourselves:

- if the Baptist, the "great", had remained alive, would have entered the kingdom announced by Jesus?

- would he be willing to become "small" as Jesus asked? To pass through the "narrow door"?
- or would he have preferred, being he "great", the "wide" route?
- would he have wanted, even at the cost of becoming "crippled, lame or blind", to take the "narrow path"?

Matthew would seem to answer this last question negatively. Jesus gives priority to all the "little ones" as the addressees of his teaching. This fact would seem to surprise John: he evidently expected from the messiah a different operating mode; a mode suitable for the "great ones", as he was, according to a "greatness" that he expected was obvious prerogative of the messiah. A "great" precursor necessarily had to spend his forces for a successor who was "great" like him. But no: the reference value, for the messiah, is "smallness". And not the Johannine "greatness" (Mt 11:2-6):

> John, who was in prison, having heard about the works of Christ, through his disciples sent to tell him: «Are you the one who must come or must we wait for another?» [...] «Go and tell John what you hear and see: the blind regain their sight, the lame walk, the lepers are purified, the deaf hear, the dead rise again, the good news is proclaimed to the poor. And blessed is he who does not find in me cause for scandal».

The Baptist sends his disciples (incomprehensibly from prison: could he therefore count on preferential treatment?) to ask Jesus if he is himself «the one who must come». Evidently, John sees in his action an obstacle (*skàndalon*). What the messiah does "scandalizes" him. He always though in a "great" way and how the "great ones" think. Jesus, instead, think in a "small" way. Using a banal but effective example, this would be tantamount to saying that a "great" long-time politician, who sponsors and supports the candidacy of a young colleague, discovers only after finishing a long and exhausting election campaign in his favor that the young man is actually the leading exponent of the opposing political group.

The words «blessed he who is not scandalized by me» show precisely how John was not blessed: the Baptist, the precursor of the "good news", who, however, strangely is scandalized by the same "good news"; which is addressed, by statute and programmatic intent, to all the "small ones". That is, to those who are not "great" as instead John is. If the Baptist (from prison) even goes so far as to send his followers to ask Jesus if he is the long-awaited messiah, then he strongly doubts it. The son of God, in fact, does things that John did not expect and that fall within the usual semantic area of "smallness". Jesus heals the sick: blind ("small" relative to sight); crippled ("small" relative to limbs); lepers ("small" relative to skin health); deaf ("small" relative to hearing). He heals also the dead ("small" in respect to life); the poor ("small" relative to wealth).

Healing the sick, raising the dead

The thread that binds all the categories that we have listed is, with all evidence, that represented by lack; deprivation; abnormality; disadvantage; conversely to fullness; abundance; normality; advantageousness; "greatness". It is those sick people who "heal"; who "rise again" (or, with a much freer translation to which we have been much more accustomed, "who are resurrected"). In summary, it is those "sick" who are the recipients of the "good news".

In the passage of Matthew that we have seen, we find a reformulation of the concepts expressed in the famous "beatitudes" in a different literary form. Blessed, then, are the blind; the crippled; the lepers; the deaf; the poor. Woe to those who have both eyes, limbs and ears. Woe to those who are "alive" and therefore cannot, like the "dead", be "raised". Finally, woe to the rich: with their load of goods, they cannot cross the "narrow door".

All these words are united by one concept: the lack of something. In the tight, pounding succession of these categories of disabled people we also find the "dead":

- are these "dead" perhaps people no longer alive?
- are the "blind" ones people who have no use of sight?
- the "deaf", individuals with no hearing?
- are the "crippled" men and women disabled in their limbs?
- are lepers human beings who have contracted leprosy?

In the case of the "dead", it would be a total deprivation. However, precisely this consideration leads one to think that a definitive condition such as death is linked to physical impairments because the word "dead" does not here indicate deceased individuals; to the exact extent that the adjective "small" does not indicate people of low stature, slim build or few years old.

Likewise, in order to "rise again" or "wake up" is not strictly necessary to be corpses. The word "dead", in its profound harshness, is there to signal that its value among impairments has the same weight as the other words. They all fall into one category, and always in the semantic area of "smallness-reduction": the indispensable, tiring, risky "reduction" that however guarantees "entry into life".

They are the "reduced in sight" those who will see fully; the "reduced in hearing" those who will fully hear; the "reduced in limbs" those who will walk without crutches; the lifeless, those who will have abundant life; the "reduced" in terms of wealth and substances, those who will be rich.

They are all deafening variants of the usual, pounding chorus: the drawback will bring an advantageous magnitude. Who becomes "small" will have the fate of the proverbial turtle that competes with Achilles, who has a fast foot. As much as he is a "great" hero, the "little" animal will have a "great" advantage over Achilles. And will triumph over him.

Let us also admit now the case that Matthew literally speaks of blind men, cripples, lame, lepers, deaf, dead. We ask ourselves:
- why should John, knowing that Jesus was healing the sick and raising corpses, have been scandalized?

- if healings and resurrections were proof of the divinity of the Christ, for what absurd reason the Baptist should have asked Jesus "are you the true messiah?"?
- were not enough evidences thaumaturgies and return to life from physical death?
- shouldn't the forerunner have rejoiced, if all these had been real miracles?

At this point, either the contradictions are admitted without explaining them; or we take into consideration the hypothesis that blind, crippled, lame, deaf, lepers, dead are anything but. Instead, these words indicate a specific category of people, whom Jesus held in great esteem to make disciples. While John did not. He is excessively "great" to understand the mysteries of the kingdom (Lk 10:21 and 12:32):

> I praise you, Father, Lord of heaven and earth, because you hid these things *from the wise and learned* and revealed them to the *little ones* [...] Fear not, *little* flock, because your Father liked to give you the kingdom.

It is crystal clear from the text that the elect recipients of the "good news" of the kingdom are the "little ones". And not the wise and learned. "Blind, crippled, lame" know things that the latter cannot know. Jesus repeatedly affirms that he did not come for this category of persons (the righteous observants of the Law), but for sinners; that is, the conscious transgressors of the Law (Mk 2:15-17):

> Many tax collectors and sinners were at table with Jesus [...] Then the scribes of the Pharisees [...] said to his disciples: «Why does he eat and drink with tax collectors and sinners?» [...] Jesus said to them: «It is not the *healthy* who need the doctor, but the *sick*; I have not come to call the *righteous*, but *sinners*».

It is not difficult to understand the proportion expressed by the metaphor:

$$\text{healthy} : \textit{righteous} = \text{sick} : \textit{sinner}$$

The healthy are related to the righteous as the sick are related to sinners. I say "healthy" but I mean " righteous"; I say "sick" but I mean "transgressor of the Law".

The protagonist of the Gospels uses a word belonging to a precise semantic area (the health of the body) to convey a meaning belonging to another semantic area (the observance of the Law). Thus, he who is healthy belongs to the area of health, as he who is righteous to that of the Law. In the same way, the sick is related to the sphere of health as the sinner is related to that of the Law.

It is these important textual spies that make us legitimately assume that, if the adjective "healthy" is used to mean "observant of the Law", and "sick" to mean "transgressor of the Law", then according to the same procedure the adjective "small", which literally translated would not satisfy any logical sense, must indicate a precise concept that, as in previous cases, is *outside* its semantic area of reference.

So, I say "healthy" but I mean "observant of the Law"; I say "sick" but I mean "transgressor of the Law". Then, when I say "small" and "least" I will mean something other than the usual meaning of such words. I will want to convey a meaning that I attribute to that precise term, which for me (and for all those to whom I want to make it known) will acquire a peculiar sense, based on an exclusive communicative code that I and I alone establish and possibly share. So,

- when the messiah "heals", does he perform miracles or is he rehabilitating transgressors of the Law?
- which of the two options is most supported by elements within the text?

One cannot be sure that Matthew really tells of individuals who regain the health of the body, and of dead people who begin to live again in the flesh. However, there is textual certainty that the messiah calls "healthy" the observants of the Law; and "sick" the transgressors, comparing himself to a doctor who takes care of them. Jesus is like a doctor who treats the sick and not the healthy. He takes care of the transgressors of the Law and not of the observants.

Mark (2:3-12) reports a very significant episode, not by chance immediately preceding the statement «it is not the healthy who need the doctor, but the sick; I have not come to call the righteous, but sinners»:

> They went to him carrying a paralytic [...] Jesus, seeing their faith, said to the paralytic: «Son, your sins are forgiven». There sat some scribes [...] «Why does he speak so? Blasphemy. Who can forgive sins, if not God alone?» [...] He said to them, «Why do you think these things? [...] what is easier? To say to the paralytic "Your sins are forgiven", or to say "Rise, take your stretcher and walk"? Now, that you may know that the Son of man has the power to forgive sins, I say to you [...] get up, take your stretcher and go to your home». He got up [...] before everyone's eyes and left.

The equivalence between the *forgiveness of sins* and the *healing of the sick* is clear. Jesus remits the sins of the transgressor, who is a cripple. We ask ourselves:

- is it by chance that, in this episode, the *transgressor* of the Law is also a *sick* person?
- if the observants do not need "doctors" while the transgressors do, would a law-abiding ("righteous") cripple be healed?

In our opinion, the answer is no and it is Jesus himself who explains the reasons:

> It is not the healthy who need the doctor, but the sick; I have not come to call the righteous, but sinners.

A righteous cripple would not be healed. The righteous cannot be sick. It would be as if a righteous were a sinner. Either one, or the other. An observant cannot be a transgressor. If he observes the Law, he does not transgress it. Therefore, sins cannot be forgiven him: he does not commit sins. He is like a *healthy* man. He cannot be healed:

he has no diseases. Those to whom sins are forgiven are like sick people who are healed:

> Son, your sins are forgiven [...] get up, take your stretcher and go to your house.

Forgiveness of transgressions is healing from an illness: that is, *it coincides* with healing. Condoning *is* healing. Forgiving a sinner *is* healing a sick person.

Absolutely in line with this equivalence – which Mark himself attributes to Jesus – is the drafting of this episode, in which a transgressor of the Law, to whom the faults are forgiven, is a paralytic who gets up and walks. The first statement ("I have come for sinners") generates the story with which the second one is expressed ("I have come for the sick"). Forgiveness is related to healing like sins are related to illness. Matthew does nothing but make Jesus the protagonist of the metaphor the messiah himself coined. He forgives the transgressor and treats the sick. What was a simple metaphorical comparison (forgiveness *is like* healing), becomes concrete fact in the story: and the metaphor generates the miracle. Healing the sick is not easier than forgiving his sins, nor more difficult. It is the same thing. It is an effort equal to the remission of sins, thus reconfirming the value of the similarity from which we started.

In numerous episodes of the Gospels, Jesus is described as a healer of the most disparate sufferers. Similarly, it is clearly stated in the text that for him the "healthy" are the righteous and the "sick" are sinners. Since Matthew reports that the messiah responded to the "scandalized" John, saying «the blind regain their sight, the lame walk, lepers are purified, the deaf hear», it follows – according to the equation "sick = sinner" – that all these are "sick"; or sinners; or violators of the Law. Jesus is dedicated to them: he is the doctor who cannot call to himself the "healthy-righteous", as John did.

The latter, a "healthy-righteous" son of blameless "healthy-righteous" who did not need any doctor, could not but be scandalized. The reason is simple: he did not have the basic requirements to be among the followers chosen by Jesus. He was "great": the opposite of the "little ones". The "little ones" were opposed to the wise and learned. It follows that John was wise and learned (with regard to the Law).

For this reason, he finds an obstacle in Jesus: the one who reveals the mysteries to the "little ones" or to his "little flock": so defined by Luke not because the sheep that form the flock are necessarily few (the evangelists also speak of crowds of followers), but because it is made up of disciples who are "small-little" as Jesus wants. And not "great" as John expected (Lk 12:32):

Fear not, little flock, because your Father liked to give you the Kingdom.

"To give you": you, "little ones". And not others. You crippled, blind, lame, deaf; and not healthy. The fact that wise and learned people were of cultural, social and doctrinal background close to the Baptist and his disciples, is shown by the passage in which it is said that the Pharisees and followers of John fasted together (Mt 9:14-17); unlike the "little ones", who did not fast at all. The followers of John adhere to protocols identical to those of the reviled scholars of the Law (Mt 9:14-17):

John's disciples approached him and told him: «Why do we and the Pharisees fast many times, while your disciples do not fast?». And Jesus said to them, «Can the wedding guests mourn while the bridegroom is with them? [...] Nobody puts a piece of raw cloth on an old-fashioned dress, because the patch takes away something from the dress and the tear becomes worse. No new wine is poured into old wineskins, otherwise the wineskins are broken and the wine is spread and the wineskins are lost. But new wine is poured into new wineskins, and so the one and the others are preserved».

The disciples of the Baptist are compared to old wineskins that cannot contain the new wine of the "good news". Despite the severity and hardness of the statement is mitigated by the use of metaphors, the concept expressed flows out of the text. As the wine that breaks the wineskins.

The doctrine of Jesus is incompatible with that of John. His disciples cannot receive it. If they try, they will split inside them, like the old wineskins. It would not be helpful. The "change of mind" (*metànoia*) would not take root: it would be wasted wine (and wasted time). Better to pour new wine in uncut wineskins; to spread the fresh doctrine among new followers. No longer "old" and "great" followers, but "new", "young" or "small":

new wineskins: *small disciples* of Jesus = *old* wineskins : *great disciples* of John

The new wineskins are related to the "little" disciples of Jesus as the old wineskins are related to the "great" disciples of John. The new (Jesus) is better than the old (John). This is how Luke expresses himself (Lk 5:36):

> No one tears a piece from a new cloak and sews it on an old cloak. If he does, the new cloak will be torn, and the piece from it will not match that of the old.

A piece of "small" and "new" cloth – literally «raw» (*àgnafos*), still unused – cannot be forcibly sewn on a "large-great" portion of cloth, on an inexorably "old" dress:

new cloth : "*small* ones" = *old* fabric : *disciples of John*

The "new" cloth is related to the "little ones" like the "old-great" fabric is related to John's disciples. In the Greek text, the verb translated with the words «it will not match» is *symfonèsei* (from the verb συμφωνέω, clearly related to the word "symphony"). The patch taken from what is "new" is not *consonant* with the "old". John and Jesus do not play the same music. This is a concept that Luke reiterates with the parable of the wineskins, adding something that Matthew had not specified (Lk 5:38-39):

> The new wine must be poured into new wineskins. No one who drinks the old wine desires the new, because he says: "The old is pleasant".

Those who are used to drinking "old" wine, will not desire the "new" one, because they will say:

- we know the "old" wine and we have always liked it, why should we *change*?
- why should "new" wine (or "small-young") be better than the "old" (or "great")? For many years we drink the usual wine and we have always had a great time.

Expressing ourselves outside the parabolic language, we will say: it is impossible that the "old-great ones" wish to change their mind (*metànoia*) and switch from the "old" to the "new". Similitude has no other purpose than to exemplify, through concrete images (changing wine), the immaterial *metànoia* (changing thought or idea). It is about changing doctrine and teacher. Virgin disciples are needed: "new" and "small" ones, who have never been "great" adhering to other doctrines before the "good news".

Literary aspects of the Gospel text

Deepening the level of analysis, we can ask ourselves from which areas originate bloody examples such as those of the foot and the hand to be amputated, or the eye to be blinded.

The invitation of Jesus to deprive oneself of limbs or eyes can only appear to the reader as an inexplicable, violent absurdity: with as much violence, it clashes with the meekness universally attributed to the protagonist of the Gospels. If, instead, we trace the expressions "cut off the hand", "cut off the foot", "gouge out the eye" *to the effects* of such actions, we get the following words:

- "maimed";
- "lame";
- "blind".

This is how one must be to "enter into life". Neither more nor less than what Matthew himself (11:5) writes:

> The blind regain their sight, the lame walk, the lepers are purified, the deaf hear, the dead rise.

"Blind", "maimed" and "lame" have a quality that the able-bodied don't have. That is, they have something *less*. They are "smaller". "Smaller" than the others. This something *less*, still vague and not well specified, guarantees an additional advantage: "the entrance into life". They are privileged with respect to all the other categories. They are sick who can be healed by a doctor exclusively: Jesus.

Without resorting to the notion of the literary quality of a text, it is difficult to understand the reasons for the protagonist's insistence on the words "blind", "maimed", "lame", "leper". The systematic redundancy of these lexical areas allows to study the text in its structural system, highlighting the key aspects. The message of the synoptic Gospels has a tight, inflexible, very logical coherence all within the text, revealed by it and strongly legitimized. It is necessary to know the communicative code in which the text is written, and how it is used. In fact, terms can be charged with a meaning that goes beyond the literal one, making the message richer and more complex (the so-called connotative level of the text).

The verse «if your hand or your foot is cause for scandal, cut it off and throw it away from you» represents the denotative (literal) level. However, it does not comply with the requirement of logical consistency. It remains obscure to the reader the reason why depriving oneself of a limb should guarantee "entry into life".

Since the sender of the message intended to give precise warnings and operating instructions, it is very likely that those words are written in accordance with a communicative code that goes beyond the superficial denotative level, to arrive at a connotative level accessible only to those who know (or «have ears to understand») the code that is being used. Only by decrypting it, will the words be loaded with meanings that, overcoming the level of the letter (level of total illogicality: deprivation of limbs and eyes), will come to an equally total and desidered logical coherence of the text.

Otherwise, we should understand that in every village or city he visited, Jesus preferably healed the blind, the maimed, the lame, the lepers; bringing back, if necessary, to a daily life lived in flesh and blood, corpses of human beings. However, the internal communicative code of the synoptic Gospels is used in such a way that the meaning of the words used is not denotative (sick = people with health problems), but connotative (sick = sinners, that is, violators of the Mosaic Law). It is one thing to have pathologies of any nature. Quite another to be transgressors of norms.

A dialogue between texts: Gehenna or the hell

Concerning the coded language of the parables, Matthew (15:15-16) refers to a significant dialogue between Jesus and Peter:

> Then Peter said to him: «Explain us this parable». And he answered: «Are you not yet able to understand?».

In the Greek text, the messiah is even harder: «Are you still *without intellect*?». Evidently, not of heart or spirit you are talking. Peter does not yet fully govern the communicative modalities of his master. It is not easy to possess them, in their entirety. This is why Jesus often makes exhortations aimed at stimulating understanding:

1. «Who has ears to hear, may he understand»;
2. «Therefore, *listen to* the parable of the sower»;
3. «*Listen* to me all and *understand* well»;
4. «Pay *attention to what you listen*»;
5. «Don't you *understand* yet and don't you *comprehend*?»

In the Gospels the function of the language most present is undoubtedly the poetic one (or "aesthetic"), in which the emphasis is placed on the message. It is exercised when you want to produce a stylistically effective statement, out of the ordinary and common language. It is enough to note the large number of similarities through which the parables are built, to realize the frequency of use. Jesus draws from it very often. An effective example is the one containing the image of the "inextinguishable fire", which refers to an extremely harsh punishment: being thrown into Gehenna. That is, to be burned.

The word "Gehenna" (in Hebrew *gē ben Hinnōm*) derives from the name of a valley southwest of Jerusalem (today's Wādī er-Rabābī), marked with anathema by king Josiah for having become the seat of the cult of Moloch: a deity that required to burn children slaughtered, for burnt offering.

The precise place where such rites were performed was called Tofet (Gr 7:31). Gehenna was later used as a collection point for human corpses that were subsequently burned, such as those of men who had fought against Israel (Is 30:33). The valley was then used as a landfill of the city's waste, which was combusted to destroy the remains and not to fail basic hygiene measures.

For all the reasons listed, the expression «to be thrown into Gehenna» must have been sufficiently explicit at the time of Jesus, especially if one takes into account what was written by Jeremiah (Jr 7:32), a prophet active in the kingdom of Judah between 626 and 586 BC:

> They built the heights of Topheth in the valley of Ben-Innòm, to burn
> their sons and daughters in the fire, something that I had never command-

ed [...] days will come [...] in which it will no longer be called Topheth nor Ben-Innòm valley, but Valley of the Massacre [...] The corpses of this people will be feed to the birds of the air and to the beasts of the earth [...] I will stop in the cities of Judah [...] the songs of joy and happiness [...] the earth will become a desert.

The imagery about Gehenna would seem clear several centuries before Jesus. Nevertheless, in Mark we will see the protagonist of the Gospels resort to the unprecedented frame of the "insatiable worm". Which is not exactly unprecedented. Isaiah had already spoken about it, around five centuries before the messiah quoted it, making it his own, in Mark. As in Jeremiah, also in Isaiah Yahweh makes known with severe admonition the fate of those who rebel against his will (Is 66:23-24):

> In every month to the new moon, and to the Sabbath of every week, every-one will come to prostrate before me, the Lord says. Going out, they will see the corpses of the men who have rebelled against me; since their worm will not die, their fire will not be extinguished and they will be an abomination for all.

An element common to Jeremiah and Isaiah is that relating to the dead violently: in fact, corpses appear in both narratives. However, Gehenna is explicitly mentioned only in Jeremiah. In Isaiah it is written simply that those who will prostrate themselves before Yahweh, will express obedience and submission to him; and they will see, with their own eyes, those who instead have rebelled end up dead and not cease to burn. Nor be devoured by worms.

In this case, the literary quality of the text consists, above all, in a precise relationship of "intertextuality": that is, the manifest presence of a text within another text (citation – with or without indication of the source from which it is quoted – or even allusion):

Isaiah (66:24)	Mark (9:47-48)
They shall see the corpses of the men who have rebelled against me: for their worm shall not die, their fire shall not be extinguishe*d*.	It is better for you to enter into the kingdom of God with one eye, than with two eyes to be thrown into Gehenna, where their worm does not die and the fire is not extinguished.

Text A (Isaiah) is incorporated in text B (Mark). The chronologically later one (Mark) is derived from an earlier one (Isaiah), by means of a procedure that can be amalgam, transformation or imitation. In this case, it is amalgam. Isaiah writes «for their worm shall not die, their fire shall not be extinguished»; Mark writes «where their worm does not die and the fire is not extinguished».

The evangelist neither transforms nor imitates the Isaiah verses. He slavishly quotes them by amalgamating them into his writing. Isaiah writes «for their worm»; Mark «where» – in the place where – their worm». This is the only deviation from the source from which Mark draws.

The quotation, taken from the imposing Old Testament, is immediately recognizable: "insatiable worm" and "inextinguishable fire" come from Isaiah. There is an undoubted dialogue between two authors. One could conclude that Jesus knew Isaiah and knowingly quoted him. Or, it was Mark who knew Isaiah, and very well: he would have put the verses of Isaiah in the mouth of him who in his Gospel speaks these words.

In this case, the author would have liked to clarify with more detail, relying on an authoritative Old Testament source, what Jesus perhaps expressed, more narrowly, with his words. Gouging out an eye is better than not to be blind and being thrown into a place called Gehenna, «where *their* worm does not die». The reader of the Gospels – who does not know Isaiah – may wonder:

- the adjective "their" ("*their* worm") to whom is it referred?
- the worm "of what" or "of whom"?
- what link between the worm in the verse and the need to gouge out one's eyes?

Everything becomes clearer if we consider the hypothesis that there may be an intertextuality. We will then understand that Mark's worm comes, through a centuries-old journey, from Isaiah. And it is directly linked to human corpses. Jesus speaks of an inexorable punishment that will be meted out to men who will become like the corpses of Isaiah:

> They shall see the corpses of the men who *have rebelled against me*: for their worm shall not die, their fire shall not be extinguished.

Precisely the adjective "their" suggests that in Mark there is a quotation from Isaiah, in which we find this word referring not to a part of the body (the eyes), but to corpses of human beings, all whole.

All this shows how it is always appropriate to consider the text not as a meteorite precipitated from the sky randomly, but as the possible result of different stratifications. It is in them that the verse of Mark we have examined acquires fullness of meaning.

Inclusion and exclusion

Having examined the relationship between Mark and Isaiah, we ask ourselves: would we be able to draw, from the synoptic text only, the precise meaning of the urgent need to become "blind", "maimed" or "lame"?

The answer is no, to the extent that Mark's worm was not enough to make us understand that Jesus – quoting Isaiah – was talking about human corpses.

The invitation to voluntarily deprive oneself of a limb or eye could be better understood by assuming that it is an intertextuality with the Old Testament. If in the puzzle of the New Testament there is a tile that falls by force among the others, perhaps it actually belongs to the Old Testament.

Mentioning in a precise order equally precise categories of impaired, the protagonist of the Gospels does nothing but establish a relationship with the Old Testament or – as the messiah says – with "the Law and the Prophets": that is, the whole Bible before the "good news". Here, in many passages, we speak of blind, maimed, lame, deaf, lepers. They are real maimed, unwelcome to Yahweh for specific reasons (Lv 21:16-23):

> And the Lord said to Moses, «Speak to Aaron, saying [...] no man of your race who has any deformity can approach to offer the bread of his God [...] neither a blind nor a lame nor a scarred nor a deformed [...] neither a hunchback nor a dwarf nor anyone who has [...] scabies or purulent sores or crushed testicles. No man of the lineage of the priest Aaron, with any deformity, shall come near to present the sacrifices made by fire in honour of the Lord. He has a defect: he must not therefore come close to offer the bread of his God [...] he will not be able to approach the veil or approach the altar, because he has a deformity.

It is inevitable to find assonances between the crippled ones of which Jesus speaks and the list of Leviticus. It is a comparison that can substantiate the bloody statements of the messiah with more acceptable logic. Also in this case, a text A (Leviticus 21) is present within a text B (synoptic Gospels); one portion of text is derived from another, chronologically earlier.

Blind, maimed and lame would seem slavishly quoted by Jesus. It is complicated to exclude *a priori* the hypothesis that they – always present in the discourses of the son of the Old Testament God – are sons (from the textual point of view) of the blind, the maimed and the lame of the same Old Testament God. And nothing else.

The fact that the evangelists have established such a strong conceptual bridge with such distant texts, shows that the bond is very close and not only formal. These words appear in succession in both texts. They are emphasized with great force by the messiah. The insistent frequency (with fixed formula: "blind crippled lame") induces to consider the quotation anything but random.

It is now appropriate to investigate whether the passages in question produce a perfect identity with Leviticus 21; or vice versa, a deviation from it. Certainly, from the text it emerges that Yahweh and Jesus, towards the handicapped, have opposite behaviors. The Father excludes. The Son includes:

Yahweh	Jesus
No man who has any deformity can approach: neither a blind man nor a lame man [...] No man [...] with any deformity will come near to present the sacrifices [...] He has a defect: he must not therefore come close to offer the bread of his God.	*It is better* for you to enter into life *maimed or lame*, rather than with two hands or two feet being thrown into the fire [...] if your eye is cause for scandal, gouge out your eye [...] *better for you to enter life with one eye.*

The formal consonance between the two texts (the words "blind", "maimed" and "lame") corresponds to a complete dissonance of the contents.

In Leviticus, the Father (Yahweh) forbids any handicapped person to offer sacrifices or the bread of God. In the Gospels, the Son (Jesus) affirms not only that those who have disabilities are privileged (the blind are those who see, the lame are those who walk...); he even says that, in the absence of them, it would be desirable to obtain disabilities. It would behoove.

Recurring words, seemingly without a specific cause, have instead a very specific weight within a text (the synoptic Gospels) whose conceptual economy is understandable only if it is compared with that work (Old Testament) without which the New would never have seen the light.

If one wants to understand how much the son resembles (or differs from) the Father, it will be necessary to examine the features of the Father, and compare them with those of the son. If for the latter blind, cripples and lame were even worthy of "entering into life", they certainly should not have had any particular problems to approach the inner parts of the temple, where sacrifices were offered to the Father. Instead, he categorically forbade them entry. Priestly service was possible only to "healthy" able-bodied.

Moreover, in Leviticus we read (Lv 22:18-20):

> Anyone of the house of Israel or of foreigners [...] will present his offer [...] must offer a male, without defect, of cattle, sheep or goats. You will not offer anything with some defect, because it would not be appreciated.

Disability, in all its types, certainly excluded. If you are a cripple, surely you do not enter. Then, a radical, unexpected 360-degree reversal happens, thanks to him who should be the son of Yahweh. The essential condition for inclusion (not to have impairments) loses the value that Yahweh had imposed on it. It flips over. Only if you are maimed, then you enter "life". And if you are not maimed, become so, if you want to enter.

This excruciating opposition between the Old and New Testament emerges with great objectivity from the text. What should be the "completion", the perfect confirmation of the Father's word, seems instead to convey the most radical reversal of perspective.

However,

- when Jesus refers to "blind, crippled and lame", does he mean what Yahweh meant?
- are these true disabilities (both according to Yahweh and Jesus)?
- or does Jesus use those sequences of terms to talk about something else?

In the case of the Father, a symbolic or allegorical reading would clash with the evidence that the same kind of treatment was reserved for animals (Lv 22:22-25):

> You will not present [...] any blind or crippled or mutilated victim [...] A large or small head of cattle that is deformed or atrophied [...] will not be appreciated as a votive sacrifice. You shall not offer to the Lord an animal with bruised testicles, or torn or cut [...] nor will you take from the hands of the stranger any of these victims to offer it [...].

Therefore, the fact that animals with defects could not be sacrificed, of what should be allegory or symbol? Simply, the physical defect and impairment in the flesh of men and animals was not pleasing to Yahweh.

The discourse radically changes if Jesus speaks about these categories. He cites them with punctuality, creating an undeniable connection with Leviticus. It now remains to be understood whether the formal bridge (the quotation) is established by the messiah to maintain bridges with the Father. Or to sever them permanently.

The Old Testament in several places seems to be repudiated by the New. Jesus seems to quote the Old (the Father), but to distance himself from it: because, in the Gospels, the text is governed not by categories themselves ("blind, maimed, lame"), but by the concept they represent: exclusion. A concept that is rooted in the semantic area of "smallness" (here related to the disease of the body).

Blind, maimed, lame, sinners

As in the case of camels, beams, midges and motes, there are good reasons to believe that the messiah is not at all commanding his auditors to cut off their limbs, or blind themselves. More simply, he tries to convince them to belong to the exclusion area. That he flips into inclusion.

The excluded of the Old Testament become for him the included par excellence, the model («better for you to be blind or lame») to imitate to "enter life":

> It is not the healthy who need the doctor, but the sick. I have not come in fact to call the righteous, but the sinners.

The communicative code with which the first sentence is expressed ("not the healthy, but the sick") is revealed immediately afterwards *by the same author of the message* ("not for the righteous, but for sinners").

The words "not the healthy but the sick" lose any literal efficacy, to be annulled by the following ("not the righteous, but the sinners").

Some other observation could be made about the use (disruptive) of formulas of sure impact, and very little ascribable to meekness, such as «better for him if a millstone was tied to his neck», «it is better for you to enter life with one eye, rather than with two eyes to be thrown into the Gehenna of fire», and the like.

It is legitimate to ask oneself in what kind of language these formulas would be placed, or how they would be defined by any reader, especially if followed by sentences such as «instead of being thrown into the fire», and so on enumerating. Of course, who pronounced them wanted to emphasize that precisely the categories excluded by Yahweh would be included. What in the Old Testament is mere chronicle (entrance forbidden to cripples and sick), in the New is reused literary in order to maintain with the Old Testament a formal consonance. But not substantial.

For Jesus the "sick" indicate *the transgressors of the Law of the Father*, on whose obedience the covenant with the Jewish people was founded. If it is correct, and respectful of the text, to say that Jesus came for sinners, it is also correct to say that he came for the blind: since the messiah himself says that the sick need the doctor, and he came for them.

Nevertheless, in some passages he urges those who are not blind to become so. However, if he came for the blind, it is assumed that this is to restore their sight. Therefore, having two eyes should represent an absolute and indispensable value. Yet, Jesus affirms that to "enter into life" it is absolutely necessary to blind oneself: how can such statements coexist, the opposite of each other?

Answering this question with formulas such as "it is a mystery" or "it is an unfathomable language", would make vain the purposes that the text has: among all, that of being understood.

Even the reader less interested in the subject would notice not only that some pieces of the Gospel mosaic are beginning to break up, but that some have never been well embedded. It has always been taken for granted they were, as it is assumed that in a song there are no dissonant notes. Until you listen to it well, and finally realize, perhaps with astonishment, the opposite.

"Jesus came to give sight to the blind" has become a proverbial expression. Not so much the exhortation to blind oneself as the only condition for "entering life". The contents remain firmly rooted in the usual concepts: "smallness" is advantageous, "greatness-fullness" is not.

If one can rightly believe that two eyes are better than one, the opposite is true for Jesus: one eye is better than two. This is, in different guises, the usual opposition between "small" and "great". From size ("small-large") you get a transition to quantity (two eyes-one eye). Instead of saying that it is necessary to become "small" to enter the kingdom, one will say that it is better to take out one eye, than to keep two and be burned in Gehenna.

Therefore, if Jesus asked his potential followers to become blind in order to enter the kingdom, evidently he gave the sight to those who voluntarily became blind; or to those who were already "blind" ("small" in relation to sight) and did not need to become so.

Now let's compare the following sentences:

a) if you are blind *you will enter the kingdom*;

b) if you are blind *you will have sight*.

In the Gospels, blindness is a disadvantage that yields a great advantage (the "sight"): and not an unfortunate handicap to be cured. If this were the case, being blind as a requirement for entry into the kingdom would never have had reason to be in Jesus' exhortations. Instead, it is the condition for entering. Only the blind can get sight. Therefore, the concepts expressed with the formulas "to enter the kingdom" and "to have sight" are equivalent. The sight (blind), the hands (maimed), the legs (lame), the hearing (deaf): these are all advantages that can have only those who are deprived. Deprived of something that is stubbornly hidden behind the communicative code with which the Gospels were written.

For example, we take two sentences:

a)   he who *loses his life will keep it for eternal life*;

b)   he who *loses his eye shall see.*

Formal assonances may hide a conceptual link. And it is precisely the fact that the message extender is transmitting the same meaning, that forces him to a variation in the form in which the message is written. If it were not so, all the parables of the Gospels would be reduced to only one.

As we know, for the followers of Jesus the deprivation of something has a precise purpose: the obtaining of something more abundant (Mt 16:24-25):

> Whoever wants to be my disciple must deny themselves and take up their cross and follow me. For whoever wants to save their life will lose it, but whoever loses their life for me will find it.

In the Gospel of John we read (12:25):

> Who loves his own life, loses it and who hates his own life in this world, will keep it for eternal life.

Similarly, in the phrase «better for you to enter life with one eye» there is a simple variation: instead of "losing life", we find "losing an eye". The consequence of such actions remains unchanged: "eternal life", "the entrance into life". Whoever loses life, will have it more abundant. He who loses his sight, will have more. For this reason, the sighted must become blind. Only the blind or those who have lost sight can see.

This concept is, with astonishing clarity and simplicity, expressed in the fourth Gospel, in the episode of the "blind from birth" (Jn 9:39-41):

> «It is for a judgment that I have come to this world, so that those who do not see, may see and those who see, become blind». Some of the Pharisees [...] told him: «Are we blind too?». Jesus answered them: «If you were blind, you would have no sin; but since you say: We see, your sin remains».

Leaving aside the fact that here the protagonist of the Gospels claims to have come to judge, while in another passage (Jn 12:47) he expressly denies it («I did not come to judge the world, but to save the world»), let us focus on an aspect now more important. The messiah says he has come so that those who do not see, may see. The Evangelist John prefers to avoid the crudeness of the synoptics authors («if your eye is a scandal to you, pluck it out»), confirming those contents: the blind will see, that is, they will be included and "enter life". The Pharisees, not at all inclined to the "change of thought", candidly ask: «Are we blind we too?». Jesus answers: «If you were blind, you would not have sinned; but since you say: "We see", your sin remains».

There could be no more radical way to explain the concept repeatedly reiterated. The semantic area of "blindness" corresponds to that of the *absence of guilt*; that is, of the absence of guilt with respect to the Law. If you are blind, you are not guilty; «but since you say: "We see", your sin remains». This alone could have been the natural and impactful conclusion of the Johannine verses. *The fault* corresponds *to sight*. "To see" is, as the synoptic authors had anticipated, an absolute disadvantage: «if your eye is a scandal to you, pluck it out». According to all four canonical Gospels, the protagonist had a clear preference for the blind (and also maimed, lame, lepers), and an equally clear rejection for the sighted (and all the able-bodied, in the broadest sense of the term).

In the Old Testament, the blind and the maimed were treated as "unclean" categories, such as lepers. In the Gospel of John, Jesus states that the "impure" (= blind) are without sin; the "pure" (= sighted) are sinners:

> If you were blind, you would not have any sin; but since you say: "We see", your sin remains.

It seems a not negligible reversal compared to what we can find in Leviticus 21, where Yahweh prevents the access to the Temple for disabled persons of any kind, stating (Lv 22:3):

> In future generations every man [...] who approaches in a state of impurity
> to the holy offerings [...] *will be removed from my presence.*

The theme of impurity is also found in testimonies related to the Qumran and Essene community. The purification rites had to be daily. Knowing this and bearing in mind the hypothesis, advanced by various scholars, about the Baptist's proximity to the Essenes and Essenism, it would be even more motivated that John doubts Jesus and is scandalized by him, just when he learns that the messiah exclusively approaches certain categories of people.

From the Qumran texts we learn, in fact, that for reasons of legal purity they were excluded from the community exactly blind, maimed, crippled, lame.

In the fourth Gospel (9:13-16) we read:

> They brought to the Pharisees the one who had been blind: it was a Sabbath [...] he said to them: «He put mud on my eyes, I washed and I see». Then some of the Pharisees said: «This man does not come from God, because he does not observe the Sabbath».

In this regard, the Essenes should be remembered precisely because they strictly observed the Sabbath as prescribed by Yahweh (the violation was punished with death, as we will see). If a beast had fallen into a ditch, or into a cistern, it could not be pulled out in that day; if a man had fallen there, one could help him but without any instrument (ropes or stairs). He could be given, to help him, only the dress.

Even in cases like this, with respect to zeal for the Law Jesus would seem not only to make an exception, but also to teach how to make a showy exception (as in the case of the blind, maimed and lame, excluded from attending the temple). In fact, a passage of Matthew (12:10-12) seems to be a reference, within a violent invective, to the Qumranian norms:

And here is a man who had a paralyzed hand. To accuse him, they asked Jesus: «Is it lawful to heal on the Sabbath day?». And he said to them, «Who of you, if he has a sheep, and this one, on the Sabbath day, falls into a ditch, does not take it and take it out? Now, a man is worth much more than a sheep. Therefore it is lawful in Sabbath day to do good».

If we recall the fact that John's disciples were strict observants and fasted together with the Pharisees – those to whom Jesus addresses himself in these verses –, we will find that with the observance of the most binding norms of the Law the protagonist of the Gospels shows a clear attitude of rupture.

In the Book of Numbers (15:32-36), Yahweh commands that the man who gathered wood on the day of the Sabbath be stoned:

They found a man who collected wood on the Sabbath day [...] they led him to Moses, to Aaron and to the whole community. [...] The Lord said to Moses: «That man must be put to death; the whole community will stone him outside the camp». The whole community led him out of the camp and stoned him; he died according to the command that the Lord had given to Moses.

In all probability, the man who tried to pull out of a ditch a sheep (indispensable, like wood, for subsistence), would not have a different end. There is no doubt that, in the words of Jesus, there is a blatant highlighting (and ridicule) of the Sabbath norm. Nevertheless, this does not alter the fact that the observance of the Sabbath was one of the most important norms of the Law, punishable by stoning by the will of Yahweh himself: who should be, according to what has long been universally transmitted, the Father of that Son who came to fulfill his Law.

When the Messiah asks who is so foolish as not to save the sheep even if the Law of Yahweh forbids it, he is stating that the exception to the norm is not only possible, but is dutiful. And the exception, however reasonably necessary it seems to save a life, always and in any case remains a transgression of the norm of that Father, whose Law the Son should have come to observe in a full and complete way.

The statement that John puts in the mouth of the Pharisees makes us understand how essential that commandment was, as we read in the Book of Exodus («Rest on the seventh day», «Do not work on the seventh day», «Do not inflict punishment on the Sabbath», «Do not go outside the city limits on the Sabbath», «Sanctify the Sabbath with Kiddush and the Havdalah»...).

The Pharisees were very reviled, as we know, by Jesus («breed of vipers», «whitened sepulchres [...] full of bones of the dead and of every rottenness», «hypocrites»). However, perhaps not everyone knows that they had the merit of having studied the texts and the biblical tradition, transmitting a vast cultural heritage that has its foundation in the Bible. They, who knew well the Law of Yahweh, wondered how there could be a derogation from such capital precepts as:

- do not erase the Torah of any commandment, in whole or in part (Dt 13:1);
- do not add precepts to the commandments of the written or oral Torah (Dt 13:1).

These commandments sealed the imperfectability of the Torah. It was already perfect. Nothing to add, nothing to take away.

The Pharisees therefore wondered where the doctrine of that man who blatantly violated the Sabbath came from. Because of this, he could not be a "righteous" according to the Law (Jn 9:24):

> They called again the man who had been blind and told him: «Give glory to God. We know that this man is a sinner».

The Pharisees affirm that Jesus is a transgressor of the Law. They therefore ask the "blind" man to bear testimony. He, who is no longer "blind", answers (Jn 9:25):

> If he is a sinner, I don't know. I know one thing: *I was blind and now I see.*

Being blind leads to seeing. This is what Jesus says to the Pharisees:

> If you were blind, you would have no sin; but since you say: "We see", your sin remains.

The "blind" man's sight coincides *with his not having sins*. If the Pharisees were "blind" like the "blind from birth", they would see: that is, they would have no fault. The problem is that they say they see: that is, they say they have no fault. It couldn't be otherwise: they are strict observants of those norms which Jesus seems, on more than one occasion, to derogate.

We can therefore affirm that, for the messiah, the most rigorous observants of the Law are transgressors; while the "blind", who is certainly not a knower of the Law, is not responsible for any transgression. To him, sins can be forgiven. Not to the Pharisees: «your sin remains». It is, therefore, not condonable. The fact that Jesus says that for the Pharisees sin remains, implies of necessity that the blind man can be taken away from sin.

Knowing that the observant Pharisees have sight, while the "blind" man has sins to be forgiven, here is what form the above verses would take:

> *If you were not observant* (= if you *had no sight*) all your sins would be forgiven; but since you say, "we are observant" (= we see perfectly), *you are sinners*" (that is, "your sin remains").

This example shows with sufficient clarity the implications of the language used by Jesus in the Gospels. For the Pharisees, the "blind" man is a sinner. For Jesus, sinners are the Pharisees (Jn 9:26-29):

> «What did he do to you? How did he open your eyes?». He answered them: «I have already told you [...] why do you want to hear it again? Do you want *to become his disciples* you too?» [...] «You are his disciple. We are disciples of Moses. We know that God spoke to Moses; but we do not know where he [Jesus] is from».

This passage is a surprising proof of what emerges from the synoptic Gospels. The fact that blindness is an advantage in approaching Jesus is revealed by the verse in which the "blind from birth" asks the Pharisees:

> Do you want *to become his disciples* you too?

It is not understood what connection there should be between healing from blindness and becoming a follower of Jesus:

- was healing the sick not a free form of compassion?
- what should the healing of a disabled person (blind, maimed, lame) have in common with any form of militant proselytism?
- did returning to health necessarily imply that the miraculous became a follower of Jesus?

The synoptic Gospels inform us that the conditions for discipleship were sufficiently stringent:

> If one comes to me and *does not hate his father, mother, wife, children, brothers, sisters and even his own life*, he cannot be my disciple. He who does not *carry his own cross* and does not come behind me, cannot be my disciple (Lk 14:26-27);

> Whoever *has left homes, or brothers, or sisters, or father, or mother, or children, or fields* for my name, will receive a hundred times as much and will inherit eternal life (Mt 19:29).

It would seem that we can deduce that the "blind" man of the Gospel of John – with all the other miraculous for which the Baptist is scandalized – should have been willing to hate father, mother, wife, children, brothers and even his own life, possibly risking death on the cross ("bearing one's cross").

The "blind" asks the Pharisees if they too want to become disciples of Jesus. The passage makes no mention except of the Pharisees and the messiah himself; therefore, we should conclude that the "blind" man healed says «will you also become his disciples?» because he who has just become a follower of Jesus is the "blind" man himself. This observation, based on textual evidence, is reinforced by the following verse, in which the Pharisees turn to the former "blind" not saying «you have been healed», but «you *are his disciple, we are disciples* of Moses»: why should they highlight their position as observants of the Law, by opposing themselves to a blind beggar – a nullity before them –, who had no means even to support himself (he could hardly have had any to study the Law)?

We will then have to return to consider the reasonable hypothesis that the words "blind", the verb "heal" and the expression "open eyes" are associated with meanings that have strong connotations, moving away from literality and adhering to a communicative code established by the one who pronounce them, and which the evangelists transmit.

Certainly, in this passage, "being healed" and "becoming disciples" are closely related; so much so that, in the text, they become inter-changeable (and the evangelist does nothing to avoid it):

You are his disciple. We are disciples of Moses,

that is:

- "Jesus *opened your eyes*, Moses *gave us his sight*"
- or "You have been healed, our eyesight is already perfect.

The evangelist John first uses the formula "open your eyes" putting into operation the code we said:

What did he do to you? How did he *open your eyes*?

Then, he uses the same code but in "outward" mode, that is in the decoding phase:

Do you want *to become his disciples* you too?

"To become disciples" is codified in the expression *"to open the eyes"*. The Pharisees ask the "blind" man how Jesus opened his eyes. He answers not talking about thaumaturgic remedies, but with an additional question:

Do you also want *to become his disciples?*

This is the warning light, which flashes drastically in the text, of the equivalence between the expressions "to open the eyes" and "to become disciples". The authorities of the Law ask the "blind" man – who evidently is not an observant of the Law like them – details on how he became a disciple of Jesus (= how his eyes were "opened"). He answers: "Do you want to know more because you are thinking of becoming his disciples you too"? Obviously, the indignant Pharisees respond: "You have become one of his followers. We remain faithful to Moses".

Summarizing:

- How *did he open* your eyes? = How *did you become his disciple?*
- Do you want *to become his disciples* you too? = Do you want *to open your eyes* you too?
- *Are we blind* too? = *Are we* also *transgressors?*
- If you *were blind* you would have no sin = *If you were transgressors* your sins would be forgiven.
- As you say, *"We see"* = As you say, *"we don't need to open the eyes* that have already been opened by Moses".

If the Pharisees had the characteristics of that "blind" man, Jesus could open their eyes: that is, he could make them become his disciples. But since they say they already have their eyes opened (= they are disciples of Moses), they can never become his disciples; nor the messiah can forgive them any guilt: they are strict observants of the Law. Therefore, they have no transgressions to be forgiven. In this lies their sin towards Jesus: not being converted to him, by becoming his disciples like the "blind".

On the conceptual assumption related to "necessary blindness" is based the use of parables to convey messages concerning the kingdom. In this regard, Mark (4:10-12) quotes Isaiah:

> When they were alone [...] they questioned him about the parables. And he said to them: «You have been given the mystery of the kingdom of God; for those who are out, instead, *everything happens in parables,* so that "they look, yes, but do not see, listen, yes, but do not understand, so that they do not get converted and be forgiven to them"».

In the language of the evangelist John we would have: «For those who are still "blind" (= *who are not yet my disciples*) everything is transmitted in parables, so that they understand how to become my disciples (= *how to open eyes*), but they do not yet know the things you know, because you have already opened your eyes; they can glimpse the content of the parables but without knowing it in detail, until they become my disciples».

As was to be expected, the link between "opening the eyes" and "becoming disciples" is confirmed in this passage of Mark, in which the programmatic contents of John 9 (episode of the "blind from birth") are expressed. Those with eyes are allowed "to look", but not "to see": this is only possible for "blind" people who are willing to open their eyes.

It is a communication based on a code of transmission of messages that is not known to all those who listen, but only to the followers of the sender. To the crowd the messiah speaks in parables, but to his disciples he reveals all the mysteries of the kingdom. It is a system of conventional words, in order not to be understood entirely, except by the faithful followers. To these words correspond meanings of which it is necessary to keep the content secret. This does not mean that those who are "out" – no expression could better reveal the exclusive (and excluding) nature of Jesus' teachings – from the narrow circle of followers, cannot in any way "see". For this to happen, the Pharisees should, in the language dear to the synoptic authors, "gouge out their eye": that is, they should stop being disciples of Moses and embrace the doctrine of Jesus. Or, alternatively, they should burn in Gehenna.

This is a concept that we find again, inexorable, in the violent invective of Matthew (23:33):

Snakes, breed of vipers, how can you escape the condemnation of Gehenna?

This is a rhetorical question that presupposes a strongly negative answer. No, the Pharisees could never have escaped Gehenna. Unless they had abandoned Moses. For Jesus, they are "sighted who have no sight". For this reason, he apostrophes them "blind and blind guides". Although their eyes have already been opened by someone else before him who made them see (Moses), they are blind to Jesus. They cannot "see" his doctrine. And they are guides of the blind because, as disciples of Moses, they procure, instructing them, always new disciples to him (and not to the messiah).

It is almost impossible to make the Pharisee, who says he has perfect vision, accept to be blinded (renouncing Moses) in order to open his eyes by turning them elsewhere (towards Jesus). The Pharisees of whom the evangelist John speaks express the same concept that the messiah, slightly varying his language, repeats in Mark (4:12), quoting Isaiah:

[...] so that "they may look and see but not perceive, and hear and listen but fail to understand, lest they be converted and be forgiven".

In John it turns out:

Since you say: "We see", your sin remains.

Replacing the words of John with those of Mark, would change nothing: "Since you say: we *do not convert*" (= we already see and we do not let our eyes be opened by you), you *will not be forgiven* (your sin remains)".

Isaiah and Jesus: two ways of "seeing" blindness

The Evangelist John, while distancing himself from the synoptic authors on the formal level, maintains their theoretical structure unchanged. It could not be otherwise, especially if we keep in mind that the words spoken by Jesus in the synoptic Gospels are a quotation from Isaiah. Mark does not make it explicit, Matthew does (13:14-15):

> The prophecy of Isaiah is fulfilled for them, that says: "You will indeed hear but not understand, you will indeed look but never see. For this people's heart has become hardened; they have stopped up their ears and they have shut their eyes, so that they might not see with their eyes and hear with their ears and understand with their heart and then turn to me, and I would heal them".

The use of the parables by Jesus would be, according to Matthew, the fulfilment of what the prophet wrote. Isaiah would refer to the crowds who would follow Jesus several centuries later, and who should not have understood (by his own will) his dark language.

However, reading the source (Isaiah 6:9-11), one can make a different idea. Yahweh says to Isaiah:

> Go forth and tell this people: «No matter how carefully you listen, you will not understand. You will continue to look, but you will not comprehend. Make the minds of this people dull; stop up their ears and close their eyes. Otherwise their eyes will see, their ears will hear, their hearts will understand, and they will change their ways and be healed». Then I asked, "How long, O Lord?" He replied: «Until the cities lie in ruins and become deserted, until the houses are unoccupied and the land lies completely desolate [...]».

It is not clear how the precise will that the people should not convert, expressed by Yahweh, can be fulfilled much later in a similarly precise will, but of the opposite sign: will of conversion. Jesus preaches blindness *to convert men to himself* (that is: to make them his disciples):

> It is better for you to enter the kingdom of God with one eye.

Isaiah is quoted using his own terminology, but the purposes are different. The purpose of parables is *to let understand the one who is willing to understand*; let see the one who is willing to see; let hear the one who is willing to hear. Since we know that the blind see and the deaf hear, it is deduced that to hear (= to understand) one must be deaf; and to see, one must be blind. If you are not, the synoptic Gospels adequately inform of what you need to do: it is necessary to take out an eye. And consequently have full "sight", that is "enter into life".

The reuse of the Old Testament source (Isaiah) is slavish in form (the word "blind", the expression "to make deaf"), but different in substance. The words with which Yahweh intends to "harden the heart" of the people should be fulfilled by the Son; but he, on the contrary, calls *to conversion* towards himself. This would be a "fulfillment" at least singular (conversion is opposed to "hardening of the heart"). For Jesus, his potential disciples, listening to the parables, must not understand. But if they have ears to understand, they must understand. For Isaiah, *the action* to be taken is "blinding"; *the consequence* of action is "not seeing"; *the purpose* is "not understanding". For Jesus, same action ("blinding"); same consequence ("not seeing"); but *opposite purpose*: "understanding".

Synthesizing the messages of Yahweh forwarded through Isaiah, we would have:

- "he who has ears shall not hear; he who has eyes shall not see".

In the exhortations of Jesus, instead, the message is reversed:

- "he who has ears must hear; he who has eyes must see".

A code that "opens the eyes"

We can better understand what Jesus says in the synoptic writings by rereading the episode of the "blind from birth", in the Gospel of John.

Who has eyes like his (not by chance he is blind "from birth"), eyes that no one, not even Moses (the Law) or Isaiah (the prophets) had ever opened and that therefore can be opened by Jesus, he himself is called to "see".

Parables prevent clear understanding, but they are the only way to transmit a code of communication that can only be intuited by the listener, but fully revealed to those who are deemed worthy. Therefore, the parables "blind"; the code reveals or "opens the eyes". It is indispensable, however, the will to open them (as demonstrated by many passages of the synoptic Gospels). This will is frequently expressed with the Greek noun *pìstis* [πίστις], generally translated with the word «faith», more literally «trust» (Mk 10:46-52):

> A blind man, Bartimaeus, the son of Timaeus, was sitting by the roadside asking for alms. When he heard that it was Jesus of Nazareth, he began to shout, «Jesus, Son of David, have pity on me». Many rebuked him and told him to be silent, but he only shouted all the louder, «Son of David, have pity on me». Jesus stopped and said, «Call him». So they called the blind man, saying to him, «Take heart. Stand up. He is calling you». Casting aside his cloak, he jumped up and went to Jesus. Then Jesus said to him, «What do you want me to do for you?» The blind man said to him, «Rabbi, let me receive my sight». Jesus said to him, «Go on your way. Your faith has made you well». Immediately, he received his sight and followed him along the road.

The passage seems to indicate that the author was not talking exactly about physical blindness:

- by virtue of what powers this man, who is at a distance from the messiah – he in fact exclaims «call him» – «jumped up» (so says the Greek text) and went to Jesus in full autonomy?
- why is he severely scolded by those around him?
- why would many people want an invalid (rendered harmless by blindness) to keep quiet and stop pleading for a cure?

Unusual would seem the request of Jesus:

What do you want me to do for you?

Being known, in the land of Israel, his qualities as a miracle worker, saying «have mercy on me» a blind man cannot ask him anything but sight. Yet, the master wants to be sure, by express declaration of the "sick", that Bartimaeus really wants to open his eyes. Only after the "blind" has done this, then Jesus can tell him that his faith has saved him.

If real blindness were involved, the episode would probably end with the words «and he immediately saw». Instead, it ends with the phrase «and *followed him* along the way».

As it happens to the "blind" of the Evangelist John, the opening of the eyes also in Mark is tied hand in glove with following Jesus. That is, with becoming a disciple. Mark writes «and immediately he saw and followed him along the way»; John writes: «"How did he open your eyes?". He answered them: [...] "Do you want *to become his disciples* you too?"».

The powerful short-circuit triggered by the word "blind", in union with verbs that do not belong to the semantic area of blindness, is even more evident in Matthew (9:27-31):

> While Jesus was gone from there, two blind people *followed him* shouting: «Son of David, have mercy on us». *Entering* the house, the blind people *approached him* and Jesus said to them: «Do you believe that I can do this?». They answered him: «Yes, o Lord». [...] «Let it be for you according to your faith». And their eyes were opened. Then Jesus admonished them, saying: «See that no one knows». But they [...] spread the news throughout that region.

Undoubtedly the verb "to follow" (*akolouthéo*) is a verb of movement: to perform this action, sight would seem indispensable. Being blind, it does not seem easy to go towards something or someone in full autonomy, that is what the two protagonists of the episode do:

- why should the messiah open the eyes to people who show that they have already opened them, first *following* him and then *approaching* him?

- why does Jesus want to be sure that they really believe he can miracle them? Is it not enough that they follow him and beg him?
- finally, why should the thaumaturgic powers of Jesus be absolutely hidden if they prove that those who have faith in him can be healed?

Having said all that, and after carefully rereading the episode, it seems reasonable to conclude that:

- if the two visually impaired people move, after opening their eyes, to leave the house;
- and if, when they still have them closed, they move to follow Jesus and approach him;

then in this episode Jesus does not perform any miracle. Before and after "healing", the handicapped perform the same actions.

Therefore, the hypothesis continues to emerge that the word "blind", for the writer of the message, has a different meaning than the literal one, which the recipient is called to decipher.

The close relationship between texts compiled at different times, between different authors who, however, use the same languages, pushes us increasingly to suppose that many tales of miraculous events told by the evangelists speak, using a peculiar message transmission code, nothing more than news events. Chronicles. Which are outside miraculous healings, but equally authentic "wonders" in Israel: that is, the fervent activity of discipleship of Jesus. It is addressed exclusively to the "blind", the "maimed", the "lame", the "lepers": all of them a substantial part of the masses that follow the messiah.

Not the healthy need the doctor, but the sick. Yet, the latter must express a clear desire to heal: as if it were desirable, for them, the paradoxical and disadvantageous alternative option: remaining sick or disabled. For this reason the authors, when they write that a large number of blind people acquire sight thanks to Jesus, most likely do not refer to human beings suffering from pathologies, but to individuals who – unlike the Pharisees who say they "see perfectly" – do not "see". They are "blind". But at least they manifest the explicit will that the messiah opens their eyes to them. With so many "blind", the seed of his word can fall on a ground made up of people willing to follow him (Mt 13:16):

> Blessed are your eyes because they see and your ears because they listen.

The disciples of Jesus never belonged to the ranks of the Pharisees or the scribes. They are "blind" to Moses. To scrupulously observe the 613 norms of the Torah, one must first know them; how to read them. Not everyone can do this (Mt 13:17):

> Many prophets and many righteous people have desired to see what you look at, but they did not see it, and to listen to what you hear, but did not listen to it.

Jesus states that the prophets «did not see»:
- so, did they not know the things which he revealed to his disciples?
- did they wish to hear such contents but not?

Although we could superficially explain these words as a desire to highlight the greater fortune of the followers of the messiah as chronologically closer to the "good news", we ask ourselves:
- if the prophets anticipated the coming of the kingdom and its full realization in Jesus – who should have fulfilled these prophecies –, how could they never have been aware of what the Lord made known exclusively to his disciples?
- how could they wish to hear the things that Jesus revealed to his followers, if they had heard them directly from Yahweh, and prophesied by centuries before Jesus?
- how could they not have known these things, if they themselves had spoken them?

Finally, it is not clear how to reconcile the quoted passage of Matthew with that of John (5:39 and 46):

> You are searching the Scriptures, thinking that you have eternal life in them:
> they are the very ones that bear witness to me [...] For if you believed in Mo-
> ses, you would also believe in me; because *he wrote about me.*

According to the Evangelist John, here Jesus would be saying that Moses – who spoke with Yahweh «face to face, as one speaks with his friend» (Ex 33:11) – wrote nothing but of Jesus himself. In fact, the whole of Scripture would testify to him.

In Matthew, Jesus himself says that the prophets – who spoke with Yahweh – would have liked to hear the things he revealed to his disciples.

In Mark (9:2-8) – as also in Matthew in the famous episode of Mount Tabor (17:1-8) – it is written that Jesus had a conversation with Moses and Elijah (the highest representative of the Law the one, of the prophets the other).

Luke (9:31) not only informs us that Jesus is conversing with Elijah and Moses, but specifies the subject of the conversation:

> They spoke of his exodus, which was about to take place in Jerusalem.

That is, the central event of the events concerning Jesus which, according to Matthew, *only the disciples should have known.* A little later, we learn not only that prophets (like Elijah) and righteous (like Moses) seem to be aware of the mysteries of the kingdom, but that vice versa just the disciples (instead of seeing and knowing, listening and understanding) see *but do not know* and listen *but do not understand* (Lk 9:43-45):

> He said to his disciples: «Remember these words: the Son of Man is about
> to be delivered into the hands of men». But they *did not understand* these
> words: they remained for them so mysterious that they did not grasp the
> meaning, and they were afraid to question him on this topic.

In summary:
- for Matthew, the prophets and the righteous of the Old Testament were not aware of the things that Jesus reveals to disciples

> (despite being these things the object of prophecies communicated by the prophets themselves);

- for Luke instead, prophets and righteous not only knew what was to happen in Jerusalem, but the messiah even talks about it with them (Moses and Elijah); while with the disciples – those who according to Matthew were the only recipients of his revelations – he cannot talk about it. Because they do not understand.

Luke would seem to wonder: "how can the Law (Moses) and the prophets not know these things?". The question would sound even more legitimate if we think that Jesus, in the Gospel of John, states that Moses wrote about Jesus himself.

It is evident that in Luke there is an attempt to resize the privilege reserved later for the disciples by the same evangelist (10:21):

> I praise you, Father [...] because you have hidden these things to the wise and the learned and you have revealed them to the *little ones.*

To the wise ones, Jesus prefers those who do not know things (as the Law) that the wise know and study. Better are those who learn directly from him the mysteries which wise and learned, originally chosen by Yahweh, cannot know. However, even of these things which are strictly revealed to them, as we have seen, the disciples, inexplicably, do not understand some of them.

The questions are these:

- how can something that is revealed (= to which the veil of non-understanding is removed) not be understood?
- what the disciples could not master with the intellect?

The fact that some content delivered to a small number of people was not understood – although they were the only recipients of this message – may appear to be a clear contradiction. Or, no contradiction if we open ourselves to another reasonable hypothesis: probably, not even the disciples knew in detail and entirely the things concerning the kingdom. For the simple fact that Jesus thought it appropriate not to reveal them completely.

Discrepancies and concordances

The evangelists Luke and Matthew agree with each other more than it may seem, and this is demonstrated by a passage of the latter, already mentioned:

> Many prophets and many righteous ones have desired to see what you look at, but they did not see it, and to listen to what you listen, but they did not listen to it.

We compare it with that of Luke (10:21-24):

> «I praise you, Father [...] because you have hidden these things from the wise and learned and have revealed them to the little ones. [...] Everything was given to me by my Father and nobody knows who the Son is except the Father, or who the Father is except the Son and those to whom the Son wishes to reveal him». And, turning to the disciples, aside, he said: «Blessed are the eyes that see what you see [...] many prophets *and kings* wanted to see what you look, but they did not see it, and listen to what you hear, but did not listen to it».

Luke adds something that complicates the speech and generates inevitable questions, namely:
- if no one knows who the Son is but the Father, in what capacity does Jesus converse with Moses and Elijah? Do they know or not that Jesus is the Son?
- if Elijah and Moses do not know who Jesus is – since only the Father knows who the Son is –, with whom do they think to dialogue when they talk to him?
- only the Son knows the Father: so Moses, with whom does he speak «face to face»?

- the prophets of the Old Testament whom did they see and know? By whom were they sent to Israel?
- moreover, if only the Son can reveal the Father, then why in the Book of Exodus is the Father to reveal himself to Moses – «I am [...] the God of Abraham, the God of Isaac, the God of Jacob» – without the need for intermediaries?

Finally, Matthew writes that «many prophets and righteous have desired to see what you see»; Luke speaks, instead, of «many prophets *and kings*», instead of «and righteous»:

- to which kings does the evangelist mention?
- which rulers should wish to hear things accessible only to the followers of Jesus, and why?
- what link should there be between alleged "spiritual" knowledge and the kings who rule the nations?
- is it likely that Luke, having grasped the uncomfortable implications of saying that those who observe the Law (the righteous) are paradoxically deprived of knowledge of the mysteries of the kingdom, avoid writing "righteous" preferring the less demanding word "kings"?

Luke legitimizes the righteous Moses and the prophet Elijah to knowledge of the mysteries that must be known only to the disciples. However, in the passage we have quoted, the followers do not understand such mysteries, unlike what happens to Moses and Elijah: the king of the righteous and the greatest prophet, who should have, according to the same words of Jesus, be second to the disciples in acquiring such secret content.

From the many contradictions one could glimpse an exit simply by considering the hypothesis that Jesus says certain things to the Pharisees; while he tells others to his disciples. He presents himself in a certain way to the former, in another to the latter. Thus there is no contradiction between the sentences listed, but coherence.

In the Gospel of John, to the Pharisees incredulous towards him he says:

> You are searching the Scriptures, thinking that you have eternal life in them:
> they are the very ones that bear witness to me [...] For if you believed in Mo-
> ses, you would also believe in me; because he wrote about me.

In the Gospel of John, Jesus says, neither more nor less, that he himself coincides with the Scriptures.

In Matthew, he states that the prophets – who compiled the books
that would speak of himself – and the righteous like Moses would have
liked to know the things that his disciples know, but did not know.

We ask ourselves: if the ancient prophets and the righteous had been
contemporaries of the messiah, would they be made able to share the
things that the disciples knew through Jesus?

According to Luke, it would seem not. The evangelist clearly writes
that the Father deliberately hid certain things from the wise and learned,
and revealed them to the "little ones". If "wise and learned" are scribes and
Pharisees, this would mean that the Father (Yahweh) has hidden to those
who study and disclose his own Law and to his prophets (who would
prophesy of his own Son) certain contents. Conversely, these contents
would be revealed, through Jesus, exclusively to a group of people (the
"little ones") who neither study nor divulge his Scriptures (those which,
according to John, would have the Son as the only argument).

Therefore, all that concerns the fulfillment of the events related to
the messiah – events already present in the Law and in the prophets
–, would no longer be the preserve of those who, until then, the Law
and the prophets had always guarded and transmitted; but of a very
small group of people, not only completely alien to the Pharisees, but in
strong opposition to them (Mt 16:6-12):

> Beware of the leaven of the Pharisees and the Sadducees [...]

The disciples answer:

> But we have not taken bread.

Jesus replies:

«How could you not understand that I was not speaking to you about bread? Instead, beware of the leaven of the Pharisees and Sadducees». Then they understood that he had not said to beware of the leaven of bread, but of the teaching of the Pharisees and the Sadducees.

Again in Matthew (15:10-14), we read:

The disciples approached to tell him: «Do you know that the Pharisees, to hear this word, were scandalized?». And he answered: «Every plant, which has not been planted by my heavenly Father, will be uprooted. Leave them alone. They are blind and blind guides. And when a blind guide another blind, both will fall in a ditch».

The acknowledged authority of the scribes derived from being experts in all that concerned the transmission of the texts and religious traditions of Israel, in the broadest sense of the term. They were cultured scholars, able to discuss legal issues. They passed the Law down by transcribing and investigating its contents. They were concerned with the formation of the observant Jew. So,

- if the heavenly Father, of whom Jesus speaks, is Yahweh, and if the transmission of the Law and prophets has always been entrusted to wise and learned people, why does the Messiah define them as plants not planted by the Father?
- they transmitted the norms of the Law underlying Israel's covenant with Yahweh, but were they unwelcome to the author of the Law, who had spoken to the prophets?
- if they were not plants of Yahweh, who had "planted" them?
- in the Old Testament the priest Ezra is called «expert in the law of Moses»: was he a plant planted by Yahweh or not?
- Baruch, the scribe of the prophet Jeremiah, who wrote on a scroll what Yahweh said to the prophet, was he "planted" by the Father or not?

But now suppose that scribes and Pharisees were plants planted by others, and not by Yahweh:

- for what reason did they have the only job of spreading the laws and prescriptions of the one who, in this case, would be an absolutely unknown Father?
- finally: what exactly does Jesus mean when he says that those plants "will be uprooted"?

The latter is an undoubtedly effective image, that seems to have a more than a slight resonance in the "parable of the murderous winemakers" (Mt 21:33-41):

> There was a landowner who planted a vineyard, fenced it in on all sides, dug a winepress in it, and built a watchtower. Then he leased it to tenants and went off on a journey. "When the time for harvest approached, he sent his servants to the tenants to collect his share of the produce. But the tenants seized his servants and beat one of them, killed another, and stoned a third. Again, he sent more servants, but they treated them in the same manner. "Finally, he sent his son to them, thinking, 'They will respect my son.' But when the tenants saw the son, they said to one another, 'This is the heir. Come, let us kill him and get his inheritance.' And so they seized him, threw him out of the vineyard, and killed him. "Now what do you think the owner of the vineyard will do to those tenants when he comes?" They said to him, "He will kill those evil men, and then he will lease his vineyard to other tenants who will give him the produce at the harvest."

The protagonists of the parable are the master of a vineyard and the winegrowers, to whom he entrusted it. However, they act as owners. This is not pleasing to the master, who after several attempts will decide to get rid with violence of those original wise and learned of vineyards. They will be replaced by other winemakers.

The text does not specify whether the latter were "wiser" or more "learned", in the matter of vineyards, than the first. Certainly, they came *after*. They are "younger". They are the "last" arrived, if compared to the "first". These "last" will bear fruit and will enjoy the flourishing vineyard. The "first" will be killed by the master.

Wise, intelligent, children

So far, we have had no difficulty in understanding which semantic area the words "wise" and "learned" belong to. But why is it not so clear for the semantic area of "smallness"?

If to the adjectives that qualify the activity of scribes, Pharisees and disciples of Jesus, we replaced the corresponding verbs, we would have:

To study and teach the Law : scribes and Pharisees = *"little ones"*: disciples of Jesus

Studying and teaching the Law is related to scribes and Pharisees, as the word "little ones" is related to disciples of Jesus. Writing, instead of the adjectives "wise" and "learned", the respective verbs with which they share the semantic area (to study-to teach), was very simple thing. While, it was not at all easy to do the same operation with the adjective "small". We do not know what exactly were the activities of the "little ones" disciples, to be classified as such. So we will continue to ask ourselves:

- what exactly does the adjective "small" mean?
- why is the sphere of action of the Pharisees and scribes always recognizable and circumscribed, while that of the disciples of Jesus is not?
- why do evangelists not simply write that the followers of the messiah are not experts in the Torah?

Once again, we find that the semantic area of reference of the "little ones" is vague. Ambiguous. The only sure thing is the usual concept: the "smallness". The words "learned" and "wise" have a meaning that is not placed under the government of a communicative code alien to the reader. The words "little ones" and "children", on the contrary, would seem so. The phrase "You have hidden these things from the wise and learned" is immediately clear to the reader. The communication code is shared by the sender and the recipient. The phrase "You have revealed these things to the *little ones*" leads one to think that they had radically opposite qualities, but not so clearly indicated. So far, we haven't found a clear decryption key for this word. We know that the disciples of Jesus are classified as "small-little ones", and that scribes and Pharisees are their antithesis. Therefore:

Small-little ones : Jesus = *great ones*: scribes and Pharisees

The "little ones" are related to Jesus as the "great ones" are related to scribes and Pharisees. Learned and scholars can only belong to the terminological area contrary to the adjective "small", with the usual, insuppressible dialectic tension that we already know (Mt 18):

> The disciples approached Jesus saying: «Who then is greater in the kingdom of heaven?» [...] «Whoever will become as *small* as this child, he is *greater* in the kingdom of heaven».

The "great ones" are bypassed by the "little ones": these are "younger" than them, who for generations were used to take care of the things of Yahweh. Which are now diverted to others (Mt 11:11):

> Among those born of a woman, no one is *greater* than John the Baptist; but one *smaller* in the kingdom of heaven is *greater* than him.

Without surprises, we ascertain that John is defined by Jesus himself as "great". Now let's see how the verses of the Evangelist John already examined would be expressed, if to the categories "disciples of Jesus" and "disciples of Moses" we applied the synoptic code:

John	John according to the language of the synoptics
"Do you also want to *become his disciples*?". They insulted him and said: "You are his disciple. We are disciples of Moses."	Do you want to *become small* you too?". They insulted him and said: "You are *small*, we are *great*".

Conversely, here is what Matthew would be like in the language of the fourth evangelist:

Matthew	Matthew in the language of John
I praise you, Father, Lord of heaven and earth, for you have hidden these things from *the wise and learned,* and revealed them to *the little ones.*	I praise you, Father, Lord of heaven and earth, for you have hidden these things from the *disciples of Moses* and revealed them to the *disciples of Jesus.*

Again, no surprise. The terminological interchangeability says a lot about the content.

Despite the diversity of the terms used, the evangelist John shows full mastery of the meanings dependent on the communicative code that governs Mark, Luke and Matthew:

- if the Pharisees were "disciples of Moses" and had something in common with those of the "great" John, this was evidently Moses and the Law: since John was a strict observant;
- therefore, if Jesus abhorred scribes and Pharisees, and they had something in common with the disciples of John, then for an obvious transitive property these were not to be compatible even with the "little ones" and with the doctrine of Jesus;
- finally, if the "little ones" could have nothing to do with either the disciples of Moses (Pharisees) or with the disciples of the "great" John (for whom Moses was indispensable), then there must be some important incompatibility between Moses and the doctrine of Jesus.

All this leads to two unavoidable questions:
- had the Father hidden revelations about the kingdom even to the Baptist, the "greatest" among the "great ones"?
- to the one who should be the "great" precursor of the master of the "little ones", had the contents of the kingdom been kept secret or not?

It should be deduced that, if the "little ones" of Jesus are "greater" than John, then they know more than he knows. So, to the precursor of the messiah such things were hidden:

- but if the Baptist, new Elijah and prophet in all respects, prepares the way for Jesus, how can he be deliberately excluded, by the will of Yahweh, from the knowledge of the ultimate truths concerning the kingdom?
- if he is the one of whom «it is written in the prophet Isaiah: "Behold, ahead of you I send my messenger"», how can he ignore, as a messenger, important parts of the message he brings?
- also: why should the "little ones" of Jesus have a higher dignity than the Baptist, and the privilege of knowing more?
- if they are "greater" than the "great" John, why does act as a precursor to Jesus one who has qualities opposed to them, who are "little ones"?
- how's that John falls into the terminological area of the "great ones" (learned and wise), highly unfriendly to Jesus, who defines them as «race of vipers»?

The expression "revealing the mysteries" the evangelist John would have expressed it with the words "opening the eyes". If he had compiled the verse of Matthew that we already know, we would have:

I thank you, Father, because you have not *opened the eyes to the Pharisees, but to the blind.*

In fact, Jesus opens his eyes to the blind, and not to the disciples of Moses. If in the fourth Gospel the "blind" man becomes disciple of Jesus, and in the synoptic Gospels his followers are called "little ones", then the semantic area of the "little ones-children" will necessarily intersect and coincide with that of the "blind-disabled".

Thus, even in the variation of a melodic line whose notes are the words "blind", "maimed", "children", "small ones", emerges in a strong way the powerful monochord conceptual harmony that connects together all these notes. To the "great" symphonies of the thought of wise and learned, Jesus continues to prefer minimalism («better to enter life *with one* eye») of "blind" and "children". These are "small", "least", "poor" notes that only his followers can hear. That's why their ears are blessed; their eyes see. The Pharisees, whose eyes Moses had opened for generations, do not see.

The mere fact that the use of the metaphor of "seeing", as a synonym of having knowledge of something, is so insistent, should lead one to wonder whether "blind" people are anything but people who voluntarily apply for a certain knowledge (Mk 10:51):

"What do you want me to do for you?" [...] "Rabbi, let me see".

In John's language it would sound:

"Rabbi, *open my eyes*" or "*Make me your disciple*".

We should conclude that Yahweh, after having entrusted his words to Moses and the prophets for centuries, literally "changes his mind". He decides that the most salient contents concerning Israel are no longer the prerogative of those who had always taken care of them, but of the "little ones" disciples of Jesus. It would be a *metànoia* in the truest sense of the term.

In this case the Father – who in translations often has the qualification of "Eternal" – would convert himself from what had happened, until then, by his will. He would take away the trust given to those who know and tirelessly study his Law, in order to give it to a small group of people who do not know it and have never studied it: if nothing else, for objective impossibility, caused first of all by the social background and origin. Moreover, they had conduct of life which, according to the same Gospels, do not seem to be in line with the "righteousness" of the Old Testament and with the observance of the precepts:

> «Lord, turn away from me, because I am a *sinner*» (that is, a *transgressor of the Mosaic law*).

This is what Peter affirms in the famous episode of the "miraculous catch", showing full awareness of his condition as a non-observant of the Law. These are concepts that the fourth evangelist would most likely paraphrase as follows:

> "Lord, turn away from me, I'm not *a disciple of Moses*"; "Fear not, from now on you will be my disciple, *who will procure other disciples*" (Peter «fisher of men»)

or:

> "Lord, turn away from me, I am *a blind man*"; "Fear not, from now on you *will have your eyes opened by me*".

It is the "blind" ones (or maimed, or lame, or lepers) like Peter who can open their eyes and then open them to other blind; who can be able to become followers of Jesus and commit themselves to finding ("catching") others. Those who are not like Peter, the observants, cannot be able to "see" or listen to Jesus and become his disciples. Unless (very distant hypothesis) they decide to become "deaf" or "blind": in this case, surely they enter life. The others, on the other hand, can burn in Gehenna. Sinners like Peter are given to know the mysteries of the kingdom (Mt 16:15-17):

> «But who do you say I am?». Simon Peter answered: «You are the Christ, the Son of the living God» [...] «Blessed are you Peter [...] neither flesh nor blood have revealed it to you, but my Father who is in heaven».

The news that Jesus was the messiah could not be acquired except by direct revelation, of which the sinner Peter is considered worthy:

> Many prophets and many righteous ones have desired to see what you look at, but they did not see it, and to listen to what you listen, but they did not listen to it.

Not wise, not learned, not prophets, not righteous according to the Law; but Peter, the transgressor, can know that Jesus is the messiah. The parables must only suggest and allude. The realities of Jesus do not lie in what he reveals, but in what he cannot fully reveal. To understand him, one must listen not to what he says, but to what he does not say. This means the protagonist of the Gospels, when he concludes the parables with the exhortative formula «who has ears, may he understand». We must pay attention to all that he does not reveal except to the most trusted disciples (Mt 16:20):

> Then he ordered the disciples not to tell anyone that he was the Christ.

The twelve all knew, outside the language of parables, that Jesus was to be the future king of Israel. But it was strictly forbidden to divulge such news outside that narrow circle. This is a ban that, if expressed in metaphors, could coincide with the proverbial warning «do not throw pearls to pigs».

Evidently, the awareness that Jesus was a candidate to be king was too precious a pearl, to be kept in the most absolute secret; although those who had "eyes to see" and "ears to hear" could catch a more than pale reflection in the parables.

As for having knowledge, the disciples always take precedence, because they are "as small as children" (Mt 18:5):

> Who will welcome only one child like this in my name, welcomes me.

Whoever receives the *"little ones* like children", welcomes Jesus himself. No better way to affirm and reiterate equality. Only one is the teacher. Among them, the disciples are all brothers. What unites them – Jesus included – is the usual requirement: being "small". The master is "small". In opposition to John, who instead is irremediably "great". If in the kingdom of heaven Jesus is king being "small", his disciples cannot be less than him and less "small" than him. This is the only indispensable requirement for the kingdom. If you are not willing to be "small", you are out. Like John. He is indeed "the greatest". But not in the kingdom.

Here, precisely because he is "great" and not "small", John would not even enter. Instead, the "little ones" not only belong to the kingdom in their own right, but as to the requirement of "smallness" they have royalty equal to the master. This is clear in the chapter 25 of Matthew – the so-called "eschatological discourse" – in which Jesus tells, speaking of himself in the third person, of how he shall sit on the throne of the kingdom of heaven (25:34-40):

> Then the king will say to those who are on his right hand: «Come, blessed of my Father, receive in inheritance the kingdom prepared for you since the creation of the world, because I was hungry and you gave me to eat, I was thirsty and you gave me to drink, I was a stranger and you welcomed me, naked and you dressed me, sick and you visited me, I was in prison and you came to see me [...] Everything you did to one of my least brothers, you did to me».

Dealing with, welcoming or not welcoming the "little-least" disciples is equivalent to dealing with, welcoming or not welcoming Jesus himself. Whoever welcomes the disciples welcomes him. Whoever rejects the disciples, rejects him. If Jesus is king and will sit on the throne, his followers are destined to do the same (Mt 19:28):

> You who have followed me, when the Son of man will be seated on the throne of his glory, at the regeneration of the world, you will also sit on twelve thrones to judge the twelve tribes of Israel.

Both Jesus and the disciples are "little". "Little ones", but who will sit on a throne (Mt 23:12):

> Who will exalt himself, will be humiliated, who will humble himself will
> be exalted.

John the Baptist, being "great" and not becoming "small", will not sit on any throne: «The one *smaller* in the kingdom of heaven is *greater* than him».

Once again we cannot fail to note the implications of this lapidary verse of Matthew (11:11), on which it is necessary to make some clarification, to underline the enormous revealing potential of what the evangelist writes.

«The *smallest* in the kingdom of heaven» (this is a superlative: the one who in the kingdom is the smallest, compared to all the others) is in particular the translation (in the Italian text appear the words «il più piccolo») present in the version edited by the Italian Episcopal Conference. But in the Greek text there is actually a comparative: *o mikròteros* [ὁ μικρότερος], «the one who is *smaller*»: smaller than someone else. Someone who? John the Baptist, as can be easily deduced from the continuation of the verse:

> The one who is *smaller* [*mikròteros*] in the kingdom of heaven is greater
> *than him.*

The fact that "smaller" is a greater than comparative (and not a superlative) could be more clearly shown in translations. The whole verse, in fact, is built *on the comparison* with the Baptist. Whoever is *smaller* than him, is *greater* than him. The second term of the comparison is openly inferred from the comparative that follows: "he who is *smaller* (than John the Baptist) in the kingdom of heaven, is *greater* than him (than the Baptist).

Therefore:

- if anyone who makes himself *small* as a child, in the kingdom is *greater* than one who does not;
- and if those who are *smaller* in the kingdom are *greater* than John;

it follows that the Baptist is not "as small as a child". All this emerges unequivocally from the synoptic Gospels. And it is at least as amazing as contradictory that who should announce the kingdom before Jesus, defects of the essential requirement to enter it:

- why did neither John nor his disciples want to become "small"?
- is John the forerunner of Jesus without sharing intentions and actions of the messiah?
- are the "little" disciples destined to sit on twelve thrones, while the envoy from Yahweh to prepare the way for the messiah – and born, like him, of the Holy Spirit – is not destined for any kingship?
- in the Gospel of Matthew, Jesus asks to be baptized by John: why does he do this, if he even believes that in the kingdom his "little ones" disciples are "greater" than John?
- why, while considering John inferior to his disciples, does he insist on being baptized by him?

Evidently, the fact that the "little" messiah had an "imprimatur" from the "great" John was something useful or indispensable to Jesus himself. According to the Gospel of Luke (9:46), his disciples were motivated by an unusual and pressing concern:

An argument started among the disciples as to which of them would be the greatest (Cei 2008).

However, in the Greek text does not appear a superlative ("the *greatest* among them"), but a comparative: literally, respecting the order of words, « which would be *greater than them*». The adjective «great» in the comparative form is followed by the second term of a comparison, "than them". The disciples are wondering if there is anyone who is *greater* than them. Jesus answers as usual, pointing out that their "greatness" resides in the opposite value, the "smallness" (Lk 9:47-48):

> He took a child, he put it close and told them: «Whoever will welcome this child in my name, welcomes me; and whoever welcomes me, welcomes the one who sent me. Who in fact is the smallest among all of you, this is great» (Cei 2008).

However, even here we are not faced with a superlative ("the *smallest* among all of you"), but with a *comparative* (one who is *smaller than* someone). There is not and could not be, by virtue of such a rigid logic, a disciple who is *the greatest* among all disciples. They, having become "small", are all in the same equal position. More literally, the Greek text says:

> Among all of you one being *smaller*, this is great.

Those who strive the most to be small (to "humble themselves"), are exalted. However, the "little ones", among them, are all brothers. The fact that there is not a disciple who is "the smallest" compared to all the others, is shown by Luke himself:

> Who will welcome this child in my name, welcomes me; and who welcomes me, welcomes the one who sent me.

Who welcomes a "little one" in the name of Jesus, welcomes Jesus himself. There could be no stronger way to deny the existence of a disciple who is "the smallest" of all. It is Jesus himself who excludes it, when he says that the "little" disciples welcomed in his name must be considered in the same way as the master. "Smallness" is the common constant. No one can, no one must claim to be "the smallest".

Conversely, what everyone must aspire to, is to become "smaller"; "lower"; "to humiliate"; to avoid being "great" and pass through the "wide" door. The disciples are "first" because they are "last". They are "great" because they are "small". They are "sighted" because they are "blind".

We understand well why Jesus dwells so peremptorily on the subject. In order to maintain cohesion in such a small group, the first thing to safeguard is a level playing field for all. So, the absence of any privileges for anyone.

We wonder:

- compared to whom the disciples must be "smaller" or must "shrink"?
- who represents the "great" measure from which they must distance themselves?

The answer is again obvious, self-evident and is given by Matthew, who uses exactly the same comparative that we have already seen (*mikròteros*):

> Among the born of a woman there is no one *greater* than John the Baptist;
> but he who is *smaller* in the kingdom of heaven is greater than him.

The Baptist is the absolute and inimitable term of comparison of "greatness". One cannot be "greater" than him, surpassing him in his own specialty. But he can be outclassed in "smallness": a quality that do not belong to him in any way.

The expression «among those born of women» identifies the area in which John excels. Which is diametrically opposed to the kingdom of heaven: that is the area in which the "little ones" of Jesus excel. On the basis of this, we will better understand that it is precisely the comparative that puts in close relation Matthew and Luke 9:

> Among all of you [disciples of Jesus], he who is *smaller* [than John], this
> is great.

Who can boast the quality contrary to John (the "littleness") automatically assumes, only and exclusively within the kingdom, the same importance that John has outside («among the born of women»), but for quality and merits "small" (Mt 23:8-1):

> But don't call yourselves "rabbis", because only one is your teacher and you are all brothers. And do not call any of you on earth "father", for only one is your heavenly Father. And do not be called "guides", because one is your guide, Christ. Who among you is *greater*, will be your servant; who instead will exalt himself, will be humiliated and who will humble himself will be exalted.

No one can boast of the title of "master": it is up to Christ alone. If there is one who is "the greatest" among all those who participate in the kingdom, it is Jesus himself.

Matthew is no exception (23:11), literally:

> He who is *greater* than you, will be your servant.

This verse is generally translated:
- «Whoever among you is greater, will be your servant» (Cei);
- «May the greatest among you be your servant» (Nuova Riveduta);
- «May the greatest of you be your servant» (Nuova Diodati).

Except that in the Greek text appears the future of the verb "to be" («*will be* your servant») and not an exhortative subjunctive, the use of the article («*the* greatest») bends to some extent the meaning towards a superlative form that in the Greek text does not appear. Instead we read again the comparative of the adjective "great" ("greater"), followed by the second term of comparison ("*than you*"). Differently, in the translations examined we find "among you": «Who *among you* is greater» and «the greatest *among you*».

The reader will soon realize that saying "the greatest among you" is not the same as saying "the one who is *greater than* you". In the first case, only and exclusively within a specific group there is someone who is "the greatest". While, in the second case, there is someone who is "greater" than all those who belong to that precise group (but he not necessarily belongs to it).

What makes us inclined to believe that we are always faced with a greater than comparative, is the following verse (Mt 23:12). Translating literally:

> The one who is *greater than you* will be your servant. He who will raise himself will be lowered, and he who will lower himself will be raised.

If in this verse Jesus were saying that the disciple who wants to be *the greatest* among all disciples should put himself at their service, why would he immediately refer to those who "rise up" and "will be lowered"? We know that those who "rise", or are "great", are *outside* the kingdom. The disciples are already "small". Precisely for this reason, they were "raised" to the rank of disciples. It is difficult to think that those who have striven to become "small", will then claim to become "the greatest" disciples among all the disciples.

If one keeps in mind that what appears in the Greek text is a greater than comparative, one can understand that the reference is to those who are *outside* the ranks of followers. So, *outside* the kingdom. Here, the Baptist is always the tiebreaker. Who is not "great" (as the Baptist is outside the kingdom), he is "small" *in the kingdom*.

We remain of the opinion that Matthew 11:11 («one *smaller* in the kingdom of heaven *is greater than* him») does nothing but reiterate, varying, the other passage of Matthew that we have seen (23:11):

> Whoever is *greater than you* will be a servant of you.

The adjective "small" in Matthew 11 («one *smaller*») has the same meaning as the noun "servant" in Matthew 23. Always the same semantic area: "smallness". He who becomes *smaller* than John, in the kingdom will be *greater* than him. Likewise, he who is *greater* than the disciples will be their *servant*. He will be in an irremediably inferior hierarchical position. If the disciples of Jesus are "smaller" than the "great" Baptist, then in Matthew (23:11) the one who is "greater" than them and will become "their servant", will be John. Once again. As the disciples, becoming "small", will become "greater" than the precursor, so the precursor, who is now "greater" *outside* the kingdom, will be "lower" (will be a *servant*) than them. Matthew 23 is therefore an inverted reformulation of Matthew 11:11.

Let us now re-read Luke (9:48):

> Among all of you one being smaller, this is great.

We find here nothing but what Matthew (11:11) says about the superiority of the disciples of Jesus in the kingdom, compared to those who are outside.

The difference is that Matthew explicitly mentions the Baptist, while Luke does not. But precisely the evident syntactic and conceptual correspondence with Matthew 11 makes us understand that Luke is talking about the same topics.

Christ "lowers himself" to become, in all respects, "brother of the disciples". "Least" among "least" disciples. While remaining king. A servant king. A ruler who, before sitting on the throne, did the things that his subordinates did: if nothing else, until they too sit on their thrones, ruling the twelve tribes of Israel.

"Small" disciples, "smaller" disciples, "least" disciples

In the Gospel of Matthew (a book that must have undoubted authority if it opens the New Testament ecclesiastical canon), the followers of Jesus are indicated, in addition to the adjective *mikròs* ("small"), with the superlative *elàchistos* [ἐλάχιστος]: «least, minimum, very small, the smallest». This author is the only one, among the canonical, to use this marked mode of definition of the disciples.

Luke writes that whoever receives a *paidìon* [παιδίον], «child», in the name of Jesus, receives the messiah himself. Matthew says that for those who will behave in a certain way with one of the «least brothers» of Jesus, it will be like having had such behavior with Jesus himself.

From the comparison, we derive that the messiah calls *paidìon* («child») a disciple, who in Matthew is a «least brother». If he defines them as his brothers, by placing himself in a clear relationship of equivalence (doing something at the "least" disciples is equivalent to doing it to him), it follows that Jesus is as "least" as they are. Obviously, the leader of the group will dissuade all other members from believing that they can be leaders for him.

Let's see now the translation of Matthew (25:40) proposed by Cei, Nuova Riveduta and Nuova Diodati:

- «All that you have done to one of my *smaller* brothers, you have done it to me» (Cei);
- «In how much you have done it to one of these my *least* brothers, you have done it to me» (Nuova Riveduta);
- «Every time you have done it to one of these *least* of my brothers, you have done it to me (Nuova Diodati).

Nuova Riveduta and Diodati translate the superlative *elàchistos* with the word «least». There can be no misunderstanding: the brothers of Jesus are called «least». The reader, while probably asking legitimate questions about why Jesus defines the disciples in this way, will have no doubt that it is a superlative.

Let's see what happens in the Cei translation:

All that you have done to only one of these my *smaller* brothers, you have done it to me.

Here the Greek superlative *elàchistos* («least») is translated by Cei as a greater than comparative («smaller»): the reader who runs into the phrase «one of my *smaller* brothers», what will he understand?

In all probability, he will understand that whoever is making this statement is referring to brothers who are "smaller" than Jesus. That is: "smaller" is a greater than comparative that has as its second term of comparison the one who is speaking: "one of my brothers smaller (*than me)*". It would be as if, in Latin, the superlative "*minimus*" we decided to translate it "smaller". In that case, we would have found in the text the comparative "*minor*", and not the superlative *minimus* ("least").

If Matthew, using the comparative *mikròteros*, writes that the one who is "smaller" than John in the kingdom is "greater" than him, then there could be a reason if the same Matthew (25:40), instead of continuing to use the comparative "smaller" referring it to the disciples "brothers" of Jesus, uses the superlative *elàchistos* ("least").

Evidently, in the first case the evangelist intends to highlight that the comparative relationship makes sense if the will to enter the kingdom is manifested: who, even outside the kingdom, shrinks and becomes "smaller" than the "great" John, manages to pass through the "narrow door" and enter the kingdom.

In the second case, however, Matthew (25:40) refers exclusively to the number of disciples: all "brothers" of Jesus and "small-little" in the highest degree ("least"). Therefore, any comparison between them loses meaning. No one is *smaller* (*mikròteros*) than another "brother".

Once again, the obstinate predilection of the protagonist of the Gospels for the semantic area of "smallness" emerges clearly, strongly reaffirmed in Matthew 25. Here Jesus, who without any misunderstanding is referring to himself (the «Son of Man»), clarifies, once seated «on the throne of his glory», what destiny awaits the "least" ones and those who have given them help and support; and vice versa, what end awaits those who are not "least" and did not give them help (25:31-34):

> All the peoples will be gathered. He will separate one from another, as the
> shepherd separates the sheep from the goats, and he will place the sheep to

his right and the goats to his left. Then the king will say to those who are on his right hand: «Come, blessed of my Father, receive in inheritance the kingdom prepared for you [...]».

If the language used can rightly be defined "parabolic" as a synonym of mysterious, enigmatic or hermetic, certainly we are not faced with a parable like others told by Jesus. Here the purpose is not to veil the contents, but to make them sufficiently explicit.

The protagonist is the messiah, who often speaks in the third person, defining himself «Son of Man» and establishing a clear intertextuality with the Old Testament (in particular, the prophet Daniel). The coming of the messiah is mentioned, together with all the angels, in the glory that belongs to him who sits on a throne.

If the word «angels» could suggest contexts not anchored to human experience, «the peoples» (*èthne*) instead refer to concrete and earthly scenarios. A large number of people are gathered in front of the «Son of Man», who has the task of separating one from the other. The following similarity («how the shepherd separates the sheep from the goats») is part of an imaginary that we find in the parables: sheep and shepherd, but also the sower who has the heavy task of separating the wheat (or *sheep*) from the weeds (or *goats*); or the fisherman, who collects in the baskets the good fish (*sheep*), and throws away the bad (*goats*).

Verse 34 introduces a change of scenery from the previous ones. Here Jesus no longer calls himself "Son of Man", but «the king». The Son of Man is a king. Who must reign over the people. Not all are worthy. Those who stand at his right hand (sheep) will have a certain fate. Those on his left (goats) will have another (25:34-36):

> Then the king will say to those who will be on his right: «Come, blessed of my Father, receive the kingdom as an inheritance [...] because I was hungry and you gave me food, I was thirsty and you gave me a drink, I was a stranger and you welcomed me, naked and dressed me, sick and you visited me, I was in prison and you came to see me».

The kingdom was prepared not for the totality of the people, but for all who had done certain things. To have been hungry, thirsty, stranger, naked, sick is the king of verse 34. This deep and claimed relationship of identity between the one who sits on the throne and the hungry, thirsty, naked, imprisoned is extremely relevant. Only by keeping it well in mind, we can fully understand the value of the question that those on his right hand ask the Lord:

> Then the righteous will answer him, «Lord, when did we see you hungry and feed you, or thirsty and give you something to drink? When did we see you a stranger and invite you in, or needing clothes and clothe you? When did we see you sick or in prison and go to visit you?».

These are questions that all sound unequivocally rhetorical:
- when can a king, seated on a throne, have ever been hungry and then fed by someone?
- having suffered from thirst?
- having needed to be hosted?
- a man in royal clothes having needed a robe to cover himself? Or even being in prison and having visitors?

Each question clearly shows the astonishment of the questioners: when and where might they have seen their king, now on the throne of his glory, in such extreme conditions of poverty?

The answer is significant and unsettling (25:40):

> Everything that you have done to only one of these *least* brothers of mine, you have done to me.

The king, occupying a "maximum" rank beyond which it is not possible to go, solemnly affirms that, before he ascended the throne, anyone who had fed, quenched, dressed, treated and visited in prison only one of his "least" brothers, it's like he did it to the king himself. The superlative "least" is part of Jesus' favourite semantic area (Mt 10:42):

> Who will have given even one glass of fresh water to one of these *little ones* to drink, because he is a disciple, in truth I say to you: he will not lose his reward.

In chapter 25, Matthew writes that the "least brothers" must be quenched. In chapter 10, those who give drinks to the "little ones", will not lose their reward. It follows that, in the language of Jesus, "small" and "least" are equivalent. In the text of Matthew, we do not read «of these brothers», but «of these my *least* brothers»». They are exclusively those whom the king calls «least», to be his brothers. Not others.

Although the association between a king on the throne and such individuals is not immediate, it is the evangelist himself who tells us that in the life of Jesus there is some connection with the above (Mt 10:19-20):

> Then a scribe approached him and said: «Master, I will follow you wherever you go». Jesus answered him: «The foxes have their dens and the birds of the sky their nests, but the Son of man has nowhere to lay his head».

The fact that the protagonist of the Gospels had no fixed abode is something that emerges clearly. The scribe, accustomed to studying the Law by leading a sedentary and comfortable life, proposes himself as a disciple to Jesus, reassuring him that he will follow the messiah everywhere. The messiah answers him that foxes and birds, having dens and nests, lead quieter lives than the one he leads.

Evidently, like all his "least brothers", he has no fixed abode. He needs to be hosted, quenched, fed (Mk 6:30-31):

> The apostles gathered around Jesus and told him all that they had done and what they had taught. And he said to them, «Come aside, you alone, to a deserted place, and get some rest». In fact, there were many who came and went and did not even have time to eat.

Welcoming and giving care, of all kinds, to the "least brothers", would seem to be the free choice of those who intended to take care of them. Not all people were intended or willing to do so. Yet, they should have done so. Anyway. They weren't just invitations. They were orders of a future king (Mt 25:41-43):

> Then he will also say to those who will be on the left: «Away, away from me, cursed, in the eternal fire [...] I was hungry and you did not give me to eat, I was thirsty and you did not give me to drink, I was a stranger and you did not welcome me, naked and you did not dress me, sick and in prison and you have not visited me».

The interrogative sentences immediately recur (25:44):

> They also will answer, «Lord, when did we see you hungry or thirsty or a stranger or needing clothes or sick or in prison, and did not help you?». He will reply, «Truly I tell you, whatever you did not do for one of *the least* of these, you did not do for me».

Those who have not rescued the "least" disciples, are destined to the inevitable punishment; the others, instead, to have part in the kingdom (Mt 25:46):

> And they will go away: these to the eternal torture, the righteous instead to the eternal life.

Entry into the kingdom or removal from it is decided on the basis of the help given not to human beings in general, but to the "least" brothers of Jesus.

That is, to his followers. Not to the followers of others.

We ask ourselves:

- if the "great" disciples of John (and not the "least" of Jesus) were thirsty, hungry and in conditions of grave need, would the people who might have received them have been destined for the life in the kingdom? Or for the torment of eternal fire?
- if the people had fed, quenched, given shelter to other human beings who had not been the "least" disciples – we assume for

contradiction the Pharisees or the scribes – would have been to the right or the left of the king?
- would they enter the kingdom or burn in the fire?

Matthew's conclusion (25:46) offers the starting point for further reflection. In this passage, only those who have offered help and support to the "least brothers" are called "righteous" and can enter life. But already in verse 37 those who had given refuge to the "least brothers" were called by the king thus:

> Then the *righteous* will answer him, «Lord, when was it that we saw you hungry and gave you food or thirsty and gave you something to drink?

Unequivocally from two precise passages, we learn that Jesus defines "righteous" exclusively those who fed, quenched and gave asylum to his "least brothers". A very clear and no uncertain meaning, attributed to the adjective "righteous", which is clearly different from the semantic context in which it was used previously: that of the observance of the Law.

This criterion must have been well known to the protagonist of the Gospels. He himself affirmed that he did not come for the righteous, but for sinners. The fact that Jesus had a concept of righteousness at least original, emerges clearly precisely from the passages of Matthew (25:37 and 46), where there seems to be no link between the "righteous" mentioned by the king and the observance of the Law. Those who are on the right of the sovereign are destined to enter the kingdom simply because they have given tangible, concrete, material support to his "least" disciples. And no one else.

The fact of being righteous does not appear in any way related to the Law or the Prophets, but to the observance of the king's precise will. Whoever respects his few commands (instead of 613 norms), is a "righteous" and will enter his kingdom. Whoever does not respect them, will be wood for Gehenna.

Therefore, the perspective in which the protagonist of the Gospels conceives the concept of "righteousness" is discreetly foreign to the Old Testament contents (Mt 10:40-42):

> Who welcomes a prophet because he is a prophet, will have the reward of the prophet, and who welcomes a righteous because he is a righteous, will have the reward of the righteous. Who will have given even a single glass of fresh water to one of these *little ones* because he is a disciple, in truth I say to you: he will not lose his reward (Cei 2008).

There is a clear contrast between "prophets-righteous" and "little disciples". It is inferred that those who welcome prophets or righteous would not be pleasing to the protagonist of the Gospels; nor to the king of the "eschatological discourse" (Matthew 25). He brings into his kingdom only the followers "least brothers". It is not in the will of Jesus that scribes or Pharisees should be accepted: they are vipers destined to the fire of Gehenna. It would be logical to think that those who had welcomed them, though thirsty or hungry, would have similar fate.

Some doubts could arouse the Cei translation of the proposed passage. With the phrase «because he is a prophet» are translated the Greek words *èis ònoma profètou* [εἰς ὄνομα προφήτου]: literally, it means «in the name of the prophet». Thus, we speak of the reception of a prophet, who comes in the name of the prophet: that is, of another prophet who sends him. It is a different thing from saying that a prophet is welcomed *because* he is a prophet: "I welcome you, prophet, *because* you are a prophet" is another thing from saying "I welcome you, prophet, *in the name* of the prophet".

In the first example, a prophet is received by virtue of his being a prophet. In the second, a prophet is received in the name of another prophet who sent him: this is what the text clearly says.

In the same way, Matthew says that whoever welcomes a righteous in the name of the righteous, will have the reward of the righteous: that is, the reward that a righteous (the sender) has prepared for the righteous sent by himself. Thus, in the other verse we read that whoever gives a glass of water to one of the "little" disciples of Jesus *in the name* of the disciple, will not lose his reward. So, whoever gives the "little one" a drink, will be rewarded because he comes *in the name* of the one who sends him.

Since we know that Jesus considers himself the brother of the "little" or "least" ones, it does not seem difficult to hypothesize in whose name the disciples should be quenched. If "little ones" and "disciples of Jesus" are equal, then Jesus is the "little brother" who sends, in his name, other "little brothers" or "least brothers" to quench their thirst or feed. It is a concept expressed in Matthew (18: 5):

> And who will welcome a single child like this *in my name*, welcomes me (Cei 2008).

Here the words of the Greek text are translated absolutely literally, with the expression "in the name of me". The reader will understand that the "little" disciple is received *in the name of* someone who sent him. The expression is in fact equivalent to the one present in Matthew 10, that we have seen ("*in the name of* the prophet"). So, why then in Matthew (18:5) that part of the text is correctly translated «*in my name*», while again in Matthew (10:41-42) we find «*because* he is a prophet», «*because* he is a righteous», «*because* he is a disciple»?

Those who receive a prophet *in the name* of the prophet who sent him, will have a certain reward. The same thing will happen to the righteous who are received in the name of the righteous. Both will have a prize that will be different from what Jesus prepares for his "little ones". He himself tells us that neither the prophets nor the righteous have been made aware of the mysteries of the kingdom.

The translation of Matthew 10 by Nuova Riveduta does not differ from the Cei version:

> Whoever receives a prophet *as prophet*, will receive the reward of a prophet; and whoever receives a righteous *as righteous*, will receive a reward of a righteous.

Nuova Diodati instead is in full agreement with what we have expressed:

> Whoever receives a prophet *in the name of* a prophet will receive a reward as a prophet; and whoever receives a righteous *in the name of* a righteous will receive a reward as a righteous. And who will also give a single glass of cold water to one of these little ones *in the name* of a disciple, in truth I tell you, he will not lose his prize at all.

Based on what is faithfully translated from the text, it is clear that there are different categories of individuals who come to the people of Israel to be welcomed: prophets, righteous, "little ones". Only the third category expresses those who are sent by Jesus. The others come in the name of someone else. If the messiah is the brother of the "little ones", the prophets and the righteous must be welcomed in the name of a prophet and a righteous man who sent them. These qualifications are fully suited to the Baptist. That he was a prophet says Jesus himself, in the Gospel of Matthew (11:9):

> What did you go to see? A prophet? Yes, I tell you, rather, more than a prophet.

As for being the Baptist a strict observant of the Law, there seems to be no doubt. This makes even more unshakable the statement of the messiah in Matthew (13:16-17), in which, once again, the "little ones" belong completely to the kingdom; while prophets and righteous people, like John, seem to be programmatically out of it:

> Many prophets and many righteous wanted to see what you look at, but they did not see it, and listen to what you listen to, but they did not listen.

The Law and the Kingdom

Chapter 5 of Matthew begins with the famous "Beatitudes", which we also find in the other synoptic Gospels. They deserve to be treated separately, but suffice it to say here that, within them, Jesus lists a series of precise qualities, that must distinguish those who are considered blessed and therefore worthy to enter his kingdom.

In verses 17 to 19, the core structures for our analysis can be identified. Here Jesus pauses to clarify his role with regard to the Mosaic Law and the prophets:

Μὴ νομίσητε ὅτι ἦλθον καταλῦσαι τὸν νόμον ἢ τοὺς προφήτας· οὐκ ἦλθον καταλῦσαι ἀλλὰ πληρῶσαι

Translating as closely as possible to the Greek text, we will have:

Do not believe that I have come to dissolve the Law or the prophets. I have not come to dissolve but to bring to fullness.

In the versions of the three translations we are examining, we find:

Cei	Nuova Riveduta	Nuova Diodati
Do not think that I have come to abolish the Law or the Prophets; I have not come to abolish, but to give full fulfillment.	Do not think that I have come to abolish the law or the prophets; I have come not to abolish but to fulfill.	Do not think that I have come to repeal the law or the prophets; I have not come to repeal, but to bring to completion.

The negative exhortation («do not think» or «do not believe») with which verse 17 opens, should in itself raise some fundamental questions, namely:

- for what abstruse reason the disciples and the crowds, who follow the messiah, should even think that he has come to abolish the Law given to Moses by him who should be the Father of Jesus?

- why does the son of the Law-giver feel the need to say that he has not come to abrogate it?
- why would disciples and crowds think that?
- what events could have led to a thought or suspicion of this undoubtedly blasphemous scope?

The Greek verb *katalýsai* [καταλῦσαι] properly means «to dissolve» (from it derives the noun "catalysis"), and is translated, into various versions, with the verb "to abolish"; which, however, would imply an action whose fruits are collected immediately. Abolishing a precept means to delete it immediately from a normative code; while in the Greek verb *katalýsai* dominate the concepts of dismemberment, disunity, dissolution.

Therefore, not a sudden abolition would seem to be, but more complicated, slow demolition. The members of the Mosaic Law are the single, numerous norms that form it. Therefore, it does not seem easy to immediately demolish a normative code composed of more than 600 precepts. Likewise, it is not easy to dismember the authority of the Prophets, whose texts make up – together with the Law – the Old Testament.

Jesus affirms that he has come to *pleròsai* [πληρῶσαι]: «to bring to fullness» both the Law and the prophets. The verb *pleròo* [πληρόω] literally means «I make full, I make to reach up to fullness».

If we compare *pleròo* with the verb that Jesus puts in antithesis to it (*katalýsai*: «to dissolve, to destroy»), we will notice that in the latter there are the concepts of subtraction, separation, dismemberment; in the first, on the contrary, those of addition, union of more elements, until you get to abundance and complete filling.

What would be better understood is in what sense Jesus speaks of "bringing to fullness"; and whether he is simply asserting that his task is *to abound* and not to destroy. If the translation of the passage takes the form we find in the versions of Cei, Nuova Riveduta and Nuova Diodati («to complete»), the meaning of the sentence would no longer be that of making abundant, but rather to make complete what was not before. Or perfect what was imperfect.

However, this would require further reflection: if Jesus came (or was sent by the Father) to make the Law perfect, would this mean that the Father gave it imperfect to Moses?

If the messiah had not come to dismember or abolish the Law, this concept would be fully reflected in the book of Deuteronomy (13:1):

> You will observe to put into practice everything I command you: you will not add anything to it and nothing you will take off.

Yahweh commands that no commandment be erased from his code of rules, either in whole or in part; neither the most burdensome rules, nor the least precepts. This would agree with what Jesus said in Matthew, about not having come to abolish: nevertheless, if he had come to complete the Law, to make it perfect because it was clearly lacking before, why then in Deuteronomy do we read: «You will observe to put into practice everything that I command: you will add nothing and take nothing away»?

If the meaning of the verb *pleròo* were "to complete what is incomplete" or "to make perfect what is imperfect", it would follow that the Law given by Yahweh to Moses was imperfect or deficient. This assumption is in manifest contrast with the solemn words spoken by Moses, by which he not only orders that every precept – no one excluded – of the Law be put into practice, but also that nothing be changed, neither by excess nor by defect (Dt 12:1):

> These are the laws and norms that you will take care to put into practice
> in the earth that the Lord, God of your fathers, gives you so that you will
> possess it as long as you live in the land.

They would not seem to be words spoken by one who believes that the Law is to be perfected (Dt 12:28):

> Observe and obey all these things which I command you, that you may be

> happy, you and your children after you, when you have done what is good
> and right in the sight of the Lord your God.

What is good in the eyes of the Lord God seems to have a fixed form already established at the time of Deuteronomy (VI-V century BC), without any need for perfecting (Dt 13:5 and 18-19):

> You will follow the Lord, your God, you will fear him, you will observe his
> commands, you will listen to his voice, you will serve him and you will re-
> main faithful to him [...] observing all his commands that I give you today
> and doing what is right in the eyes of the Lord, your God.

There would seem to be no room for more late refinements or accomplishments.

If, instead, the meaning to be attributed to the verb *pleróo* was, rather to a greater extent, that of "to bring to realization", we would ask ourselves:

- was Moses not sufficient to carry out the legislative intentions for which he had been chosen and designated?
- was he not sufficient to give full enforcement to the Law?
- was his work incomplete?

Finally, if the meaning of *pleróo* were "to ratify" the Law, this would mean that Jesus confirms in all its parts the Mosaic Law. "To ratify" means to make valid, confirmed; to approve something that has already been done by others. In this case, the Law would already be fulfilled by Moses. But if so,

- what necessity would there be for Jesus to ratify it?
- was it not already valid in itself?
- the fact that the lawgiver was Yahweh (the Lord God) was not enough?
- was it therefore paradoxically necessary to ratify or validate an "eternal" will expressed by an "eternal entity"?

«*Heaven and earth will pass away*»

Continuing his programmatic discourse, in verse 18 of Matthew 5, Jesus utters some words that seem to confirm a clear will to ratify the Mosaic Law:

ἀμὴν γὰρ λέγω ὑμῖν, ἕως ἂν παρέλθῃ ὁ οὐρανὸς καὶ ἡ γῆ, ἰῶτα ἓν ἢ μία κεραία οὐ μὴ παρέλθῃ ἀπὸ τοῦ νόμου, ἕως ἂν πάντα γένηται.

Translating as closely as possible to the Greek text, we will have:

Verily I say unto you, until heaven and earth have passed away, let not a single iota or one apex pass from the Law, until all things are done.

If we take into account the presence, in the Greek text, of the particle *àn* [ἂν] (ἕως ἂν, "until when": it gives the phrase meaning of possibility and eventuality), and the reinforcing negation ("ever"), the translation closest to the Greek text will sound like this:

Verily I say unto you, until heaven and earth [eventually] have passed away, shall not a single iota or one apex ever pass from the Law, until everything is done.

The concept expressed by the Greek verb *parèrchomai* [παρέρχομαι] is sufficiently clear. From the Mosaic Law not even an iota (the smallest letter of the Greek alphabet, probably representing here the Aramaic letter *jodh*) or an apex (*keràia*, a small sign resembling an acute accent) can pass, pass over, perish or fall. Therefore, here Jesus would be affirming that the Law is, and will always be, untouchable. Unwavering in all its parts. Even minimal. Unless (that is «until») a precise eventuality occurs: that the heaven and the earth "pass away". And another eventuality, more vague: «until everything has happened, is done».

In the usual three translations we have:

Cei	Nuova Riveduta	Nuova Diodati
Verily, I say to you, until heaven and earth have passed, not even an iota or a sign from the law shall pass, *without all being fulfilled.*	Verily, I say to you, until heaven and earth have passed, not even an iota or a sign from the law shall pass, *without all being fulfilled.*	For verily I say unto you, until heaven and earth have passed, not even an iota or a peak of the law shall pass *without all being fulfilled.*

About the translation of the verb that concludes the verse («without all being fulfilled»), the reader who does not know the Greek text might believe that the verb *pl…

 o* is repeated here ("to bring to completion, to fulfill") and that Jesus is referring to the fulfilment of the Law; while in the original language appears quite another verb, *ghènetai* [γένηται]: «to become, to happen, to be done». Therefore: «before everything has happened / have become / is done».

The concept expressed is that something, not well specified, happens. Until everything has happened (that is: until heaven and earth have passed), not a single dash falls from the Mosaic Law:

- but if the possibility of heaven and earth passing away occurred, what would happen?
- would the Mosaic Law remain in force?

As long as heaven and earth stand, so do the Law and the prophets. Problems arise, instead, when heaven and earth are "passed away". As for this, the protagonist of the Gospels seems to have very clear convictions, if in other passages of the synoptic Gospels the exhaustion of heaven and earth, rather than an eventuality, would seem a certainty, or a hope, prophetically expressed with great asseverative force (Mt 24:35; Mk 13:31; Lk 21:33):

Heaven and earth will pass away, but my words will not pass away.

On this translation agree Cei, Nuova Riveduta and Nuova Diodati. However, in the clause introduced by the adversative conjunction "but" («*but* my words will not pass»), in the Greek text appears a verb expressed in the subjunctive mood (an hortatory subjunctive: not indicating, therefore, an action that will take place in the future). So, more literally, we will have: «but may my words never pass!». It is completely identical to what we have already encountered in Matthew 5. Jesus' words must not "pass away" like heaven and earth. It must not be inevitable or fatal that they pass away.

At the conclusion of this discourse, we ask ourselves: how can the Messiah perfect (or ratify it in all its parts) a Law to which he himself, in his most effective programmatic discourse, sets a precise deadline («*until* heaven and earth *have passed*»)?

Old word, new meaning: the semantic neologism

In light of the considerations we have just made, we must begin to examine the hypothesis that when Jesus uses the verb *pleròo* to say that he came to "bring to fullness" the Law, the messiah – precisely because he is sure that it will last as long as there is heaven and earth – means that the Law is about to be fulfilled. In other words, the Law ends with him, who is bearer of a new announcement. However, until the Law and the prophets pass away, one must know or believe that Jesus is *fulfilling* the Law. It is fulfilled until it lasts, that is: as long as the Law and prophets exist.

In this regard, Matthew (5:19) has a peremptory clarity, equal to that of the one who utters these words:

ὃς ἐὰν οὖν λύσῃ μίαν τῶν ἐντολῶν τούτων τῶν ἐλαχίστων καὶ διδάξῃ οὕτως τοὺς ἀνθρώπους, ἐλάχιστος κληθήσεται ἐν τῇ βασιλείᾳ τῶν οὐρανῶν· ὃς δ᾽ ἂν ποιήσῃ καὶ διδάξῃ, οὗτος μέγας κληθήσεται ἐν τῇ βασιλείᾳ τῶν οὐρανῶν.

The evangelist writes that, until heaven and earth will pass away,

who has eventually violated only one of these least commandments and

211

> has thus instructed men, he *will be called least* in the kingdom of heaven;
> instead, who has put them into practice and taught them, he *will be called
> great* in the kingdom of heaven.

The concepts expressed are entirely consistent with what is written in verse 18: until the passing of heaven and earth, the Law remains intact, including iota and apics. In fact, it is to them that a reference is made, immediately after, when *the least commandments* are mentioned. In such a period of time (that is, until the passing of heaven and earth) two obvious eventualities may occur: the commandments are broken or observed. The rules are either violated or put into practice.

In this regard, verse 19 of Matthew 5 contains nothing new. Since the Lord had delivered the set of precepts to Moses, they could be observed or violated. However, it is what comes immediately after, in the text, to constitute a significant novelty:

> Who therefore will transgress only one of these least precepts and teach
> others to do the same, *will be called least* in the kingdom of heaven. Who
> will observe and teach them, *will be called great* in the kingdom of heaven.

As it happens when, after many and repeated listenings to a piece of music, you notice a dissonant note passed until then unheard, in these verses there is something alienating, that risks not being seen. Something that at first glance is not understood and that instead, listening more carefully to the conceptual melody, turns out to be a note spectacularly foreign to the Old Testament score. There is dissonance, and one can grasp it only keeping in mind that Jesus here speaks of the Mosaic Law. So, he speaks of what the Jewish people had known for centuries. For a long time the Law was observed or violated, and words already existed, in the Hebrew language, to indicate transgression and transgressors, observance and observants.

The transgressors were called "sinners"; the observants "righteous". So,

- why then does Jesus introduce a new terminology concerning transgressors ("least" ones) and observants ("great" ones)?
- why should those, who for centuries in the Old Testament had been called "sinners", now be called by Jesus, in a precise period of time indicated by himself, in a different way ("least")?
- according to what criteria should those who in the Old Testament are called "righteous", change their name and be called "great" (instead of "righteous"), from Matthew 5:19 up to the "passing of heaven and earth"?

Surely Matthew is illuminating in the use of the superlative "least". Technically, it constitutes what is called a semantic neologism: that is, the addition of a new meaning to an already existing word. It allows you to express concepts already known, by naming or otherwise qualifying them.

It is quite clear what the protagonist of the Gospels does:

> Whoever therefore transgresses only one of these least precepts and teaches others to do the same, *will be called least* [...] who instead observes and teaches them, *will be called great.*

The "least" is the transgressor, the "great" is the righteous. So we will have:

$$least\ ones\text{: sinners} = great\ ones\text{ : righteous}$$

The "least" are related to the sinners as the "great" are related to the righteous ones. In the language of the kingdom, the word "least" is to indicate *the sinner* of the Old Testament; the word "great" is to indicate *the righteous* of the Old Testament.

Let us now see how a well-known passage of Matthew himself would sound (9:13), if the words "sinner" and " righteous" were replaced by the neologisms of Jesus:

> I did not come to call the righteous, but sinners

it would become:

> I did not come to call the *great* ones, but the *least* ones.

This is not surprising. As usual, preference is given to those within the semantic area of "smallness" ("small, "little", "least"). Jesus did not come to call John and those "great" like him. He came to call the "least": but why in Matthew (9:13) does the messiah, speaking with the Pharisees, use the "righteous-sinners" opposition and not the "great" and "least" neologisms?

Because with those who strive only and exclusively to prevent entry into the kingdom, it would make no sense to use a language and terminology that are equally *exclusively of the kingdom*. They must not be made aware of the language of the kingdom, nor in particular of the two neologisms of crucial importance, since they invest in all respects the action of the Pharisees: which is to promote *knowledge* and *observance* of the Law.

In Old Testament terminology, the meaning of "transgressor of the Law" was transmitted by a word ("sinner") that shared entirely with the verb from which it derived ("to transgress") the semantic area related to "transgression". There was no possibility of misunderstanding.

With the neologisms, instead, the action relating to the observation or transgression of precepts *loses its reference word*. The action of "transgressing" is no longer performed by the "transgressor" (just as the "runner" is the one who performs the action of "running"). Now, the action of transgressing the Law is accomplished by the "least": that is the superlative of an adjective ("small") which could be referred to anything. Then, it could enter into any semantic family. Everything can be "small" or "least". While the semantic area of "transgression" is a closed and restricted set, that of "smallness" is open and enlarged. And, above all, "least" is a superlative that appears to us totally detached from the semantic area related to the concept of "transgression".

Use of slang and marginal categories

By formulating a banal example, you can understand the effects that the neologism we have said could produce, both in listeners who know it and in those who do not know it at all:

> Yesterday we hosted our *least* friends in our house.

Who was not aware of the meaning exceptionally attributed to the word "least", might think that a group of children at an early age was in the home of a family, at a party. Those who are aware of the substantial shift in meaning, caused by the neologism, will understand very well that some individuals have hosted adults transgressors of norms in their home.

The (old) word is "least". The (new) meaning is "transgressor of the Mosaic Law", which until then had been expressed by the word "sinner".

A particular language spoken exclusively by a well-defined group of people is called jargon: that is, a form of language proper to certain social groups (such as religious sects, people of the same trade, and even vagabonds, criminals, prisoners, etc.), used to avoid understanding by people outside the group. It consists in the systematic substitution of words of the common language with others, with changed and allusive meaning, or deformed or altered.

Bearing in mind this definition, we read Mark (4:33-34):

> With many parables of the same kind he announced to them the Word, as they could understand. Without parables he did not speak to them but, *in private, to his disciples he explained everything*.

According to the author, Jesus spoke to those who went to listen to him (and were out of the group of disciples) literally «as they could hear». It was not allowed to understand all that he said; but, as long as they *could* understand. No further. The measure and the limit of understanding were decided by the one who extended the message: in a deliberately cryptic form, in order not to make people understand completely; but with some margin, granted in order to make them partially understand (Mk 4:24):

Pay attention to what you listen.

In other words: Jesus explained what he said to those outside his group using his jargon, that is, in the cryptic-parabolic language. The Greek verb translated with «explained» is *epèlyen* [ἐπέλυεν], literally "he melted": the messiah melted the tangle of the parables, decoding, for the benefit of the disciples, what was strictly codified to the outside.

All these aspects are addressed, in a simple and very effective way, by the linguist and scholar Roman Jakobson, when he explains that whenever the sender and the recipient have to verify if they use the same code, the speech is centered on the code. This statement is easily verifiable in the Gospel text:

- Have you understood all these things? (Mt 13:51);
- You do not understand this parable, and how will you understand all the parables? (Mk 4:13).

This last passage is the maximum expression of what has been said so far. There is a communicative code of access to the parables told by Jesus, established by the sender. If you know it, you access all of it. Otherwise, none.

Jakobson, in his essays entitled *Linguistics and Poetics*, uses an example to help the reader understand this concept as fully as possible. He asks him to imagine an exasperating dialogue like this:

A. "The *bean* has been rejected".
B. "But what does "rejected" mean?
A. "Rejected" means the same as *torpedoed*".

B. "And torpedoed?"

A. "Torpedoing means *failing a test*".

B. "But what is a bean?" (the interlocutor ignores the student jargon).

A. "A bean is (or means) a *college student* who is in his second year".

All these equivalent expressions convey information exclusively on the lexical code.

Finally, Jakobson's most interesting considerations concern the ambiguity of the message, which is typical of any cryptic language. According to the scholar, it is an inalienable, intrinsic character of every message concentrated on itself. Therefore, the predominance of the poetic function over the merely referential function of language does not cancel the reference, but makes it ambiguous. In simpler terms, the fact that the poetic function of language (expressed with metaphors, similarities, jargon, etc...) is used to a greater extent than that of ordinary communication, does not cancel the concrete object of the message sent by the sender, but simply does it obscure, as in the following example:

> And if your eye is a cause for scandal, take out your eye and throw it away from you. It is better for you to enter life with one eye, rather than with two eyes being thrown into the Gehenna of fire.

The recipient will understand that behaving in one way will be much better than acting in another. Nevertheless, the poetic function («It is better for you *to enter life with one eye*») prevents the immediate reception of the contents that you would have instead in ordinary communication.

"Jargon" is a term used to indicate a variety of languages with a specific vocabulary, that is used by particular groups of people, in certain situations, in order not to make communication transparent to strangers, and to emphasize, conversely, the belonging to a very precise group (Mt 11:25):

> You *have hidden* these things to the wise and the learned, and you have revealed them to *the little ones*.

This language, incomprehensible outside the group that makes use of it, becomes nothing more than a secret code. It excludes from communication those outside the group, but strengthens the bonds of the group that speaks it, whose members share activities and ways of life.

According to the definition of Mika Halliday, which fits very well to the context we are examining, the jargon is used by social categories defined as marginal; it has a value of opposition to the language of normal and institutional society, and is therefore configured as "anti-language", which expresses a counter-culture of opposition and resistance to codified norms and values. The fact that the "little ones" represent marginal categories is clearly evident from the Gospel text:

> Lord, get away from me, because I am a *sinner*.

Applying the neologisms of Jesus, this sentence would result:

> Lord, get away from me, because I'm *least* (= transgressor of the Mosaic Law, who in turn teaches to transgress the norms, according to the definition by Jesus in Matthew 5:19)

After centuries, in which the transgressor had always been called a "sinner" and the observant "righteous man", imposing a new name on these categories undoubtedly represents an opposition to codified values. The intent is not to reveal the contents, or to make them secret: it is "cryptolalia", a Greek word that means "hidden talk". Those who use it are well aware of the need for secrecy, that often makes necessary the imposition of silence. Of this last aspect, there are significant traces in the Gospel text:

- The impure spirits, when they saw him, fell at his feet and cried out: "You are the Son of God". But he *strictly ordered them not to reveal* who he was (Mk 3:11);

- She took the child's hand and said: «Talità kum», which means: "Girl, I say to you: get up". And immediately the girl stood up and walked [...] And he urged them *that no one should know* (Mk 5:41-43);
- They brought him a deaf-mute [...] He took him aside [...] he said: «Effatà», that is: «Open up». And immediately his ears opened, and the knot of his tongue was untied, and he spoke correctly. And he *commanded them not to tell* anyone. But the more he forbade it, the more they proclaimed it (Mk 7:32-36);
- He ordered the disciples *not to tell anyone* that he was Christ (Mt 16:30).
- «But you, who do you say I am?». Peter answered: «The Christ of God». He strictly *ordered them not to report* it to anyone (Lk 9:18-21).

The need for secrecy also emerges in other ways (Mk 6:30-33):

The apostles gathered around Jesus and told him all that they had done and what they had taught. [...] «Come aside, you alone, in a deserted place, and get some rest». In fact, there were many who came and went and did not even have time to eat. Then they went by boat to a deserted place, in the background. But many saw them leave and understood, and from all the cities they ran there on foot and preceded them.

Several questions could arise:
- the "many" people of whom the evangelist Mark speaks, where were they headed?
- what was the purpose of the continuous "coming and going" of the many apostles?
- was the evangelizing activity of invitation to "conversion" a rapid coming and going?
- exactly, what activities did the followers of the messiah carry out, so that they had no time to eat?

Jesus invites the apostles – «you alone» – to rest, even if for a while, but «in a deserted place» and «aside» (*kat'idìan*, «privately, in secret»):
- why is the disciples allowed to rest as little as necessary, but only in a deserted place and on the sidelines, or in secret?

- were they not allowed to stay a little in the places where they were received, rather than having to go to deserted places?

Mark points out that many «saw them leave and understood, and from all the cities rushed there» – in the deserted place – «on foot and preceded them»:

- in particular, what did the inhabitants of the cities «understand»?
- did they understand that Jesus and the disciples were going to a lonely place?

The reaction of the crowd is clearly described as that of someone who sees someone else leaving; and the latter does not want to be seen in such a situation. Therefore,

- what need did Jesus and his people have not to be seen in preparing to leave for a place, that evidently had to remain secret?
- if evangelization was directed at the crowds, why in this passage is clearly understood the desire to escape the crowds, trying to hide the departure by boat?

"To call" or "to consider"?
Discordant translations of Matthew 5:19

About the fact that *"least"* and *"great"* are neologisms deliberately coined by Jesus, all translations are agreed, including Nuova Riveduta and Nuova Diodati. That of the Italian Episcopal Conference, however, is radically different (Mt 5:19):

> Who therefore will transgress only one of these least precepts and teach others to do the same, will be *considered* least in the kingdom of heaven. On the contrary, who will observe and teach them, will be *considered* great in the kingdom of heaven.

What will the reader understand? He will understand that the transgressors will be *considered, judged* very small, minimal, least; therefore, of the least value; individuals in the last places in the kingdom of heaven.

The difference is not insignificant. It is substantial.

It is one thing *to call* an individual "least"; another is *to consider* him such. Using a simple example: being called "zero" is not necessarily equivalent to "*being* a total zero" only because some people call us that. We do not know the motivation or intent of the person who imposed that name on that particular individual.

For Nuova Riveduta and Nuova Diodati, "least" and "great" are the neologisms that Jesus introduces into the kingdom of heaven. The "least" transgresses, the "great" observes. If the "great" is the observant of the Law, the "least" is the transgressor. And therefore, he is an iniquitous man.

This new terminology *does not appear in the Cei translation*. Here, the words "least" and "great" express not a new way of calling transgressors and observants, but the judgment, expressed by Jesus, on them: whoever transgresses, *will be considered* least; who observes, *will be considered* great.

However, we ask ourselves: if, according to Cei, the transgressors are *considered* least, how is it that, in Matthew, Jesus himself always says that «one *smaller*» ("small": the same semantic area of "least") than John in the kingdom of heaven is «*greater* than him»?

Let us see what meaning the passage of Matthew (11:11) would assume, in the light of the concepts expressed, according to the Cei translation, by the same evangelist (Mt 5:19). Here, with all evidence, the semantic area of transgression is matched by the adjective "least"; while the semantic area of observance by the adjective "great". We will have:

> Among those born of a woman, no one *more observant* than John the Baptist has arisen; but the one who is *more transgressor* of precepts, in the kingdom of heaven is more observant than him.

Knowing – always following the Cei translation – that the observants are *considered* "great" while the transgressors "least", we will have:

> Among those born of women, no one has arisen who is considered greater than John the Baptist; but he who is considered smaller in the kingdom of heaven, is considered greater than him.

John, although to be considered "great" – because observant – in the kingdom according to Cei, is presented as the greatest among those born of women, *but not within the kingdom*, where judgement yardsticks seem to be different («one *smaller* in the kingdom is *greater* than him»: greater than him, who is *out of it*):

- if, according to Cei, the observants are considered "great", why then in Matthew (11:11) is the Baptist clearly ascribed to the area of the «born of women» and not to that of the kingdom?
- in the kingdom it has no place for the "great" ones?
- is there room, in the kingdom, for both "least" and "great"?
- or only for one of these two broad categories?

Without a doubt, Matthew reinforces the conviction that the formula "kingdom of heaven" expressed not an indefinite eschatological expectation, but a reality that is coeval with Jesus, and already in progress during his work. A reality that included a specific and restricted category of individuals, inaccessible to most people for programmatic intent, which also included the use of a verbal language whose communicative codes were strictly and exclusively known to members of the "kingdom of heaven". And therefore, not to those "born of women".

The objective problem, in this case, is represented by the fact that there is no one "greater" than John: who is a perfect observant of the Law. Being "smaller" than him means being "less great". That is, less observant. And being less observant means transgressing in some measure the precepts.

Moreover:

- if the one who observes the norms, and teaches to observe them, is considered "great" in the kingdom, does this mean that John occupies the same place «among those born of women» and in the kingdom?
- why, then, does the whole structure of the phrase in Matthew (11:11) unequivocally denounce an irremediable difference between the "born of women" (of whom John is the most authoritative exponent) and the members of the kingdom?

We will then have to consider the hypothesis that those who, among the "born of women", would be considered "great", are not at all in the kingdom; which is neither more nor less what Matthew relates:

> Among those born of a woman, no one is greater than John the Baptist; but the one smaller in the kingdom of heaven is greater than him.

Among the "born of a woman" the yardstick is "greatness". In the kingdom of heaven, instead, "smallness". According to the Cei translation, John is called "great" because Jesus considers him such: a rigorous observant. Therefore, he should occupy the first places in the banquet of the kingdom; while instead, always according to Cei, in Matthew (11:11) Jesus states that in the kingdom there are those who are "greater" than John, who is already "great". So,

- is there anyone who can surpass John in the kingdom in relation to observance of the precepts?
- if so, does this mean that John was, to some extent, a transgressor of the rules?
- if the "competition", so to speak, within the kingdom is all about "greatness" (that is observance), why would Jesus introduce the opposite category of "smallness" as an indispensable requirement for entry into the kingdom?

Continuing to keep in mind the Cei translation, we can only wonder about the position of scribes and Pharisees with respect to the kingdom. We know that, as for being observant, the Pharisees are observant. Therefore, according to Cei, they should be *considered* "great" in the kingdom. However, Jesus considers them strongly antithetical to it; the first obstacle to the entry of any of his disciples (Mt 23:13):

> You close the kingdom of heaven before the people; in fact you do not enter, and do not let in even those who want to enter.

Conceptual dissonances and stridors seem to be many. If the Pharisees are observants who teach to observe, according to the translation Cei we would deduce that, as observants, they will be considered "great" in the kingdom; while in Matthew (23:13), the same observants Pharisees paradoxically block the entry to the kingdom. They don't get in and they don't let in those who want to enter: but if they teach the rules of the Law, how can they prevent entry into the kingdom?

Jesus, in Matthew (23:2 and 4), states:

> The scribes and the Pharisees sat on the chair of Moses [...] They bind heavy and difficult burdens to carry and place them on the shoulders of the people, but they do not want to move them even with a finger.

Scribes and Pharisees appear as heirs of Moses in the work of transmission and disclosure of the Law. And this is all too obvious. What is not at all obvious, is the fact that the messiah seems to say here that the teaching of the Law is equivalent to imposing heavy burdens (to enforce the numerous rules) on the shoulders of the people, despite scribes and Pharisees do not want to move them even with the finger (they would not really want to observe the rules).

In essence, in a passage of the text wise and learned of the Law would be "promoted" (considered "great" according to Cei); in this other, decidedly rejected. Everything we have seen comes from the textual evidence that in Matthew (5:19) the translation Cei attributes to the Greek verb *kalèo* [καλέω], «I call, I name», the meaning that belongs to the so-called verbs "of judging", or "estimative verbs" («to estimate, to judge, to consider»); while the verbs "appellative" or "of naming" («to call, to define, to name, to appellate»: this is the case of *kalèo*) answer to the question "how?" ("*How* will transgressors be called? *Least*"). It is immediately clear that all the listed meanings of *kaléo* are ascribable to the verbs "of naming", and not to those "of judging" («I believe, I judge, I consider»).

We now list below, for scrupulously exemplifying purposes, the passages of the text in which the verb *kalèo*, in its various forms, appears in the synoptic Gospels and in which it is translated "to call, to give the name" in the same version Cei:

1. Mt 2:23: He will be *called* Nazarene.
2. Mt 21:13: My house will be *called* a house of prayer.
3. Mk 11:17: My house will be *called* a house of prayer for all nations.
4. Lk 1:32: He will be great and will be *called* the Son of the Most High.
5. Lk 1:35: He will be *called* the Son of God.
6. Lk 1, 60: But his mother intervened: «No, it will be *called* John».
7. Lk 2:23: Every firstborn male will *be said* to be sacred to the Lord.
8. Mt 2:15: From Egypt I *called* my son.
9. Mt 1:25: He *called* him Jesus.
10. Mt 4, 21: Saw two other brothers [...] and *called* them.
11. Mt 25:14: He *called* his servants.
12. Mk 1, 20: And immediately he *called* them.
13. Lk 14:16: A man gave a great supper and *called* many.
14. Lk 1:59: They wanted *to call* him by the name of his father, Zechariah.
15. Mt 27:8: Therefore that camp was *called* "Field of blood".
16. Lk 2:21: He was *given the name* Jesus.
17. Mt 22:43: Why then does David, moved by the Spirit, *call* him Lord?
18. Mt 22:45: If therefore David *calls* him Lord.

19. Lk 14:13: When you give a banquet, you *call* the poor, the crippled, the lame, the blind.

20. Lk 20:44: David therefore *calls* him Lord.

21. Mt 23:7: To be *called* "rabbis" by the people.

22. Lc 1, 62: They asked his father what he wanted *his name to be*.

23. Lc 1, 61: There is none of your kinship that is *called* by this name.

24. Lk 2:4: He went up to Judea to the city of David *called* Bethlehem.

25. Lc 6, 46: Why do you *call* me: "Lord, Lord"?

26. Mt 9:13: I have not come in fact to *call* the righteous, but sinners.

27. Mt 22:3: He sent his servants to *call* the wedding guests.

28. Mk 2:17: I have not come to *call* the righteous, but sinners.

29. Lk 5:32: I have not come to *call* the righteous, but sinners.

30. Mt 2, 7: Herod, secretly *called* the Magi [...]

31. Lk 7:39: The Pharisee who *called* him said to himself [...]

32. Lk 14:9: He who *called* you and him [...]

33. Lk 19:13: *Called* ten of his servants [...]

34. Mt 22:9: All those whom you find, *call* them to the wedding.

35. Mt 23:9: And do not *call* any of you a father on earth.

36. Mt 1, 21: You will *call* him Jesus.

37. Lk 1:13: You shall *call* him John.

38. Lk 1:31: You will give birth to him and *call* him Jesus.

39. Mt 20, 8: *Call* the workers and pay them.

40. Mt 1, 23: He will be *given the name* of Emmanuel.

41. Lk 1, 36: It is the sixth month for her, which was *called* barren [...]

42. Lk 8:2: Mary, *called* Magdalene.

43. Lk 10:39: She had a sister, *named* Mary.

44. Lk 7:11: Jesus went to a city *called* Nain.

45. Lk 9:10: He withdrew to a city *called* Bethsaida.

46. Lk 6:15: Simon *called* Zelotes.

47. Lk 19:29: The Mount *called* "of Olives".

48. Lk 21:37: The Mount *called* "of Olives".

49. Lk 22:3: Judas, *called* Iscariot.

50. Lk 23, 33: When they came to the place *called* Skull [...]
51. Lk 19:2: A man *named* Zacchaeus.
52. Mk 3, 31 Standing outside, they *called* him.
53. Lc 14, 10: When you are *called*, go and put yourself in the last place, because when the one who has *called* you comes, he says: "Friend, come further".
54. Lk 14:12: He then said to the one who had *called* him [...]
55. Lk 14:24: None of those men who had been *called* [...]
56. Mt 22:8: The wedding feast is ready, but those *called* were not worthy.
57. Mt 22, 4: Tell the people *called*: Here, I have prepared my lunch.
58. Lk 14:17: He sent his servant to *call* the guests [...]
59. Lc 14, 8: When you are *called* to a wedding by someone [...]
60. Lc 14, 7: Noting how the people *called* chose the first places [...]
61. Lk 15:19: I am no longer worthy to be *called* your son.
62. Lk 15:21: I am no longer worthy to be *called* your son.
63. Lk 1:76: You will be *called* the prophet of the Most High.
64. Mt 2:23: He went and dwelt in a city *called* Nazareth [...] "He shall be *called* Nazarene."
65. Mt 5:19: He will be *called* least in the kingdom of heaven.
66. Mt 5:9: Blessed are the peacemakers, for they will be *called* sons of God.
67. Mt 23:8: But do not be *called* "rabbi" [...]
68. Mt 23:10: And do not be *called* "guides" [...]
69. Lk 2:21: He was *given the name* Jesus [...]

Moreover, in addition to the approximately 70 times it is found in the canonical Gospels, the verb *kalèo* is also present in the other texts that make up the New Testament. In total, it appears 148 times. In more technical terms, it will be said that it has 148 occurrences. However, against all 148 verses —we emphasize – in which it is repeated and always unequivocally translated by Cei "to call" or "to give the name", *the only two times* in which – according to the same Cei – such verb should be translated with a totally different meaning ("to consider", "to estimate"), would be – *only and exclusively* – those of Matthew (5:19):

> [...] he will be *considered* least [...] he will be *considered* great.

Nevertheless, even the Latin translation of the Vulgate confirms the belonging of *kalèo* to the verbs "of naming" (and not "of judging"):

> [...] minimus *vocabitur* [...] magnus *vocabitur*.

That is, «*will be called* least [...] *will be called* great». The Latin verb used is *vocare*: there is no doubt that it can only be translated "to call", and certainly not "to consider": the latter is a meaning that in Latin would be expressed by a completely different verb.

Therefore, the translations of Nuova Diodati and Nuova Riveduta would seem more consistent with the text: in these versions, the superlative "least" is simply the name that Jesus gives to those who transgress and teach to transgress the precepts. Since this word, referring to human beings, occurs only twice more in Matthew, we will now examine the passages involved (25:40 and 45), to try to ascertain whether the term is used in the same sense.

Reward and punishment in Matthew 25

Chapter 25 of Matthew proposes, in various degrees, the opposition "prize *vs* punishment". At the beginning of the passage, two parables (so-called "of the ten virgins" and "of the talents") are enunciated.

The first one occupies verses 1 to 13. To the couple "reward *vs* punishment", the evangelist adds the couple "wise *vs* foolish". The wise virgins, who have kept watch at night waiting for the bridegroom, will be admitted into his dwelling. But fools will remain locked out (Mt 25:1-12):

> Then the kingdom of heaven will be like ten virgins who took their lamps and went out to meet the bridegroom. Five of them were foolish and five wise; the foolish took their lamps, but they took no oil with them; the wise [...] also took oil in small vessels. Because the bridegroom was late, they all fell asleep. At midnight a cry arose: «Behold the bridegroom. Go meet him». Then all those virgins woke up and prepared their lamps. The fools said to the wise: «Give us some of your oil, because our lamps go out». The wise women answered: «No, so that we and you may not miss it; go instead to the sellers and buy it». Now, while they went to buy the oil, the bridegroom came and the virgins who were ready entered with him at the wedding, and the door was closed. Later the other virgins also arrived and began to say: «Lord, Lord, open to us». But he answered: «Truly I say to you: I do not know you».

The second parable (verses 14-30) is constructed according to the same scheme, with the variant consisting of the binomial "faithful and productive servant *vs* unfaithful and unproductive servant". The trusted servants are rewarded by the master; the subordinate who had not put to good use the talent, is destined to bitter end (25:14-36):

> Again, it will be like a man going on a journey, who called his servants and entrusted his wealth to them. To one he gave five bags of gold, to another two bags, and to another one bag, each according to his ability. Then he went on his journey. The man who had received five bags of gold went at once and put his money to work and gained five bags more. So also, the one with two bags of gold gained two more. But the man who had received one bag went off, dug a hole in the ground and hid his master's money. After a long time the master of those servants returned and settled accounts with them. The man who had received five bags of gold brought the other five. "Master", he said, "you entrusted me with five bags of gold. See, I have gained five more". His master replied, "Well done, good and faithful servant. You have been faithful with a few things; I will put you in charge of many things. Come and share your master's happiness". The man with two bags of gold also came. "Master", he said, "you entrusted

me with two bags of gold; see, I have gained two more". His master replied, "Well done, good and faithful servant! You have been faithful with a few things; I will put you in charge of many things. Come and share your master's happiness". Then the man who had received one bag of gold came. "Master", he said, "I knew that you are a hard man, harvesting where you have not sown and gathering where you have not scattered seed. So I was afraid and went out and hid your gold in the ground. See, here is what belongs to you". His master replied, "You wicked, lazy servant. So you knew that I harvest where I have not sown and gather where I have not scattered seed? Well then, you should have put my money on deposit with the bankers, so that when I returned I would have received it back with interest. So take the bag of gold from him and give it to the one who has ten bags. For whoever has will be given more, and they will have an abundance. Whoever does not have, even what they have will be taken from them. And throw that worthless servant outside, into the darkness, where there will be weeping and gnashing of teeth.

If the parable of the ten virgins begins with the words «then the kingdom of heaven will be like ten virgins», and that of the talents with the words « it will be like a man», in the following verses 31-46, however, no veiled similarity is established between the man who tells (Jesus) and the bridegroom or master, protagonists of the parables. There is a relationship of identity between the one who speaks (the messiah) and the protagonist of the story (Mt 25:31):

When the Son of man comes in his glory, and all the angels with him, he will sit on the throne of his glory.

Since we know that the protagonist of the Gospels often loves to speak of himself as the «Son of Man», we can say that in Matthew (25:31) Jesus affirms that he is the one destined to the throne. In the first story, the messiah speaks of an unidentified spouse; in the second, of a rich master. In the third, we immediately feel the difference compared to the other two. Suddenly, a tear opens in the parabolic veil. And he speaks of himself.

In fact, there can be countless men who marry; as many can be the protagonists of any story, who play the role of masters. But there is only one Son of Man. The fact that he is the one to give rewards and punishments, should dispel any doubt about the identity that, out of parable, have the groom and the master. It is up to them to reward or punish, just like it is up to the Son of Man (25:32-33):

> All the peoples will be gathered in front of him. He will separate one from the other, as the shepherd separates the sheep from the goats, and he will place the sheep on his right and the goats on the left.

The coded language is decoded by the same extender of the message. Husband and master are but the Son of Man. He separates those who have fulfilled his will all of it, from those who have not done it or have done it imperfectly. "Virgins" and "servants" are all the nations gathered before him.

As the bridegroom separated the virgins and the master separated the servants, the messiah divides the people according to precise criteria, as the shepherd does with the flocks. He defines himself as king. The Son of man is bridegroom. Is master. Is shepherd. He is king. He disposes of the destiny of his subjects. At his right hand are the sheep. To the left are the goats. They cannot mix with sheep: the only ones to belong to the shepherd. Metaphors aside, they are human beings blessed by the Father:

> I was hungry and you gave me to eat, I was thirsty and you gave me to drink, I was a stranger and you welcomed me, naked and you dressed me, sick and you visited me, I was in prison and you came to visit me.

The messiah is therefore saying that he suffered from hunger and thirst. He claims to have been a stranger; naked; sick; in prison. All quite atypical living conditions for a king: before he was king, what kind of life did the protagonist of this story lead?

This and other questions would be natural and licit. In fact, they correspond neither more nor less to those that the subjects to the right (sheep) address to the Son of Man; questions that have the obvious purpose on the one hand to emphasize the objective wonder of the subjects before a list of actions that do not befit a king; on the other hand, to emphasize the precise merits for which the subjects to the right could inherit the kingdom (25:37-39):

> Everything that you have done to only one of these *least* brothers of mine, you have done to me.

These things must have been extremely important tasks, if their performance is the yardstick for admission to the kingdom. Or to be definitively excluded:

> Then he will also say to those who will be on the left: «Away, away from me, cursed, in the eternal fire [...] I was hungry and you did not feed me, I was thirsty and you did not give me to drink, I was a stranger and you did not welcome me, naked and you did not dress me, sick and in prison and you have not visited me [...] all that you have not done to one of these *least*, you have not done to me».

Not doing these things is a sin that cannot be forgiven (25:46):

> And they will go away: these to the eternal torture, the *righteous* instead to the eternal life.

The adjective "righteous" we had already found in verse 37:

> Then the *righteous* will answer him: «Lord, when did we see you hungry and feed you, or thirsty and give you drink?».

What risks going unnoticed is the meaning in which the adjective "righteous" is used here. In the Old Testament and in the Gospels themselves it designates, as we know, the observant of the Law. At the same time, we also know that Jesus says:

I have not come to call the righteous, but the sinners.

Therefore, we should no longer have found the adjective "righteous" in reference to people called by Jesus. Whereas, we find it in Matthew 25, just in reference to the people chosen and preferred by him (those on his right). Jesus uses the adjective "righteous" in a radically different way than the meaning known until then. For the protagonist of the Gospels is "righteous" not who generally observes the precepts, but who feeds; hosts; protects; eventually cares and visits in prison his "brothers" followers. To such "righteous" are opened the doors of the kingdom.

If we defined those on the king's left with Old Testament terminology, we would call them "sinners". It follows that for the king the "sinners" are not the transgressors of the Law, but exclusively those who have not fed; hosted; protected; cured; visited in prison his "brothers" followers. He receives a reward who does these actions not in general towards needy human beings, but only towards the disciples of Jesus.

In the same way, are chastised not those who refuse to do the same things to any human being who asks for help, but those who refuse to do them only for the benefit of the "brothers" of Jesus. From all this, we will deduce that righteousness according to the Law – that is, the observance of the norms of the Torah – seems to take a clear second place in the fulfilment of that precise list of actions for the benefit of the followers of the messiah (Mt 12:31):

Any sin and blasphemy will be forgiven to men, but the blasphemy against the Spirit will not be forgiven.

The fact that Jesus claims that «any» transgression of the Law and «any» blasphemy (only to Yahweh it could be addressed) will be forgiven by him, but not blasphemy against the Holy Spirit, implies that the Old Testament righteousness has given way to a new righteousness: to do the will of the disciples, that is, of Jesus himself.

Therefore, the Son of Man also forgives any blasphemy against the one who would be his Father (with all the objectively blasphemous potential that such a statement might carry within Jewish society). But he does not forgive blasphemy against the Spirit at all. This last word is inextricably linked, together with "fire", to the proselytizing activity of Jesus; and radically differentiates it from the "water" of John the Baptist. The messiah forgives the transgressors (sinners) towards the Law. But he will never absolve him who has been unrighteous to those who have the Holy Spirit and have been baptized in it: that is, Jesus and his disciples.

The righteous according to the Law are irrelevant with regard to the concept of righteousness of which Jesus is the bearer. For him, one is righteous (or not) only in relation to his will and, equally, to the will of his disciples. The discrimination between righteousness and unrighteousness appears only this.

The fact that transgression against the Spirit is a sin that can in no way be forgiven, is clearly stated in Matthew (25:46; 12:31):

Matthew 12:31	Matthew 25:45-46
Any sin and blasphemy will be forgiven to men, but blasphemy against the Spirit will not be forgiven.	Everything you haven't done to one of these least, you haven't done to me. And they will go away: these to eternal torment, the righteous instead to eternal life.

The fact that between the irremediable lack of absolution and torture – not by chance it is an «eternal torment» – there is a clear relationship, is deduced from the continuation of Matthew (12:32):

> He who speaks against the Son of man shall be forgiven; but he who speaks against the Holy Spirit shall not be forgiven, neither in this century nor in the future.

So, according to Jesus you can also speak against Jesus (and if you speak against someone, it will not be nice words). But whoever is guilty of guilt against the Spirit, can in no way obtain mercy. Neither now, nor ever. This is a concept undoubtedly expressed also by Mark (3:28):

> All will be forgiven to the sons of men, sins and even all the blasphemies they will say; but whoever has blasphemed against the Holy Spirit will not be forgiven forever: he is guilty of eternal guilt.

Equally eternal and irrevocable will be the penalty imposed: neither more nor less than that expressed by Matthew (25:46). Those who have not fed, given asylum, cared for and visited in prison the disciples "brothers" of Jesus, will have the same fate: perennial punishment. Or, they will not have forgiveness forever (Mark). The unforgivable guilt towards the Spirit coincides with the punishment of Matthew 25.

The fact that the offense against the Spirit entailed a definitive penalty, and without any discount, is witnessed by the episode that in the Acts of the Apostles (5:1-11) involves the beloved disciple Peter and the spouses Ananias and Sapphira, elderly married couple belonging to the first Christian community in Jerusalem. Regarding all the followers of the community, we read immediately before (Acts 4:32-35):

> Nobody considered what belonged to him as his property, but everything was common among them. [...] Those who owned fields or houses sold them, brought the proceeds [...] they laid it at the feet of the apostles; then it was distributed to each according to his need.

Within these contexts, the story of Ananias and Sapphira constitutes a very significant episode:

A man named Ananias, with his wife Sapphira, sold a piece of land and, having kept it for himself, in agreement with his wife, a part of the proceeds, handed over the other part to the apostles. But Peter said: «Ananias, why [...] did you lie to the Holy Spirit and withhold a portion of the proceeds of the field? Before selling it, was it not your property and the amount of the sale was not perhaps at your disposal? [...] You did not lie to men, but to God». Hearing these words, Ananias fell to the ground and died. A great fear spread to all who listened. The young men rose, wrapped him up, took him out and buried him [...] about three hours later, his wife came in, unaware of the incident. Peter asked her: «Tell me: is at this price that you have sold the field?». And she answered: «Yes, at this price». Then Peter said to her: «Why did you agree to test the Spirit of the Lord? Here at the door those who buried your husband: they will take you away too». She instantly fell at Peter's feet and died. When the young men entered, they found her dead, took her outside and buried her next to her husband. A great fear spread throughout the assembly and in all those who came to know these things.

The passage did not fail to arouse more than one perplexity even many centuries ago, for example by the philosopher Porphyry of Tyre, who had no difficulty in identifying in the excess of zeal and in the armed hand of Peter the ultimate cause of the death of the two elderly spouses:

The famous Peter is accused of injustice also on other occasions: in fact a man called Ananias and his wife called Sapphira, because they had not laid down the entire value of their land [...] Peter made them die without having committed any evil. For what did they do wrong if they did not want to give all their possessions? If in fact the gesture was considered wrong, it was necessary that he remembered the precepts of Jesus, who had taught him to forgive sins up to four hundred ninety times, and forgive them for that one fault, if the episode could really be considered a sin [...] he himself had not only lied by swearing that he did not know Jesus, but he perjured and despised the coming judgment and resurrection (quoted by Macario, 2009, at page 221).

Jerome, the Doctor of the Church already mentioned, answers indirectly to the philosopher in an epistle addressed to the Roman virgin Amna Demetriade, on the occasion of her consecration:

> The apostle Peter had in no way invoked the death of Ananias and Sapphira, as falsely accuses the fool Porphyrius (quoted by Muscolino, 2015, at page 189).

However, the author of the translation of the Vulgate presumably should not have been in possession of the unshakable certainty of such a statement, if he himself referred, in another letter (epistle 109, 3), to «*Petri severitatem Ananiam et Sapphiram trucidantis*» (quoted by Porphyry, 2009, at page 219): which means the «hardness of Peter in the slaughter of Ananias and Sapphira».

It is a sufficiently transparent statement through which Jerome, proclaimed a saint by the Church and author of the Latin translation of the Gospels – on which the theological imaginary, in the broadest sense, of the West was built – would be here stating that Peter, the "stone" at the base of the future *ekklesía* (assembly) of Christians, was a murderer.

The events involving Anania and Sapphira were the subject of a relatively recent dialogue between Jorge Mario Bergoglio and the Lombard seminarians, received in audience on Tuesday, October 16, 2018, in the Clementine Hall of the Apostolic Palace, next to Saint Peter's Basilica in Vatican City (the transcript is published in the «Bulletin of the Holy See Press Office» No. 0758 of 16.10.2018, available online at https:///press.vatican.va/content/salastampa/it/bollettino/public/2018/10/16/16/0758.pdf.).

On pages 7 and 8 of the official document we read the verbal exchange between a deacon of the diocese of Milan, whose name is reported (David), and the current Pontiff:

> Holy Father [...] in recent months we have witnessed serious events that have shaken from the inside the boat of Peter [...] How to stand authentically in front of the scandals that afflict us and involve even the consecrated? How to help the faithful not to lose hope [...]?

Immediately below is the Bishop of Rome's answer:

> "There must be scandals", says Jesus. The scandal is from the beginning of
> the Church: think of Ananias and Sapphira, those two who wanted to cheat
> the community: a scandal. Peter clearly resolved the scandal, in that case: he
> "cut off the head" of both.

However, since transcribing an oral speech is not possible to place on words, for obvious reasons, graphic signals so strongly distinctive as the high quotation marks between the verb "to cut" and the noun "head", one wonders: why should the transcriber of the dialogue unlawfully do so?

In light of this, the correct transcription would be as follows:

> Peter has clearly resolved the scandal, in that case: he cut off the head of both.

Therefore, in the meeting with the Lombard seminarians received in audience on Tuesday, October 16, 2018 (the contents of which are transcribed in the «Bulletin Press Office of the Holy See»), the Bishop of Rome, successor of Peter, would have said that Peter was an assassin.

Moreover, the «scandal» represented, according to Bergoglio, by «those two who wanted to cheat the community» and to whom the sword of Peter would put an end, makes appear the "fraud" of Ananias and Sapphira – not having given all the goods to those who forced them to donate goods – a guilt and a scandal greater than the double murder committed by a human being against other human beings.

Nevertheless, even assuming that Peter was not responsible for their deaths, we still have confirmation from the text that the offense or blasphemy against the Holy Spirit was undoubtedly not forgiven. Exactly as written in the evangelical passages examined.

Therefore, with respect to what was said by Porphyry on the fact that Peter needed to remember the precepts of Jesus on forgiveness up to 490 times, we would answer that, in reality, the work of Peter is adherent precisely to the evangelical prescriptions:

> Whoever has blasphemed *against the Holy Spirit* will not be forgiven forever: he is guilty of eternal guilt.

Peter knew well that he had to "forgive up" to seventy times seven (calling to himself as many transgressors as possible). But the only true fault – that against the Spirit – could not and should not be forgiven in any way: for such a fault was found on those who were not willing to do all that Jesus and his disciples imposed. Those who opposed the Spirit did not give all their goods to the *ekklesía* (assembly) of the disciples and, like the "rich young man" from the famous Gospel episode, could not therefore enter the Kingdom. The episode of Ananias and Sapphira confirms this.

"Elàchistos" [ἐλάχιστος]: the perfect disciple of Jesus

The superlative form of the adjectives "little-small" ("least"), in Matthew (5:19) is once referred to the norms of the Law:

> Who therefore will transgress only one of these *least* precepts.

In the other cases it has to do with human beings:
- He will be called *least* in the kingdom of heaven (5:19)
- Every time you have done these things to one of my *least* brothers (25:40)
- Every time you have not done these things to one of these *least* (25:45)

In these last two cases, instead of "least", in the Cei translation we find «*smaller*». So, what should the reader understand if he has no access to the Greek text?

He will understand that there are some individuals "smaller" than Jesus. Hearing, for example, the sentence "if you do not treat these *smaller* children well, you will be punished", we would understand that there are children *smaller* than the one who pronounces the phrase; or smaller than others, within a certain group or set of children. However, the context of Matthew 25 does not help to understand in what sense Jesus' brothers would be "smaller". In the Nuova Riveduta and Nuova Diodati versions we find "least", and not "smaller".

According to the grammar of the Greek language, an absolute superlative appears unequivocally in the text.

We ask ourselves:

- if, as we have already seen, according to Cei the "least" are those whom Jesus "considers" as such (thus expressing a judgment of minimal value on men who will be far from the kingdom), why does he consider them, at the same time, their "brothers" in Matthew 25?

- if, according to Cei, there is someone who is «considered great» by Jesus (as the Baptist was defined), how is it possible at the same time that the messiah defines his "brothers" those he himself *considers* "least" within the kingdom?

- should it not be the exact opposite, that is to say that his "brothers" are considered "great"?

- John the Baptist, precursor and by Jesus himself defined «great», would be considered by Jesus a "brother" or not?

At least, we should be able to answer this last question. If for Jesus the one who in the kingdom is "smaller" than the "great" John is superior to John himself, then evidently the Baptist cannot be among those whom Jesus defines as brothers in the kingdom.

All the questions (unanswered) that can be asked, are justified in the Cei translation of Matthew (5:19). Here the Greek verb *kalèo* is translated as a "verb of judging" ("to estimate", "to consider"). However, in no grammar or dictionary of the Greek language this verb is classified among the "verbs of judging ", but among the "verbs of naming", as clearly reported by Nuova Riveduta and Nuova Diodati. In these versions, Jesus *calls* the disciples "least", and defines them unequivocally his "brothers".

This is a passage that Matthew could not have written if the messiah had defined his "brothers" as the people he *considered* "least".

In addition:

- why should denying anything to those whom Jesus himself *considers* "least", amount to denying it to himself?
- so does the messiah have has at heart the fate of those he himself *considers* "least" in the kingdom?
- shouldn't it be much more obvious that denying something to those whom Jesus "*considers* great" (according to the Cei translation), is equivalent to denying it to himself?
- is Jesus "great" or "least"?

All the questions arise from a translation defect at the beginning. Simply, Jesus does not "consider" least, but he *calls* his brothers "least".

To understand precisely what Jesus means with this superlative, we must remain in Matthew's text, chapter 5, where we learn that "least" are *those who violate the norms of the Law and teach to violate them*. The question now is whether there is any relationship between the repetitions (occurrences) of this superlative. If in fact, within a text, appears a superlative form with the clear explanation of the meaning attributed to it by the sender himself of the message; and later we find the same superlative repeated twice, there is the very high probability that they are conceptually related.

So let us return to Matthew (25:40):

> Every time you have done it to one of these my *least* brothers, you have done it to me.

The usual problem recurs: "least" exactly what does it mean for Jesus? It will suffice to return to Matthew 5:

> Whoever therefore *will transgress* only one of these least precepts and teach others to do the same, will be *called least* in the kingdom of heaven.

This is the definition that Jesus himself gives of the word "least" in Matthew. Here the evangelist points out that the superlative is directly linked to the kingdom of heaven (the fact that in chapter 25 we are talking about the kingdom is obvious: the protagonist is a king seated on a throne).

To re-number now all the hypotheses on the possible meanings of the superlative "least", would be completely useless. These would be personal interpretations; while the messiah himself explains it, in his own words, in the Gospel of Matthew. Therefore, in order to have a clearer idea, it remains only to replace the word "least" (Mt 25:40) *with the corresponding meaning that Jesus himself attributes to it*, always in Matthew (5:19).

In the left column we put the word ("least"); on the right the meaning that Jesus himself gives to this word:

Word examined ("least")	Meaning of the word examined according to Jesus
Everything you've done to one of my *least* brothers, you've done to me.	Everything you've done to one of these brothers of mine *who have broken only one of these least commandments and have taught men this way*, you have done to me.

Repeating the operation in Mt 25:45, you have:

Everything you have not done to one of my *least* brothers, you have not done to me.	Everything you have not done to one of these brothers of mine *who have broken only one of these least commandments and have taught men this way*, you have not done to me.

It is enough to violate one single commandment of the Law, even a minimal one, to be a follower of Jesus. He who does not transgress the Law, cannot be his disciple. He came to call sinners, not the righteous.

We can therefore easily ascertain, and with the full support of the text we can affirm that in the Gospel of Matthew – which opens the ecclesiastical canon of the New Testament – it is clearly written that the messiah defines his "brothers", destined to the kingdom, the transgressors of the Mosaic Law. Who, in turn, teach to transgress it. Thereby, procuring new disciples transgressors.

In the Cei edition, in a footnote relating to the translation of Matthew (25:40), we read:

> «By the word "little ones" we mean here all those who, in various ways, are in need».

However, this interpretation («we mean») is not supported and is not legitimised by the text. It has no internal verifiability elements. It is one of many, free interpretations possible. While in Matthew the same Jesus unequivocally states:

> Whoever therefore transgresses only one of these least precepts and teaches others to do the same, *will be called* least.

In this very precise way he will be called the one who is most committed to transgressing the Law: a precise meaning, attributed by the author of the message, which is not to be understood – as if there were not enough textual evidence – according to a usual, customary, habitual, common interpretation; but in its sense completely unusual. Not predictable. Out of the ordinary. Absolutely peculiar.

Therefore, being generally «needy» is not the meaning to arbitrarily attach to the adjective "small-little" and "least". If anything, it is the obvious *consequence of the meaning that Jesus assigns* to it, that is: extreme and constant destitution, caused by living in constant danger. The result of the voluntary hiding of individuals systematically committed to transgression.

The justice of the Kingdom

At this point, the lighthouse of the comparison between the passages of Matthew should have put light in the fog of the text. And the thick fog should begin to clear.

Within the kingdom, Jesus gives preference not only to the transgressors of the Law, but to those who produce an important surplus (or "talent"); that is, to those transgressors who, in addition to transgressing the Law, teach to transgress it. And therefore, procure new transgressor disciples (new "talents").

Having ascertained, within the text, how Matthew's passages are substantiated by content of an undoubted subversive nature, one can understand more clearly how neologisms ("little-least") are useful to cover up what cannot be openly said. If in public discourses the messiah had affirmed that sinners would enter the kingdom – and not the observants of the Law –, the preaching of Jesus would have stopped immediately (or almost). For obvious, serious reasons. The fact that the Pharisees sought him to catch him, is indicative of his project radically hostile to the Law and its knowledge and dissemination:

- And the Pharisees, gone out, immediately held counsel with the Herodians against him, to make him die (Mk 3:6);
- Then the Pharisees went out and took counsel against him to make him die (Mt 12:14);
- Meanwhile, some inhabitants of Jerusalem said: «Is he not the one they're trying to kill?» (Jn 7:25)
- They tried then to arrest him, but nobody was able to get their hands on him, because his time had not yet come [...] Therefore the chief priests and the Pharisees sent guards to arrest him (Jn 7:25-32);
- Some of them wanted to arrest him, but nobody laid hands on him. The guards then returned to the chief priests and the Pharisees, and they said to them, «Why have you not brought him here?» (Jn 7:44-45);
- They tried to capture him again, but he slipped out of their hands. He

then returned again beyond the Jordan, to the place where John first
baptized, and here he remained (Jn 10:39-40).

It would not be a stretch to wonder what the common reader might
or should think about reports of attempted arrests and escapes, if he
simply ignored the identity (Jesus in our case) of the wanted man we're
talking about. The common reader would think, in a very motivated
way, that the character of which we speak is a man who has done such
actions, that it was necessary for him to be arrested.

Returning now to the "least brothers", not universal magnanimity is
mentioned in Matthew 25, but the obvious and natural consequences of
being violators of norms. Those who transgress them will most likely be
fugitives. They will need food; water; hospitality during their absence, being fugitives. They will need clothes, care, visits to prison at worst.

An eventuality, the latter, which is obvious if you let Matthew say
what Matthew wanted to say: the disciples of Jesus were transgressors.
As such, they risked ending up in prison. This is a word ("prison")
that is incomprehensible if we want to silence the text and arbitrarily
attribute to the superlative "least" the meaning of "innocent children,
innocent as pure children", and so on. The children, precisely because
"innocent", with prisons would strictly logically have very little to do.
While, any transgressor who procures further transgressors to a movement of transgressors, with detention he should have, rightly and until
proven otherwise, many more conceptual ties.

Not having hosted the "least" is equivalent to not having taken
care of the future king of Israel. Just like them, for a long time he had
nowhere to lay his head, living in the open, often being an unwelcome
guest in the many villages he visited with his disciples. Those villages,
having refused him, should have had, according to his own words, a
worse fate than that of the Old Testament cities of Sodom and Gomorrah: swept away by an incinerator fire. People who do not accept
to be conniving with transgressors are punished. Those who are con-

niving, will have an adequate reward in the kingdom («they will not lose their reward»).

Language of the Old Testament
and use of neologisms in comparison

Having seen the latest textual discoveries, we believe that the probabilities that the "least" (those who transgress) of Matthew 5 have different meanings than those of Matthew 25, are equal to zero. Otherwise, Jesus would coin the neologism "least" to indicate the transgressors of the Law and then, a little later in Matthew 25, would use it with a meaning *outside the communicative code established by himself* just before.

Now we can ask ourselves: why, in the Cei translation (Matthew 5:19), the superlative *elàchistos* is correctly translated as superlative ("least") like Nuova Riveduta and Diodati, while in chapter 25 it is translated by Cei "*smaller*" (as a comparative), unlike the versions of Riveduta and Diodati which correctly translate "least"?

From these last two translations, the relationship of identity between the disciples of Jesus and the transgressors of the Law clearly and powerfully stands out. Here is what happens, instead, in the version of the Italian Episcopal Conference:

Mt 5 (Cei)	Mt 25 (Cei)
«Chi dunque trasgredirà uno solo di questi minimi precetti e insegnerà agli altri a fare altrettanto, sarà *considerato minimo* nel regno dei cieli». ↓ Therefore, whoever transgresses only one of these **least** precepts and teaches others to do the same, will be *considered* **least** in the kingdom of heaven.	«Tutto quello che avete fatto a uno solo di questi miei fratelli *più piccoli*, l'avete fatto a me [...] Tutto quello che non avete fatto a uno solo di questi *più piccoli*, non l'avete fatto a me». ↓ Everything that you have done to one of these **smaller** brothers of mine, you have done to me [...] Everything that you have not done to one of these **smaller**, you have not done to me.

In the left column, the word "least" is the correct translation of the Greek superlative *elàchistos* (according to Riveduta and Diodati). It appears identical in Matthew 25, but this time it is translated by Cei "*smaller*" instead of "*least*". The reason appears simple.

The compilers of Nuova Riveduta and Nuova Diodati have not intervened on the text, although it clearly says that Jesus makes followers only among the transgressors of the Law ("least": those who transgress and teach to transgress), and requires them to do so in their turn.

The translators of the Italian Episcopal Conference version, on the other hand, having clearly understood the heavy implications of translating "all that you have done to only one of these *least* brothers of mine (= transgressors of the Law) you have done to me (transgressor like my brothers)", intervene with overt censorship purposes, heavily, on the text, replacing "least" with "smaller". This happens not once, but twice.

Thus, as can be seen in the table above, the translation of the adjective *elàchistos* ("least") present in both columns according to Nuova Riveduta and Diodati, since it allows the reader to finally understand who the disciples of Jesus are and what they do, is drastically altered. Therefore, the potential reader of the Gospels in the translation Cei will not come to understand that the "least" transgressors of Matthew (5:19) are none other than the followers "least" (and not "*smaller*") of Matthew 25. They will receive the eternal prize. Eventually, to understand this relationship can only be the reader of the Gospels in Greek, ascertaining that in those crucial passages always appears, and only, the same superlative: "least".

The same kind of censorial intervention is found, of course, in the other passage of Matthew (5:19), and always relative to the superlative "least": authentic "scandal" or maximum obstacle for those who do not want to translate the text faithfully, for what it is and intends to mean: denying the evidence that the Messiah *calls*, imposes the name of "least" to the transgressors of the Law. While, inexplicably, in the Cei version we read that he "*considers* them least".

Reading, instead, that the transgressors are *called* least – since this and only this is written in the Greek text – there could be the too concrete possibility that the reader of the Cei text understands that these are the same "least" transgressors of Matthew 25. Instead, if the reader will find in the text that Jesus "*considers* least" the transgressors, certainly he will not come to understand that the messiah *can not* absolutely "consider" them least: since they are *exactly the same* that he assigns to the kingdom, in Matthew 25. Even more so, he will not understand it because in Matthew 25 the Cei version crosses off, twice, from the text the superlative "least", replacing it with the comparative "smaller". Who reads, therefore, has the road blocked twice, both in Matthew 5 and 25; or, the passages in which Jesus explains:

- who are the "least";
- what they do;
- for what reason they will enter the kingdom while the "great" will not.

Manipulations and substitutions all take place around the superlative *elàchistos*: a forbidden adjective, that magnificently expresses the semantic area of "smallness", on which the whole message of the synoptic Gospels is implanted. If around this word there is a censorship so massively; precisely; stubbornly carried out in the opposite direction of what we read in the Greek text, then there is a good chance that it reveals what the parables conceal.

However, in the "narrow door" of this revelation will not mathematically be able to pass the naive, honest and confident reader of the Cei version. Instead, it may be that, since the entry of the Cei translation has been blocked, any eventual reader who will take the trouble to pass through the eye of the needle of the Greek version, can be able to see what the text wants to reveal.

The "least" transgress, the "great" are observant:

> Among those born of women there is no one *who observes and makes the Law be observed* (= one who he is *great*) more than John the Baptist; but he who in the kingdom of heaven *violates the Law* (= one who is *smaller*) *and teaches to violate* it is *greater* than him.

Perhaps in no verse of the Gospels the communicative code of Jesus' neologisms is more clearly operative. John observes and enforces the Law. Jesus does not. The many blatant violations of the Sabbath, a very important norm of the Law, which he enacts, are a clear spy of very different intentions. Dramatically different from those of John. Jesus preaches the kingdom and its implementation. Here the violation of the norms applies. For those who followed him and not John, there was a higher prize than what the Baptist could guarantee.

Let us now suppose that Jesus, in Matthew (11:11), had spoken *outside the terminological code* he himself coined, and had wanted to use, instead, the Old Testament terms. Here's what we would have:

> Among those born of women there is no more *righteous* ("great") than John the Baptist; but he who is more *sinful* ("small") in the kingdom of heaven is *more righteous* ("great") than him.

This is no wonder to us. It corresponds in every way to Matthew (25:37-40):

> Then *the righteous* will answer him, «Lord, when did we see you hungry and feed you, or thirsty and give you something to drink? » [...] «All that you have done to one of my *least* brothers, you have done to me».

It is a very clear example of the coexistence of the two terminologies relating to violators and observants. The "righteous" are those who feed and give shelter to the "least" transgressors. The righteousness of the kingdom is not substantiated by observance, but by transgression:

> Everything you have not done to one of these *little ones*, you have not done to me.

This is a concept expressed, by the same evangelist, in another passage (5:20):

> If your righteousness does not exceed that of the scribes and the Pharisees, you will not enter the kingdom of heaven.

The righteous of Jesus are "more righteous" than the righteous of the Old Testament, that is, the observants like the scribes and the Pharisees. The "righteous" of Jesus must overcome the "righteous" of Moses: but how can one overcome in terms of righteousness those who are already scrupulous followers of the Law?

It will be enough to make the usual test of terminological interchangeability, and the answer will appear clear.

Jesus calls "great" those who observe and teach to observe. Likewise, the word "greatness" will therefore be the substitute neologism of "righteousness". So:

Matthew 5:20	Matthew with neologism
If your *righteousness* does not exceed that of the scribes and Pharisees, you will not enter the kingdom of heaven.	If your *greatness* does not exceed that of the scribes and Pharisees, you will not enter the kingdom of heaven.

In order to overcome the "greatness" of the scribes, of the Pharisees and of John himself, it is necessary to take a new perspective and practice a deep *metànoia*. Reasoning according to the Old Testament schemes, neither scribes, nor Pharisees nor the Baptist can be surpassed in "greatness" or in observance of the precepts. To be "greater" than them, we must place ourselves in the perspective of the kingdom: it is necessary to be "smaller"; less "great"; therefore, less observant; less righteous; consequently, more sinners or more transgressors.

This is a sharp reversal with respect to that Law and those Prophets of which John was the greatest exponent. A reversal that explains the dramatic question of the precursor once he became aware of the methods used by Jesus:

> Are you the one who must come or should we wait for another?

To be "greater" than the great John, it is necessary to become "as small as children":

> If you do not convert and do not become like children, you will not enter the kingdom of heaven.

More literally, «if you will not *turn back*», from the Greek verb *strèfo* [στρέφω]: «To turn, to turn around; to turn away; to turn back».

If we were not lucky enough to be able to see the Greek text, we would think that the words «if you will not *convert*» are the translation of the verb *metanoèo*, connected to the word of reference *metànoia*. While, that it is a different verb is shown by several passages:

- But he, *turning*, said to Peter [...] (Mt 16:23);
- Jesus admired him and, *turning* to the crowd [...] (Lk 7:9)
- And, *turned* towards the disciples, aside, he said [...] (Lk 10:23)
- Do not give dogs what is sacred; do not throw your pearls to pigs. If you do, they may trample them under their feet, and *turn* and tear you to pieces (Mt 7:6).

To the Greek verb *strèfo* corresponds the meaning of "turning", "turning back". The request for conversion (*metànoia*) would presuppose the "change of mind" forward, that is: towards something new, and not back and towards something old (childhood).

Therefore, in line with all the Cei translations just seen, we believe that in Matthew (18:2-4) Jesus, to illustrate to his closest followers the functioning of language he used, indicates the age of the child as an essential condition that adults need to "turn back": in order to recover it, if they want to enter the kingdom.

This does not mean that they have to rejuvenate and then become children; but, to become *like* children. For the Messiah, that age has something indispensable, which can be restored by his disciples, despite being adults (Lk 22:24-27):

> The kings of the nations govern them, and those who have power over them are called benefactors. But you shall not do so; but he who is *greater* among you shall become as the *younger*, and he who rules as the servant. For who is greater, who is at the table or who serves? Is not he who sits at the table? Yet I am among you as the one who serves.

The disciples want to know who, among them, can be considered *greater*, evidently attributing to this adjective the meaning of "more important" or "more prestigious". For his part, Jesus responds by using his own communicative code, which opposes to the concept of hierarchical "greatness" something belonging to a completely different sphere of meaning: that delimited by the Greek adjective *nèos* ("new" and, if referred to human beings, "young").

In the request of the disciples, a communicative code different from the common one is not put into operation; in the answer of Jesus, instead, it is active. If in this dialogue the disciples spoke to an interlocutor who uses their own communication code, the question should be: "Which one of us is *greater*?". The answer should be: "the *older* one".

Logic, in fact, would like a superior hierarchical position to be filled by those with more experience. According to Jesus, instead, it is necessary that who wants to be "great" becomes like who is *younger* (or "smaller"):

- does this mean that those who are younger (concerning the age) and have less experience, will be above those who have more?
- or that those who have little merit stand above those who have many, against every principle of fairness and justice?

The alienating illogicality of the phrase remains standing, if to the adjectives "small" and "great" we attribute meanings that belong to the common language, so that what is "smaller" cannot be above what is "great". If in an apparently paradoxical way, in the language of Jesus, this happens, it is not because he reverses the logic of common sense to which he himself refers («when a blind man leads another blind man, both will fall into a ditch»), but because to the adjectives "great-old" and "small-young", he assigns a peculiar meaning. It must not be made clear to everyone, and is hidden by words that are anything but peculiar: they are, vice versa, common and universal. In fact, everything can be "great" or "small". And this is exactly what would happen in any language, if X intended to transmit content reserved for Y without Z understanding this content.

Returning to the disciples, we ask ourselves:

- if they were devoted exclusively to dealing with "spiritual" realities, rejecting any ambition for earthly domination that might have provoked internal rivalries, why do they dispute over who among them is greater?
- how does one reconcile the anxiety of primacy with the sovereign disinterest in worldly things, which is supposed to have those who have embraced a certain model of life?

Again, in Luke (22:26) Jesus states:

Whoever governs [shall become] like the one who serves.

However, in the same Gospel he says (22:30):

And you will sit in throne to judge the twelve tribes of Israel.

It seems difficult to reconcile the invitation not to sit at the table but to stand to serve, with, conversely, the invitation to sit as governors over thrones, in order to judge the twelve tribes of Israel. The image of the servant who stands is undoubtedly strongly antithetical to that of the governor on the throne; just as it is antithetical to the role – to be exercised over the tribes of Israel – entrusted to the disciples. They appear in all things as governors who judge, and thus dominate. Namely, they exercise those functions by the same Jesus abhorred few verses before:

> *But you shall not do so*; but he who is greater among you shall become as the younger, and he who rules as the servant.

We should conclude that the disciples must not be like the "great" ones. That is, they are not to rule over anyone. On the contrary, they must become "young"; therefore, they must not dominate anyone. However, then they become paradoxically "great" and do something that coincides precisely with what the "great ones" do over other nations: exactly what it seemed that they had to avoid at any cost. Yet, they will judge the tribes of Israel, by sitting on a throne.

We can now better understand the logic of the synoptic Gospels: we become "small" (servants) not because we must not be "great" (rulers of nations), but because *the way* in which the disciples must be "great" is radically different. The "great ones" on whom Jesus points the finger are already "great". They do not need to become so. They already sit at the table. They are used to being served. The disciples of Jesus, instead, are not "great" (dominators). But they can be, becoming "small": therefore, having opposite qualities to those of the "great" ones.

"Little ones" and servants

A comparison of all three synoptic Gospels is now particularly useful:

Lk 22:25-26	Mk 10:42-44	Mt 20:25-27
The kings of the nations govern them, and those who have power over them are called benefactors. But you shall not do so; but he who is greater among you shall become as the younger, and he who rules as the servant.	Those who are regarded as the rulers of nations dominate them and their leaders *oppress* them. But among you it is not so; but whoever wants to become great among you will be your servant, and whoever wants to be the first among you will be a slave of all.	You know that the rulers of the nations rule over them and the leaders *oppress* them. Among you it will not be so; but he who wants to become great among you will be your servant, and he who wants to be the first among you will be your slave.

In Luke's Gospel, Jesus states that those who exercise power over nations call themselves "benefactors". In Mark and Matthew, to submit nations to their dominion are the "great" ones.

The structure of the phrase is identical: if in Luke to be called "benefactors" are those who exercise dominion over nations, and in Mark and Matthew to be called "great" is he who has power over them, then in Luke Jesus defines "benefactors" those he calls "great" in Matthew and Mark. "Great" and "benefactors" ("operators of good") in the language of Jesus are synonymous. In the first case the evangelists use the adjective ("great") as it is peculiarly used by the messiah; while Luke reveals *the consequence* that being "great" (observant of the laws) has: to be benefactors.

If, on the other hand, the one who administers power at the highest levels violently flouts the laws and teaches their subjects to do so, he would certainly not be an "operator of good" but, on the contrary, a ruler with all probability despotic. Or, in the worst case, a bloody tyrant.

This is what seems to be the protagonist of Luke's parable (19:11-27), similar in part to Matthew's "parable of the talents". In the Cei version, the story is entitled "Parable of the ten servants", in other "of the ten mines" (coins or talents): although it is immediately clear that the protagonists are not the servants who have received orders, or the money entrusted to them. The protagonist is the one who gave it to them, in order to make it fruitful during his absence, while he is traveling to a distant region to be proclaimed king. A king not very merciful, who would justify, as we will see, for the story the title "Parable of the merciless king and the ten servants".

The structure of the parable replicates that of the "banquet". The beginning consists of words relating to the imminence of the kingdom of heaven, in conjunction with the approach of the messiah to Jerusalem:

> While they were listening to these things, he said another parable, because *he was near Jerusalem* and they thought that the kingdom of God should be manifested from one moment to the next.

Predictably, the theme of the kingdom is declined in a way of veiling what cannot be openly uncovered:

> He then said: «A man of noble family left for a distant country, to receive the title of king and then return. Called ten of his servants, he delivered them ten talents of gold, saying: «Make them fruitful until my return».

It is an episode similar to that of the Gospel of Matthew (the "unfaithful servant" who does not yield talent). However, Luke frames it within a context of events (a "before" and an "after") illuminating, absent from Matthew. The protagonist is a man who leaves for a distant country, where he aspires to have a title of king that he cannot receive in his city: evidently, the previous rulers have always ruled residing in a larger city. Therefore more important. Like a capital. However, he does not want to reside there permanently, but to receive there the title of king, and then return to his city and from here govern. During his absence, ten servants shall yield ten gold coins. But the departure of the man who wants to become king is hindered by his own countrymen:

> But his citizens hated him and sent a delegation behind him to say: «We do not want him to come to reign over us».

Therefore, he has already begun his journey, when a delegation of fellow citizens join him, to communicate to his trusted men that they do not want him at all as king. However, the pretender's royal ambitions come true, and he returns home as promised:

> After receiving the title of king, he returned and had those servants called to whom he had handed the money, to know how much each had earned. The first one showed up and said, «Lord, your gold coin has yielded ten». «Well, good servant. Because you have shown yourself faithful in the little, you receive the power over ten cities». Then the second came and said: «Lord, your gold coin has yielded five» [...] «You too will be at the head of five cities».

The protagonist of the story immediately wants to verify if those servants, to whom he had entrusted the talents, have made them yield or not. It is significant that the number of coins multiplied by the servant (ten) corresponds to an equal number of something infinitely greater: the cities over which he shall rule.

This is very reminiscent of what Jesus said about the disciples: servants who are destined to govern. It is what happens to the servant of the parable: he will no longer be a servant, but a ruler.

Therefore:

$$servant : coins = king : city$$

The servant is related to "the little" (coins) as the king is related to "the much" (city). If the servant is faithful in the little, the king will be faithful in the much towards him. If the servant bears fruit, the king will multiply what he has yielded.

The story takes a dramatic turn during the dialogue of the sovereign with the subordinate who had been entrusted with only one talent:

> «Lord, here is your gold coin [...] I was afraid of you [...] because you take what you did not deposit and reap what you did not sow» [...] «From your same words I judge you, wicked servant. You knew that I am a severe man [...] why then did you not deliver my money to a bank? On my return I would have collected it with interest [...] Remove the gold coin and give it to the one who has ten». [...] «Lord, he has already ten» [...] «To those who have, it will be given; instead to those who do not have, it will also be taken away what they have».

The one who is destined to rule over ten cities, is entrusted with one more city. It does not matter if he already has ten. He has made more coins. He was more faithful to his master. Therefore, he takes precedence over all. The other servants must be silent. The master decides who and how much must be rewarded. If a criterion of redistribution of wealth, based on equity and justice, supposedly wants the "coin-city" to go to the one who has yielded five, this does not interest the king at all. The superabundant prize goes to the most faithful and capable.

Meanwhile, the other countrymen have always remained enemies of the future king:

> And my enemies, who did not want me to become their king, bring them here and kill them in front of me.

The king peremptorily ordered his servants to kill in his presence those who wished to avert his accession to the throne. The irrevocable intention to proceed with summary execution, carried out by an equally summary procedure, is clearly expressed. The king is a despot. A tyrant who does not have to account for the massacre of his countrymen. The violence that pervades the verse is further amplified by the evangelist: the executions must take place in the presence of the king. He wants to be a privileged spectator.

Cei, Nuova Riveduta and Nuova Diodati do not entirely do justice to the Greek text by translating «kill them in front of me». In fact, there are several ways of taking life, and the verb "to kill" usually contains them all. Here, however, the evangelist intends to specify by what kind of punishment the enemies must die. The Greek verb *katasfàzo* [κατασφάζω] properly means «to slash», «to butcher». That is, to slit the throat by cutting the carotid artery and trachea:

> *Bring them* here and *cut their throats* in front of me.

Two imperatives from which exempts the violent and despotic nature of power; its abuse; the satisfaction of the sovereign in wanting to witness the bleeding of men, whose only fault was to express their opposition to his royal investiture. Here is described a bloody settling of accounts, far superior to the dramatic episode of the servant unable to put to use the talent. In that case the coin was removed. In this, the life is taken.

The Gospel of Luke has more or less always been known as "the Gospel of mercy". It is a concept also extended to all four canonical Gospels by Jorge Mario Bergoglio, in the General Audience on April 6, 2016 (the transcript is readable online at https:///www.vatican.va/content/francesco/it/audiences/2016/documents/papa-francesco_20160406_udienza-generale.html):

> [...] A mercy that he has always expressed, realized and communicated, in every moment of his earthly life Jesus makes visible a love open to all: no one excluded! Open to all without borders [...] Yes, the Gospel is truly the "Gospel of Mercy", because Jesus is Mercy!

With this premise, why does Jesus, who should be mercy, use in the "Gospel of mercy" a language so brutally connoted, telling a parable whose protagonist performs actions not merciful but, on the contrary, actions of unprecedented, inhuman, ruthless, gruesome ferocity?

Certainly, in the parable – Jesus' preferred mode of communicating the "good news" – there is absolutely no content attached to piety. All lead back to its opposite: revenge. He who, according to Bergoglio, is to be identified with the very essence of mercy, tells of a man who has no compassion for his servant. And instead of forgiving his enemies by turning his cheek to them, he prefers to have their throats cut.

At the conclusion of the parable, Jesus does not tell the disciples "that king had no mercy, but you be merciful to your enemies". The king decides the moral of the story: "slaughter them in my presence".

We ask ourselves:

- if we would take into account, absurdly, another literary work with a protagonist who was not called Jesus, could be called "book of mercy" if it had within even just an episode similar to the one cited?
- the parable, having a sender, has a recipient and a message: which message?

- if it is veiling what cannot be clearly revealed, what exactly does it mean?
- is it the result of only narrative creativity, detached from any historical and biographical context, or does it have specific references?

Jesus tells the parable when he moves from Galilee to reach Judea, where he will be acclaimed king. According to Luke (19:40), if the disciples do not acclaim him, «the stones will shout» that he is king:

- can this have a slight, distant consonance with what happens in the story to the man who sets out from his city to arrive in a distant land, where he will be made king?
- if, absurdly, the protagonist of the Gospels had managed to become king of the Jews, would he have reigned residing in Jerusalem or in a city in Galilee?

In various historical periods there have been several leaders, religious and politicians, who have become the protagonists of a preaching on the practice of mercy and non-violence, including, in the twentieth century, the charismatic Mohandas Karamchand Gandhi, political and moral leader of the independence movement of India:

- if, again absurdly, in his speeches to the crowds, he had inserted one full of violence and revenge like the parable narrated by Jesus, among the recipients of his message would have caused a stir or not?
- would they be shocked at such a glaring contradiction to his non-violent preaching?
- why should the parable of the "merciless king" be perceived as absolutely dissonant when told by Gandhi, while consistent and timely when told by Jesus?
- finally: why a reader of Gandhi's speeches would most likely be assailed by numerous doubts after encountering a story similar to that of the "merciless king", while, with equal probability, it would not constitute a problem for a reader of the Gospels of Christian-Catholic faith?

Benefactors and malefactors

Human history certainly does not lack examples of organized and violent movements, through which a new social or political order is established. It is very likely that the one who is not "great" – therefore who has no power over anyone – wants to become so. If he does not have the means to become so, he will choose to violate the rules of the law; and, above all, to teach to violate them to as many people as possible, so as to have enough supporters to get to hold that power, for a long time the preserve of others. This is the most usual way chosen by anyone who tries to overthrow a system of power from below: transgressing the norms that the power system has imposed (Lk 22:25-26):

> The kings of the nations govern them, and those who have power over them are called benefactors. But you shall not do so; but he who is greater among you shall become as the younger, and he who rules as the servant.

It cannot be omitted that the text of Luke clearly says that those who have dominion over nations are called benefactors; and that for the disciples of Jesus *it must not be so* at all. He cites the "great" ones (observants) and the benefactors that such "greatness" exerts, and then asserts that the disciples *should not behave like the "great" and the benefactors.* So,

- how is it possible that law-abiding and operators of good constitute for Jesus a negative model that the disciples should not follow?
- if the messiah says that for his disciples it should not be so (they must not be operators of good), for what actions should they have been distinguished instead?

What we want to highlight is the scope of this programmatic statement. Matthew (20:25-26) writes:

> The leaders of the nations, as you know, dominate over them and *the great ones* exercise power over them. This must not be the case among you (Cei 1974).

Mark (10:42-43) reads:

> You know that those who are considered leaders of the nations rule over them, and their *great ones* exercise power over them. But among you it is not so (Cei 1974).

In the Greek text of Matthew we find the words *òi megàloi* [οἱ μεγάλοι], "the great ones". The same thing we find in Mark. According to the translation Cei 1974 of Matthew, the "great ones" are the ones who exercise power over the nations. Yet, the important textual spy that relates unequivocally Matthew to Mark, and which testifies with fidelity the translation Cei 1974, disappears in Cei 2008:

Mt 20:25-27 (Cei 1974)	Mt 20:25-27 (Cei 2008)
The leaders of the nations, you know, dominate over them, and the *great ones* exercise power over them. This is not to be among you.	You know that the rulers of the nations rule over them and the *leaders* oppress them. Among you it will not be so.

If Matthew writes "great ones", it is probably because he intends to use that very adjective, which both Matthew and Mark make Jesus say: so,

- for what reason the correct translation «the *great* ones exert on them the power» of Cei 1974 changes, in the 2008 edition, and becomes «the *leaders* oppress them»?
- why is the Greek adjective *mègas* ("great") translated with the words "leaders"?

Matthew and Mark use the adjective "great" precisely because it is Jesus who determines its meaning. The messiah will be at the head of a kingdom, and will have people who will depend strictly on him (they will eat and drink at his table). Like him, they will sit on a throne to judge the twelve tribes of Israel. A ruler above all, twelve faithfuls who will be judges of the tribes of which the nation is formed. They will be accountable to him. We ask ourselves:

- why then does Jesus say to the disciples "do not act like them" referring to the "great ones", if the pattern he intends to follow is the same?

Simply, the disciples will each exercise dominion over each tribe of the nation. But they will not do so as the "great ones" do. His followers are, and must remain, "small" and "least". They must reign in the opposite way to that of the "great ones".

Highlighting other differences between the translations, we note that, according to Cei 1974, some individuals *exercise power* over nations; while according to Cei 2008, the same individuals *oppress* nations. However, to exercise authority over someone is quite different from oppressing someone. The exercise of power is legitimate and necessary (a teacher exercises his power or authority in the classroom and does not necessarily oppress pupils).

So, how is it possible that translations of the same passage exist, so radically different from each other?

Certainly, the exercise of power within the limits of the law benefits citizens (or subjects). Abuse, on the other hand, enslaves them:

Mt 20:25-28 (Cei 2008)	Mk 10:42 (Cei 2008)	Lk 22:25 (Cei 2008)
The rulers of the nations rule over them and the leaders *oppress* them.	Those who are considered the rulers of the nations rule over them and their leaders *oppress* them.	The kings of the nations rule them, and those who *have power* over them are called benefactors.

This of Matthew, Mark and Luke is clearly the same editorial content:

- but why is the same verb translated "to oppress" in Matthew and Mark, while "to exercise power" in Luke?

- according to which criterion a positive meaning is assigned in one case (so much so that the one who performs the actions expressed by that verb is called *benefactor)* and absolutely negative ("to oppress") in the other two cases?

Luke's passage is a clear sign that the valence of the verb used is entirely positive. This can only be the case in Matthew and Mark: the evangelists refer to kings or princes who use governors-administrators. They govern by exercising their powers, with the purpose of pursuing the good for their subjects. The confirmation of this comes not only from the fact that Luke defines them as "benefactors", but also from the fact that Matthew and Mark inform us that Jesus defines "great ones" those who exercise power over nations (instead of "oppressing" the nations).

We know well that in the language of the kingdom, with that precise adjective ("great") Jesus means those who observe and teach to observe the Law. It is therefore obvious that such individuals operate for the good. However, in all three synoptic Gospels the Messiah reiterates to the disciples that they must behave neither as good workers or "great", but as "small" or "servants".

If the "big ones" command, to be "small", in common language, would mean to be servants, and therefore, subject to someone: however, if this were to be the entire Gospel message, why are there passages in the text that are totally opposite (that is, "you will sit on twelve thrones and rule")?

"Great" rulers, "little" servants

Another element of reflection is offered by the comparison between two passages of Luke:

Lk 10:26-27	Lc 17:7-10
He who is greater among you shall become as the younger, and he who rules as the servant. For who is greater, who is at the table or who serves? Is not he who sits at the table? Yet I am among you as the one who serves.	Which of you, if he has a servant to plow or to graze the flock, will tell him when he returns from the field: Come now and sit at the table? He will not tell him rather, Prepare me to eat, roll up your robe and serve me, until I have eaten and drunk, and then you will eat and drink too? Will he consider himself obliged to his servant because he has carried out his orders? So also you, when you have done everything that has been ordered to you, say: «We are useless servants. We have done what we had to do».

In the passage of Luke 10, Jesus says that the disciples must not govern but be servants: therefore, they submit to someone.

In Luke 17, Jesus himself addresses the disciples, referring not to servants but, on the contrary, to persons who have servants.

The logic of Luke 10, according to which not who is at the table is greater but who serves, is in contrast with Luke 17, in which the figure of the servant who is seated at the table appears in a questioning phrase that has the function of showing the complete illogicality of promoting a servant to a degree equal to that of the master. The servants are treated as servants. It is necessary to give orders to them. What master would make a servant sit at his table? Who is at the table gives orders. The servant remains a servant. He does not become like the master. He feeds only after having served and satiated his master. The latter has no duties or obligations towards him. He must not promote him. The servant, moreover, did what he had to do: he has been a servant. Therefore, he should not expect any reward. He must be silent. And obey.

The same must apply to the disciples, the servants of Jesus: «So also you, when you have done everything that has been ordered to you, say: "We are useless servants. We did what we had to do"».

As the servant rolls up his sleeves and serves the master as long as he is satisfied, without making any demands, so also the disciples, once they have done all that was ordered to them by Jesus, must say: we have carried out all the orders. We are servants who have nothing more to do. Obviously, waiting for the next orders.

All this, if read in the light of the continual requests of the disciples regarding their hierarchical position in the kingdom, says much about the intentions, and especially about the methods used by Jesus towards them. The phrase "and after you will eat and drink also you", addressed to the servant of the parable, would seem to have much in common with the destiny of the followers (Lk 22:28-30):

> I prepare for you a kingdom [...] so that you eat and drink at my table in my kingdom.

Linking programmatic statements and parables, we will not struggle to understand that the place of honor at the table belongs to landlord: Jesus. The servant-disciples will eat and sit at the same table. But not in the same place. They will eat only after he has sat down to drink and eat Jesus; if and only if the disciples will have carried out, without discussing or making demands, all the orders given by their leader. An eventual award will come only at the end of the work.

In Luke 10 the messiah says: «I am among you as the one who serves». He therefore reaffirms the primacy of those who are at table, while specifying that he is among the disciples as the one who serves: a concept that is not expressed in Luke 17, where those who sit at the table give orders exclusively, and are not equated with a servant: what then is the difference between Luke 10 and Luke 17?

The latter does not contain the key words of the Gospel vocabulary ("great-little-young"), which are instead present in Luke 10. In the first case, we have a servant and a master: the message does not need to be decoded. In the second case, the terms "great" and "little-small" appear. Therefore:

$$great : \text{housekeeper} = small : \text{servant}$$

The "great ones" are related to the rulers as the "small ones" are related to the servants (or subjects). The rulers are put in relation to the word "great", to which Jesus attributes a particular meaning. The same will happen for the "servants": since they are related to the word "little-small", they will assume a particular meaning that distinguishes them from the "servants" of Luke 17.

The transition from rulers to servants is equivalent to the transition from "great ones" to "young ones", that is "little ones". The disciples are not destined to be servants, but to sit on twelve thrones. From this we infer that, while in Luke 17 they must serve Jesus in the sense that belongs to the normal semantic area of this verb (and therefore they must carry out all his orders), in Luke 10 they must be "servants" and not "rulers": to the exact extent that they must not be "great", but "small".

The "great ones" wield power in one way. The "small ones" will do so in another. We know that the "great ones" are related to the rulers as the "small ones" to the servants: we will have then, de-codifying the code, that he who observes and makes the law be observed is in relation to the ruler as he who violates it and causes it to be violated is in relation to the servant: that is, to the disciples "little ones".

As was widely understood, the opposition "rulers *vs* servants" could not but depend strictly on the opposition "great" vs "small" that firmly governs the synoptic Gospels.

"Great" benefactors, "small" evildoers

From all that has been seen so far, a value system is gradually emerging, a real "philosophy of the exercise of power", which opposes kings or principles – who exercise power by enforcing laws – to subjects who would overturn it, violating and teaching to violate the laws.

If the "great ones" are good operators, the "small ones" who transgress will be, of necessity, *bad* or *evil operators*. The latter term corresponds to the Greek word *kakoùrgos* [κακοῦργος]: «evildoer», «criminal».

In the Gospels, the Greek word *amartolòs* [ἁμαρτωλός] specifically designates the transgressor of the Mosaic Law in any of its norms: that is the reason why it is not said that he must necessarily be a criminal. The word *kakoùrgos*, on the other hand, unequivocally designates a criminal. He is wanted for the crimes – serious and very serious – he has committed. Presumably, he was not to be pleasing to either the Jews or, of course, the Romans.

The term *kakoùrgos* is repeated three times in the Gospels, all three in Luke (23:32; 23:33, 23:39). Coincidentally, it is the same evangelist in which we find the opposite term ("benefactors"). By this author are defined *kakoùrgoi*, "malefactors", individuals condemned to death by the cross together with Jesus (23:32):

Ἤγοντο δὲ καὶ ἕτεροι κακοῦργοι δύο σὺν αὐτῷ ἀναιρεθῆναι.

This below is the literal translation of the Greek text:

Were led also two other evildoers together with him to be crucified.

Based on the elements that emerged, we should have already come to assume a fair congruence between everything that concerns the individuals "small" or "least", and the extreme consequences of the equally extreme actions committed by criminals; by malefactors that the religious imagination, in a broad sense, has always portrayed as strangers to Jesus and his events. It would therefore be two criminals who, being the Romans engaged in crucifying an innocent man who has nothing to do with them, are condemned to the death penalty, at the same time, by pure chance; and not because maybe the two men have something to do with the excellent convict.

Luke clearly reports that not only two evildoers were led, but «*also two other* evildoers». That is: the two, who were to be hung on the cross, were not the only evildoers. There was another than them. As they were "others" compared to him.

Exemplifying:

X went to Golgotha. Two other criminals also went with him.

We'll assume that individual *X* is a criminal. Otherwise, there would have been no need to accompany the noun "criminals" with the adjective "other". Regarding what are the criminals "two others" compared to the individual *X*? Regarding being criminals. Therefore, *X* must certainly be a criminal.

A few simple examples are enough to verify how the meaning of a sentence changes radically with the presence or absence of an adjective or a conjunction. And it is precisely the numeral adjective "two" that nails the translation to a cross from which it cannot move a millimeter. In spite of all the "interpretations" that go beyond what the passage candidly says: they were led to be executed two *other* criminals. There was a malefactor with two other malefactors. If the condemned person had a name different from the one he has, no one would try to interpret what does not need to be interpreted. But everyone would say that the one who is sentenced to death is a criminal.

Here is the latin text of the Vulgate:

Ducebantur autem et alii duo nequam cum eo ut interficerentur.

Below is the translation:

> Also two other criminals were led along with him, so that they could be executed.

The latin version slavishly reproduces the original Greek text that we have already examined.

Cei 1974 translates:

> *Two criminals* were also brought together with him to be executed.

The adjective "other", that in the Greek text accompanies the noun "evildoers", disappears in the translation Cei 1974: "Also two evildoers" instead of "Also two *other* evildoers".

This is not a translation error, that is, an incorrectly translated word. It is an obvious omission. Or, using the metaphor of the "lost sheep", it can be said that, in the long journey from the Greek to the target language, a sheep would seem to be lost. What is present in the source text, is omitted in the target text. Perhaps for unconscious, blameless lapse.

Thirty-four years later, the adjective "other" that had been lost, almost like a "prodigal son" was found again in the version Cei 2008:

> Together with him were led to death also *two others, who were criminals.*

However, we note that to the restored word are added two unexpected entries in the text, compared to the 1974 version: one concerning punctuation, the other syntax. From «two evildoers were brought together with him to be executed» (1974), we move on to «together with him were led to death also *two others, who were evildoers*» (2008). In Cei 2008 appears a comma after the numeral "two", which in the original text immediately follows the noun "malefactors". In addition, what in the Greek text is a simple and incontrovertible union of a noun and an adjective numeral ("two evildoers"), is broken, as well as by a comma, also by the addition of a relative pronoun ("who", referred to the evildoers) and a verb ("were"). Both, relative pronoun and verb, are absent from the Greek text, which instead simply reads:

> Two other evildoers were also led.

We ask ourselves:

- why is a comma inserted, in Cei 2008, to separate the noun "criminals" from the adjective "two"?
- why are two fundamental parts of a sentence, such as a relative pronoun and even a verb ("*who were* criminals"), inserted while being both absent from the Greek text?
- if it did not seem appropriate for the author, in such a simple and linear sentence, to make use of a relative pronoun and a verb, why should those who translate that sentence do so?

Of course, by translating "two others, *who were* malefactors", the reader will hardly think that individual X is a criminal. While, if it is faithfully translated from the Greek text ("even *two other* criminals"), the reader will have no doubt that X is a criminal.

The translation of Nuova Riveduta reads:

> Now, *two other, criminals,* were led to be put to death together with him.

The conjunction "also" ("*also* two other criminals") is omitted, which in the Greek text refers to the addition of two criminals to the first condemned to capital punishment; two commas are also placed to separate the numeral "two" from the noun "criminals" and the noun "criminals" from the rest of the sentence ("now, two other, criminals,"). This results in the sought-after effect of creating a clear separation between the first condemned to death and the other two.

The extreme ease in the placement of punctuation clearly shows how the translation suffers distortions when it is the will to force interpretation to blindly guide it, leading to the genesis of a hybrid alien to the original Greek enunciation.

In Nuova Diodati we read:

Now *two criminals* were brought with him to be put to death.

As in Cei 1974, we note the omission of the adjective "other" referred to the evildoers.

Finally, a quick look at other translations reveals the existence of versions of the same content:

Now *two others, both criminals,* were led away with him to be executed (New American Bible).

The conjunction "also" ("*also* two other criminals"), present in the Greek text, is omitted; we also find the usual manipulation of punctuation.

The French version:

Ils emmenaient aussi avec Jésus *deux autres, des malfaiteurs,* pour les exécuter.

The usual two commas ("deux autres, des malfaiteurs,", that is "other two, malefactors,") are inserted.

The general preference given to translations in which something inexplicably loses its way or is arbitrarily added, suggests that what the Greek text would say if translated literally does not coincide at all with what is expected to be said. And this seems to be equivalent to the unsuccessful attempt to find other possible solutions of the operation "2+2": the result of which can hardly be different from 4.

The fact that from this important passage of Luke, as well as from the numerous references to the "least" followers of Jesus, gradually emerge the contours of a movement of sedition dedicated to violent actions, is an evidence that is added to corroborate what has been written by many, important authors. They – while fully respecting any "mysteries of faith" in a broad sense projected by anyone on the text – have instead glimpsed, in these writings, seething the magma of messianism and zealous struggle, violent and uncompromising, against the current ruler. A new magma: that of Jesus. Unprecedented, if compared with the previous one of John the Baptist. A magma that flows from the pages of the Gospels, like new wine that smashes old wineskins.

Messianism and sedition

The fact that the "historical Jesus" had, at least, an incongruous profile with the "Jesus of faith", was already evident in the eyes of the Anglican priest Samuel Brandon, author of the fundamental essay entitled *Jesus and the Zealots*. Ascertained how violence was the common denominator of the events concerning Palestine of that era, Brandon himself wrote that the problem implicit in the narratives of the synoptic Gospels was posed by the fact that these documents agree in presenting Jesus as if he were completely alien to the political ferment that profoundly stirred up Jewish society contemporary with him. The story of the trial of Jesus, in which Pilate, governor appointed by Rome to the government of the most rebellious region of the empire, is presented by the evangelists as a useful idiot and passive executor of the will of a people on which he should instead firmly decide, is paradigmatic in this sense.

The hypothesis that, in our opinion, from the analysis carried out so far can be formulated, is that the synoptic authors in part attempt to present the protagonist as alien to the ferments of which it has been said; for the remaining part, they veil the news content, using a cryptic communicative code but decryptable by the recipient who has (and especially wants to have) ears to understand. To understand that, within that great movement of hope and national exaltation called messianism, Jesus is, in all respects, an atypical messianist. Radically different.

In fact, he invites the Jewish people to transgress the Law and not to observe it; while the movement of the extremist zealots fought against the Romans in the name of the Law of Yahweh.

After all, messianism had several facets. There were many leaders and false leaders of the time, who made royal demands. This is clearly written in the Gospels (Mt 24:4-26):

> Beware that nobody deceives you. In fact many will come in my name, saying: "I am the Christ", and many will be deceived. [...] Many false prophets will arise and deceive many [...] Then, if someone will tell you: "Behold, Christ is here", or: "He is there", do not believe him; because false Christs and false prophets will arise [...].

This "messianic competition" was not at all hidden by the evangelists. They wanted to operate, as Riccardo Calimani writes with an effective formula, an operation of «necessary cosmetic»; which however, according to the author, does not prevent us from understanding, between the lines and in backlight, that the facts, beyond the contradictions and interpretations, took place differently from the official, suffered and controversial truth of the Gospels.

In this regard, two hypotheses in our opinion could be made:
- the first one:
  having to work on a matter as incandescent as monothematic, and not being refined writing experts, the authors could not have full control of the matter narrated. And so – as in the case of the "other two evildoers" – they would have inadvertently left out details that inevitably collide with what we know today as the "Jesus of faith".
- the second one (for which we are more inclined):
  the evangelists did not let themselves escape, but consciously *wanted to leave* traces and clues. The example of Matthew's "least brothers" is, in this sense, the most striking. Precisely because the term is repeated several times, it is very difficult to be-

lieve that the evangelist, inadvertently, let slip the news that the followers of the messiah were transgressors of the Law. Instead, it is much more likely that he consciously wanted to leave the news inside the text. So that he who had ears to hear, might understand. And he who had eyes to read, might not close them.

«The Law and the Prophets until John»

Further searching the synoptic Gospels to see if there are direct references to the use of force within the kingdom of heaven, in Matthew (11:7-15) we read:

> Jesus began to speak of John to the crowds: «What did you go to see in the desert? [...] A man dressed in luxury clothes? Behold, those who wear luxurious clothes are in the palaces of kings. [...] A prophet? Yes, I say to you, rather, more than a prophet. He is the one of whom it is written: "Behold, ahead of you I send my messenger, ahead of you he will prepare your way". Verily I say to you, among those born of women there is none greater than John the Baptist; but a smaller one in the kingdom of heaven is greater than him. From the days of John the Baptist until now, the kingdom of heaven has been subjected to violence and the violent take it over. Indeed, all the prophets and the Law have prophesied until John. And, if you want to understand, he is the Elijah who must come. Who has ears, may he hear.

John is not the one who will be covered in soft regal robes. He "prepares the way" for the future king. The possible, even legitimate kingly claims by John, fall into the void. The Baptist is only a prophet. He is not king. He will never be.

Interesting for the analysis are the words spoken by Jesus after the nod to the "violent ones":

> From the days of John the Baptist until now, the kingdom of heaven has been subjected to violence and the violent take it over. *Indeed,* all the prophets and the Law have prophesied until John.

The conjunction "indeed" places in clear relation the activity of the Baptist with the observance of the Law. We ask ourselves:

- what is the relationship between the action of the violent ones on the kingdom and the fact that John is a recognized representative of the Law and prophets?
- does the phrase «all the Prophets and the Law have in fact prophesied until John» mean that the Law and the prophets are in force *until* John?
- and what should happen *after* John?
- how is it that the concept of the duration of the Law and the prophets, until the specified time limit represented by John, is clearly linked, through the conjunction "indeed", to the entrance of "the violent"?
- does this mean that, as long as John was present, precisely because of his observance of the Law the violent who yearned to abduct the kingdom by force found in him the greatest obstacle?

At this point, it does not seem a gamble to assume that there is a link between:

1. the action of the violent ones;
2. the sudden departure of the Baptist;
3. the fact that this departure is defined by Jesus "the opportune moment" that has arrived.

Therefore:

- if in Matthew Jesus claims to have come not to abolish but to give fulfillment to the Law and the prophets (so, they should never have any term), why here does he say instead (putting a strict, indubitable cut-off period) - «all the Prophets and the Law have in fact prophesied *until John*»?
- if the Baptist is the last stage of the action of the Law and prophets, what should remain to be done to Jesus?

According to the translations, it would appear to be common ground that:

1. the Baptist is in a leading position (he is "great");
2. however, in the kingdom of heaven there is someone who questions his primacy and manages to take it from him;
3. as long as there is John, there are also the Law and prophets;
4. nevertheless, while he is still active, violent people enter the scene, who want to take possession of a kingdom by means that are not lawful (therefore, not according to the Law).

We know that the purpose of the neologisms ascribed to Jesus is to prevent immediate understanding. So, what would have happened if here the messiah had made clear the meaning that he ascribed to the words "great" and "small"?

A considerable number of people would have been made aware that within the kingdom (still to be established but already present in the intentions of the one who wanted to establish it), to violate and teach to violate the norms – in force for many centuries in Israel – was to be preferred to the observance of the same. Sinners were *more righteous* than the observants. That is, more righteous than the righteous (Mt 5,20):

> If your righteousness does not exceed that of the scribes and Pharisees, you will not enter the kingdom of heaven.

This expresses neither more nor less what was said in Matthew (11:11):

Mt 11:11	Mt 5:20
Among those born of women there is none greater than John the Baptist; but one smaller in the kingdom of heaven is greater than him.	If your righteousness does not surpass that of the scribes and Pharisees, you will not enter the kingdom of heaven.

Both verses are governed by a concept: that of "overcoming". The righteousness of the scribes and Pharisees is linked to (and derived from) the Law. According to Jesus, we must be "more righteous"(or "greater") than they are: and how can one be "greater" than the "great" observants Pharisees and John the Baptist?

He lets us know it candidly Matthew (11:11): we must be "smaller". To overcome the observance of the precepts, one must transgress and teach to transgress them. There can be no greater righteousness than that which has an individual observing and teaching to observe the whole Law. It is already a full, accomplished righteousness. The only way to overcome it is to exalt the opposite quality. Using neologisms, we would have:

> I have not come to transgress and abolish the Law (= *to be "least"*), but *to be "greater"* than scribes and Pharisees.

This sentence, if understood in the perspective of one who is "great" (observant), should mean that Jesus proposes to be even more observant than the one who is already "great". This would mean, being even "greater" than the "great" John.

However, it is Jesus himself who tells us that none, among those who are born of women, is "greater" than the Baptist. Neither is Jesus himself. In fact, if he had wanted to affirm this, what difficulty would he have had to say "I am *greater* than John"?

But in the synoptics Gospels we never find this statement. Instead, Jesus claims to have (and to teach his disciples) the opposite quality to "greatness". And it is precisely by virtue of it that takes place the overcoming of John; of the scribes; of the Pharisees.

When the messiah says "I have not come to abolish, but to complete", he uses words *outside the slang code*: therefore, devoid of neologisms. Instead, *the explanation* of this sentence is strictly expressed *in jargon*:

> Among those born of a woman, no one is *greater* than John the Baptist; but the one *smaller* in the kingdom of heaven is greater than him.

The phrase "I have not come to abolish but to complete", not being expressed in code, will be understood, by those who listen, as a message absolutely in line with the Law and prophets. Jesus, in this case, figures as the one who brings the Law to fullness, reassuring those who listen to him that he does not intend to transgress and teach transgression.

However, in Matthew (11:11) he states *the exact opposite*: there cannot be someone who brings the Law to further fullness. If John is the maximum representative of the Law and of the prophets, one cannot be greater than the maximum. This crucial message is transmitted using a communication code that has the function of cushioning and encrypting the enormous subversive potential of the statement. Who transgresses and teaches to transgress *is more observant*: not of the Law and the prophets, but of the new law that is in force in the kingdom. The law of the "little ones". The law of the violent ones.

Communicating this kind of project without filters, in such a strident contrast with the numerous norms that had always constituted the life and history of the people of Israel, would have been extremely counterproductive. To state in public that the precepts of the Law were to be transgressed if one wanted to enter the kingdom, would have meant revealing the contents of a subversive action that provided for the dismissal of an already recognized and established leader (John); and of a political-priestly-intellectual establishment that, while not recognizing itself in the work of the Baptist, shared however his position towards the Law and prophets: that is, the observance and transmission of the Law itself. Certainly, not the systematic transgression of it.

Violence told in code

The discourse just addressed is of disconcerting, very logical, dramatic coherence. If those who violate and teach to violate prevail over those who observe, then the reference to the kingdom that is subjected to violence is logically consequent and should not surprise. Between the "little-least" disciples and the violent ones who take over the kingdom, there is a relationship of identity.

In verse 11 of Matthew 11 ("who is *smaller*... is *greater*"), transgression and violence are concepts expressed *in code*. Immediately after in verse 12, instead, they are expressed *in the common language* of the so-called "born of women". Therefore, we will have:

> The kingdom of heaven suffers violence and *the violent* (instead of "*the least ones*") take possession of it.

They take it from someone to whom that kingdom was supposedly destined. This is why the violent enter the scene "from the days of John *until now*":

- they were already violent when the Baptist was active;
- they continued to exercise violence even after he was imprisoned, *until now*, in the present time, in which Jesus speaks and in which they continue to exercise it.

If verse 11 of Matthew were not in code, and openly spoke of transgressors who in the kingdom prevail over the righteous John, it would be immediately apparent that the next verse (verse 12), that speaks of the violent ones who take over the kingdom from John onwards, is not a cryptic allusion to an unknown group of violent, but simply the decoding, *in common language*, of what was written just before in code: those who are "smaller-least" (*code word*) surpass John in the kingdom; or, the *violent* (*decoding* the word "smaller-least") kidnap the kingdom.

If in a community, rigidly regulated by a set of norms, it was elevated to the prime value, making it known to all, the violation of the same norms, in the event that the transgressors had a project to carry out in a violent way they would find numerous obstacles from all the "great" ones (= observants of the Law). Only those who are part of the project will know about it. Eventually, those who, since the project began, have shared purposes and methods with the leader, will play a leading role (Mt 19:28):

You too will sit on twelve thrones to judge the twelve tribes of Israel.

The formula "the Law and the Prophets *until John*" indicates a clear, unattainable expiration date, reiterated by verse 14:

And, *if you want to understand*, he is that Elijah who must come.

The Israelites awaited a new Elijah, who would restore the highest fidelity to the ancient covenant of the Jewish people: the covenant founded on the precepts and their observance. Jesus, in the above-mentioned verse, states that the "new Elijah" that the Israelites were waiting for, was John: the last link in that long chain called "Law and prophets". It is useless to expect in Jesus the new Elijah. The Law and the prophets end with John: the last of the "great" ones. Who gives way to the first of the "little ones".

"Trying to make something" or "being forced to do something"?

The evangelists Matthew and Luke agree that there is something different, separating what comes *before* John the Baptist from what comes *after*. What comes before is represented by the Law and by the Prophets; what comes next, by the advent of the kingdom (this clearly suggest that Law and prophets are one thing, the kingdom another).

Mt 11:12-13 (Cei 2008)	Luke 16:16
From the days of John the Baptist until now, the kingdom of heaven has been subjected to violence and the violent take it over. All the Prophets and the Law in fact prophesied until John.	The Law and the Prophets until John: from then on, the kingdom of God is announced and everyone strives to enter it.

Keeping in mind the translation Cei 2008, according to Matthew after the time of the Baptist the kingdom suffers violence from some not better specified "violent" ones. For Luke, instead, after John the kingdom is "happily announced" (*eu-anghèlion*), and everyone "strives" to enter it.

Therefore:

- for Matthew, the violent take over the kingdom;
- for Luke, violence would seem to be totally absent from it. Indeed, the kingdom is happily announced (therefore, without violence?), and everyone makes an effort to become part of it.

This may already contain a contradiction in terms: something that is announced with joy should not require efforts to be shared. According to Matthew, after John something very bad happens; according to Luke, instead, something very nice:

- why do they have opposing views about the kingdom of heaven, even though they speak of the same content?
- for what reason, while agreeing that the Law was applied until John, are they not at all in agreement about what comes *after* John?

Both evangelists use the same Greek verb, *biàzo* [βιάζω], «I force, I violent»: the etymological root is common to the noun *bìa*, which in Greek indicates brute force, violence. The same form is found in the verse of Luke, which Cei instead translates «everyone *strives* to enter».

Therefore, in Matthew the verb *biàzo* would unequivocally mean "to suffer violence, to be taken by force"; while in Luke it would mean "to strive" to do something, or "to commit, to make an effort". So, in Matthew the verb would have a harshly negative valence; in Luke the perspective would be reversed in a completely positive sense:

- can this be an indication that they are saying different things?
- is it not more reasonable instead that, precisely because they both speak of the Law, the prophets and the kingdom using the same verb, they are expressing exactly the same concepts?

The translation of Nuova Riveduta is closer to the Greek text:

> The Law and the prophets lasted until John; from that time the good news
> of the kingdom of God is announced, and each one *enters by force*.

Summarizing:
- according to Cei, everyone is committed to doing something, striving to achieve a certain result;
- according to Nuova Riveduta, everyone enters the kingdom by force, or unwillingly (because obviously someone is forcing him).

However, between "striving to enter" and "entering by force" there is a substantial difference. Therefore,
- how is it possible that the same passage, by the same author, written in a Greek syntax whose level of difficulty could be classified in the beginner category, is translated with such different meanings?
- what can the opinion of the common reader be?

In the Greek dictionary, about the translation of the verb *biàzo* we read:

> I make violence; I constrain; I force; I oblige; I impose with violence; I violent; I abuse; I use violence; I go to force.

These are all meanings that would not seem to be subject to extensive interpretations, nor to be able to have dilutions enough to be transformed, to the point where it comes to mean "to make an effort of good will to do something". A comparison of Luke's translations (14:15-24), containing the famous "parable of the banquet", may be useful in this regard:

Cei 1974	Nuova Riveduta	Nuova Diodati
One of the diners, having heard this, told him: «Blessed is he who will eat bread in the kingdom of God». Jesus replied: «A man gave a great supper and made many invitations [...] But all, unanimously, began to apologize. [...] On his return the servant reported all this to the master. Then the landlord, irritated, said to the servant: "Go out immediately through the squares and the streets of the city and lead here poor, crippled, blind and lame". The servant said: "Lord, it was done as you ordered, but there is still room". The master then said to the servant: "Go out into the streets and along the hedges, *encourage them* to enter, so that my house may be filled"».	One of the guests, heard these things, told him: «Blessed is he who will eat bread in the kingdom of God». Jesus said to him: «A man prepared a great supper and invited many [...] They all began to apologize together [...] The servant returned and reported these things to his lord. Then the master of the house became angry and said to his servant: "Go quickly to the squares and streets of the city, and bring the poor, the crippled, the blind and the lame here". Then the servant said: "Lord, it was done as you commanded and there is still room". The lord said to the servant: "Go out into the streets and along the hedges and *force them* to enter, so that my house is full"».	Now one of the guests, hearing these things, said to him: «Blessed is he who will eat bread in the kingdom of God». Then Jesus said to him: «A man made a great supper and invited many; [...] But they all began to apologize in the same way. [...] So that servant returned and reported these things to his lord. Then the owner of the house, full of indignation, said to his servant: "Quickly, go to the squares and streets of the city, bring here the beggars, the mutilated, the lame and the blind". Then the servant told him: "Lord, it was done as you commanded, but there is still room". Then the lord said to the servant: "Go out in the streets and along the hedges and *force them* to enter, so that my house is full"».

The theme of the parable is the kingdom, and Jesus declines it according to the usual parabolic modes, using the metaphor of the banquet. When dinner is ready, the master sends a servant to call the guests.

They unexpectedly decline the invitation. There are those who do it for business reasons («I bought a field», «I have five pairs of oxen»); or because they have just married and must fulfill their conjugal obligations («I have taken a wife and therefore I cannot come»).

These aspects of the story would already reveal, in a sufficiently clear way, how the word "banquet" is a code word that denotes something else:

bread : kingdom = *dinner* : landlord

The bread is related to the kingdom as the great supper is related to the landlord who organizes it. However, the accession of an invited person is severely hindered by the money he owns and the use he makes of it. He buys a field. Therefore he will have the burdensome task of administering it. Having a lot of economic resources can be a big obstacle to the positive response to the invitation. In fact, a rich person can hardly pass through the eye of a needle.

Even taking a wife is a problem and an obstacle of no small importance. Being tied for life to the spouse is something absolutely incompatible with what, metaphors aside, is the kingdom and its implementation:

- The sons of this world take wives and take husbands; but those who are judged worthy of the other world and of the *resurrection from the dead* [= *healing of the disease*] do not take wives or husbands (Lk 20:34-35).

- If one comes to me and does not *hate* his father, his mother, *his wife* [...] cannot be my disciple (Lk 14:25-33).

To participate in the "banquet", you must free yourself from any impediment of a professional nature. From any bond of a sentimental nature. Otherwise, the landlord will decide to divert the numerous invitations to completely different types of people. Not businessmen and professionals. Not husbands with heavy parental responsibilities. But, exclusively, "poor, crippled, blind, lame". They, and not others:

None of those men who were invited will taste my supper.

The invitation is not extended. Nor is the refusal of the first guests forgiven. No second chance is given. All they will be categorically excluded from the banquet.

We ask ourselves:

- but why, then, did John marvel at Jesus' works for the benefit of the blind, the crippled, the lame?
- did he think that the only suitable guests were those from the first round of invitations, that is to say, those who unanimously refused?
- is the servant who calls the first guests the same one who calls the second (blind, crippled, lame)?
- metaphors aside, when John went in search of followers and disciples, did he receive refusals? If so, how did he react?
- the Baptist was an active part of the proclamation of the kingdom but did he not know that Jesus addressed himself exclusively to the blind, the crippled and the lame?
- was the Baptist the "servant" who had been entrusted with the task of bringing to the "banquet" guests who were everything but blind, crippled and lame?
- is John the "servant" to whom was candidly answered "no, thank you"?

If it is true that John prepared the way for Jesus who invited the blind, crippled and lame to the "banquet", this should mean that the precursor began to do (= to bring blind, crippled and lame) what Jesus would finish doing (= to bring blind, crippled and lame). On the contrary, we have seen how John with "blind, crippled and lame" has little to do.

Surely, from the parable we infer that the announcements are two. Chronologically distinct. The second is a "happy announcement", in the perspective of those invited to the "banquet": in fact, cripples, blind and lame from the first round of invitations were excluded. Those first guests, not maimed and therefore "healthy", took the place of those who, before, were *last*. And those who were *last*, disabled individuals and therefore "sick", now occupy the place that should have been of the first. All this because Jesus is not the physician of the healthy, but of the sick.

Since it is quite clear from the parable that the second round of invitations is announced because the first has failed dramatically, it is reasonable to think that, being radically different the type of guests, the servant who sends the invitations is not the same for both rounds, but there are two different servants.

Even leaving aside the evidence that in the Greek text does not appear the phrase "the landlord said to the servant he had sent before", or "said to the same servant", or "to that servant", but simply "*to the servant*", it is just a comparison with Matthew to reveal that the invitations to the banquet or to the kingdom are made in two distinct moments, by two distinct individuals: if John sends words to Jesus, saying that the messiah calls *exclusively* blind cripples and lame, the Baptist evidently was not aware of it.

In this regard, they are very interesting the news provided by Robert Eisenman in his work *James the Brother of Jesus*, about the "Roll of the War" (found in the excavations in 1947), one of the most important texts of Qumran, where the rules of extreme purity, in force in the fields in the desert, are indicated (we refer to sites that recent findings have confirmed as actually existing). The passage we propose is very significant:

> No boy or woman will enter these camps from the moment the holy warriors leave Jerusalem to go to war. No one who is a blind, a cripple, or has a plague in his flesh or has his body plagued by contamination [...] all those who *voluntarily* want to enlist, must be perfect in spirit and body. No man who is sexually impure on the day of war can go with them.

To comment, the scholar writes that this is the description, given in the texts of Qumran, of the "desert fields". According to Eisenman, we have to keep precisely in mind that the categories banned by these "holy camps" (blind, lame, crippled and sexually impure), are exactly those that Jesus often frequented, at least according to the canonical Gospels. The author observes that in the Gospels the Messiah has in great consideration blind, crippled and lame individuals: that is, those who were forbidden to enlist – according to the Roll of the War – in the messianic army that should have engaged in the holy war against foreign oppressors.

What can now allow access to a higher level of analysis is an investigation:

- into the structure of the message;
- into the code by which it is transmitted;
- into the semantic areas of concern: *exclusion* and *inclusion*.

We will get that:

1. Yahweh has an attitude of exclusion with regard to blind, crippled, lame and other human beings deemed unclean for various reasons;

2. according to the Roll of the War, the same categories of handicapped persons should be excluded from training camps for holy war, again for reasons of impurity; moreover – it goes without saying – hardly blind, crippled and lame could have successfully formed the ranks of a messianic army;

3. the messiah not only frequents, as Eisenman writes, the individuals affected by such impairment, but "heals" them. From unclean, makes them pure. That is, for him they are pure. They are already well. He is a physician of sinners, not of the righteous;

4. John the Baptist, who until his arrest works in the desert – where the training camps according to the Roll of the War are located –, is surprised that Jesus "heals" blind, crippled, lame and lepers.

We are convinced that only in the case of Yahweh and the Roll of the War is made mention of actual physical impairment. In the case of Jesus and John, instead, the terms related to the semantic area of illness are, from the evangelists, transferred to the area of transgression: is the reason why the Baptist is amazed at the innumerable "healings of the sick" (that is, *the forgiveness of sins and sinners*).

Is the truth in the code?

The fact that, in the parables, the "servant of the landlord" must (so it would seem) appear unique, is reflected and explained in the programmatic discourses of Jesus. When he is put in difficulty by the disciples of John, who ask him if he is "the one who must come", the messiah does everything to convince the crowds that between him and the Baptist there is full unity of intent. As they were both the only servant of one landlord:

> He is the one of whom it is written: "Behold, ahead of you I send my messenger, ahead of you he will prepare your way".

Quoting Isaiah, the messiah seems to want to reassure the crowd that he and John are two "servants" of the landlord, motivated by the same aims. However, in the kingdom for which the Baptist would prepare the way, he who is "smaller" than John is "greater" than him. This sentence is in itself sufficient, for the listener or reader, to perceive that there is some difference between Jesus and John. Knowing now well the meaning of neologisms, we could say that the message "John prepares the way for Jesus" is for use and consumption of many who do not know the code by which the messiah encodes his messages. Only a few ears will know, instead, that the "great" John, precisely because of his "greatness", cannot open the way to the "little" Jesus, who works in the opposite way to him (Mt 11:16-19):

> But to whom shall I compare this generation? It is similar to those children sitting in the squares who turn to their other companions and say: "We played the flute and you did not dance, we sang a lament and you did not cry".

The generation of Jesus behaves like children who have received two different calls to attention. A lament was sung and they did not cry. A flute was played, with melodies evidently "happy" if they could be danced, and they did not dance. The calls were two: a sad one (the observance of 613 norms was not to be a cheerful thing), and nobody answered. The second one was a "happy announcement". However, neither one nor the other pleased the "first" recipients of the invitations.

If it is not sufficiently clear that Jesus refers to two servants of the landlord who act towards the guests in ways that are irreconcilable with each other (weeping *vs* laughter), he himself gives light in this sense (Mt 11:18-19):

> John came, who does not eat or drink, and they said: «He has a devil». The Son of Man, who eats and drinks, came and said: «Here is a glutton and a drunkard, a friend of tax collectors and sinners».

John strictly followed the prescriptions of the Law. However, he was not accepted. He played a lament. Fasting and not drinking alcohol are actions that belong to the semantic area of mourning, sadness; while eating and drinking – actions that Jesus ascribes to himself as a yardstick of difference from John – get along with the flute and dance that accompany the "happy announcement", of which music and dance are frank expression.

If we explained in other words the verses in which Jesus affirms that John has prepared the way, we should say that a faster, willingly abstaining in accordance with strict protocols, prepared the way for a man who, even as willingly, did not fast. And consumed without hesitation alcoholic beverages, having as his drinking companions publicans and sinners: that is, violators of the Mosaic Law. It would be like saying that an intransigent and disciplined ascetic prepares the way for the one who demolish the same discipline; that a faster baptizes a glutton; that a teetotaller promotes a drunkard; that a strict observant of the Law paradoxically favors the one who is friends of transgressors and feasts with them.

All this leads us to think that on the one hand the evangelists must necessarily present the Baptist as the precursor of the future king; however leaving within the text abundant clues to understand that things did not go this way at all; to understand that Jesus has overthrown, with his methods more than convincing, the one who before him had applied to be king.

For this reason, having established that the doctrine of the Baptist had nothing to do with that of Jesus (observance *vs* transgression), it is difficult to continue to believe that he baptized encouraging happily the *metànoia* towards the messiah: since it is now clear that Jesus preached the "change of mind" precisely in relation to John. The "way of thinking" had to be changed with respect to his doctrine: no longer *purification* from sins, but complete *forgiveness* of sins. This is a very good "news" compared to the previous one. Good for all sinners: the crippled, the lame, the blind that Jesus sought.

Therefore, it seems much more reasonable to assume that the large number of people who proclaimed the transgressions had not brought them John, who had to do with the righteous, but another person. Both wanted to achieve certain goals, with the difference that the Baptist followed the above-mentioned Qumran protocols, relating to the enlistment of the righteous under the Law to wage holy war against the oppressors. This hypothesis was evidently not so much pleasing to Herod Antipas: he in fact arrested John, who with reasonable probability in the "desert fields" of which Eisenman writes was not only a peaceful fasting ascetic who abhorred alcohol.

On the contrary, Jesus, endowed with a political and operational intelligence clearly superior to that of John, had well understood that, addressing the observants of the Law, he would never have achieved much in terms of numbers. All of them, the invited of the first round (observants), would desert the banquet. They would not follow the Baptist.

They had better things to do: to work, to think about buying fields and oxen, to get married and start a family.

Less than ever would have endorsed the work of John the Pharisees: they too, endowed with strong political intelligence as well as with simple and pragmatic common sense, knew well that, however numerous the possible messianic army might be, to defeat the strongest army in the world (until then known) was a discreetly distant eventuality. If it had not been realized – as we read in the Gospel of John (11:50): «Better that one man [Jesus] die for the people and not the whole nation perish» – an entire nation would have paid the terrible penalty, going towards an end not different from that of the protagonists of the famous Spartacus' revolt: crucified – thousands of men – in the long journey between Capua (near Naples) and Rome (in Lazio).

Even more distant was the possibility that disorganized and heterogeneous crowds of "blind, crippled and lame", gathered in the villages, in the streets and even in the bushes, had some hope of overthrowing the power of the Roman rulers: perhaps even risking death on the cross to allow an unscrupulous leader to become king of Israel. For this reason, the Pharisees have answered "no, thanks" to John. And "no, thanks" to Jesus. They have not sung a lament. And they didn't even dance to the flute.

The authors of the Gospels can not leak all this information about the real messianic intentions of John and Jesus, openly and from the beginning of their writings: this would not help at all to the shaping (according to the Pauline doctrine?) of an imaginary to be based granitically on the indispensable presupposition of the "suffering messiah", who is put on the cross (by the Romans) by the will of the "perfidious Jews": whose will would impose itself on that of Pilate (also known to the chronicles of the time, on the contrary, for his brutality towards peoples subjected).

However, to those who have ears to understand, it can always be suggested, through the parables, that things did not go exactly like that. Instead, immediately making known the finality – all earthly – of the work of John and Jesus, the structure of the entire narrative would be immediately lost. And it would turn into a thin, very short report.

It is in the similarities coined by the messiah that we find clear indications of his will: on the one hand, with words outside the jargon code, the will to be credited as the one to whom John left the fulfillment of a precise project; on the other, through the code language, to send out a message that cannot, because of its harshness and the scandal it would provoke, be openly disseminated. John and Jesus are actually two bitterly antithetical personalities. Irreconcilable. Adversaries. They address different people. With equally different intentions and methods. Among them we must choose: those who opt for the "great", cannot be with the "small". And vice versa. Those who sing the lament cannot dance to the sound of the flute. Or lament, or dance. With Jesus or with John. With Jesus or against Jesus («with me or against me»). Being with the Baptist meant going against the messiah.

The evangelists tell us about the ways in which, in the times and places of which they write, two highly charismatic personalities took turns:

- both sent invitations to their people, who had long been suffering the setback of foreign domination;
- both turned to different kinds of people;
- both obtained refusals and denials.

However, on this last aspect the second charismatic personality was much more rigid, promoting a "zero tolerance" towards opponents:

- If someone does not welcome you [...] shake the dust from your feet [...] on the day of judgment the land of Sodom and Gomorrah will have a more bearable fate than that city (Mt 10:14-15);

- Some came to him and told him about those Galileans, whose blood Pilate had made flow along with that of their sacrifices. [...] Jesus said to them: «Do you believe that those Galileans were more sinners than all Galileans, for having suffered such a fate? No, I tell you, but if you are not converted, you will all perish in the same way. Or do you think those eighteen people, on whom the tower of Siloam collapsed and

> killed them, were more guilty than all the inhabitants of Jerusalem?
> No, I say to you, but if you do not convert, you will all perish in the
> same way» (Lk 13:1-5).

Refusal implies the use of violence: «If you are not converted, you will all perish». We can have a further idea of what methods the servant of the "second call" – described in the "parable of the banquet" – used:

> The servant said: "Lord, it was done as you ordered, but there is still room".
> The master then said to the servant: "Go out into the streets and along the
> hedges, push them to enter, so that my house will fill" (Cei 1974).

More faithful to the Greek text appears Nuova Riveduta: «*Force them* to enter».

Not dissimilar Nuova Diodati: «*Force them* to enter».

Cei 2008, correcting Cei 1974, is perfectly in line with Riveduta and Diodati: «*Force them* to enter».

Many blind, crippled and lame people were called and responded positively. But there is still room in the banquet hall. The landlord is peremptory and won't listen to reason. So that the room overflows with guests, they will have to be collected from the streets. Found in the hedges. And *forced* to enter (from the Greek verb *anankàzo* [ἀναγκάζω]: «I make it necessary; I force; I oblige; I constrain, by force, threats, by persuasion or other means»).

From Cei 1974 to Cei 2008 there is a difference of no little significance: "pushing" someone to do something does not exactly correspond and necessarily *to forcing* him to do it. This is a relationship similar to that we have identified between "striving to enter" and "entering by force". Guests at lunch, being forced, are no longer *invited* to attend. But, they *are forced* to attend. If they answer "yes, ok", fine. If they answer no, it is the same. They will be forced.

We ask ourselves: is there a relationship between the "least" disciples (violent transgressors) and the compulsion to enter the kingdom?

The "little" disciples entered villages and cities, and the messiah himself contemplated the concrete probability that they were not welcomed:

- in order not to be welcomed, the disciples exactly what kind of activities did they carry out?
- what should the inhabitants do to receive them in an appropriate way?
- what words of the followers of Jesus did they not want to listen?

The wise unrighteousness

According to what we have noted so far, the following proportion could hardly be incorrect:

$$\text{Law} : \textit{observants} = \text{Kingdom} = \textit{violent}$$

In the code language of Jesus, the proportion would take the following form:

$$\text{Law} : \textit{"great ones"} = \text{Kingdom} : \textit{"least ones"}$$

The Law is related to those who observe it and make it be observed, as the kingdom is related to violence and to those who exercise it. Law is for the observants. Kingdom is for the violent. In the first case, it is necessary to abide by rules. In the second, the opposite is necessary: the kingdom must be seized by force. This is the only way to obtain it. The only law to be observed if one wants to reach the goal (Mt 6:33):

First seek the kingdom of God and *his righteousness.*

The kingdom has its own intrinsic righteousness. It is taken with violence and the violent take possession of it precisely because the Law is no longer observed. A conduct of life permeated by the observance of shared norms collides inexhaustibly with the taking possession of a kingdom. Or you take it by force, or you can not take it.

In the "parable of the banquet" there are those who bought a field, those who bought oxen. They are working individuals:

> For six days you will work, but the seventh will be for you a holy day, a day of absolute rest [...] Whoever in that day will do some work will be put to death.

If you work, there is no time for "dinner" or "banquet". Observance of the norm (working six days a week and resting on the Sabbath) prevents participation in the banquet of the kingdom.

The same can be said of the use of money earned through work and aimed at the possession of goods. Yahweh wanted the righteous to enjoy it, as clear in the book of Deuteronomy (14:25-26), which mentions the conversion of tithes into money:

> You will employ that money to buy you everything that your heart desires: oxen, sheep, wine, alcoholic beverages, or whatever you may like more; and there you will eat in the presence of the Lord your God, and you will rejoice with your family.

In Luke (12:16) we read the following parable:

> The campaign of a rich man had given an abundant harvest. [...] He said, «I will demolish my warehouses and build larger ones and gather all my grain and goods there. Then I will say to myself: "My soul, you have many goods at your disposal, for many years; rest, eat, drink and have fun"». But God said to him: «Foolish, this very night your life will be required of you. And what you have prepared, whose will it be?». So is he who accumulates treasures for himself and does not get rich before God.

The Israelite of whom Deuteronomy speaks, with full favor and according to the will of Yahweh, does what the rich man of Luke 16 does. Having accumulated goods by the sweat of his brows, he rests, eats, drinks, gives himself to joy: all actions harshly condemned by the protagonist of the Gospels. The Old Testament God blesses the abundance of riches; the God of whom Jesus speaks, instead, he calls foolish who behaves in the way that Yahweh blessed.

Luke (12:20-2) also writes:

Foolish, this same night your life will be required of you. And what you have prepared, of whom will be?

In Matthew (12:29) we read:

How could one penetrate the house of the *strong* man and kidnap his things, if he does not bind him first?

It would be questionable if there could be some consonance between the fool whose life will be required, and the unspecified individual willing to enter the house of a strong man to rob him; tying him up first, so he can make a full haul.

To be translated «foolish» is the Greek word *àfron* [ἄφρων], which means «person without sense»; it is the opposite of *frònimos* («sensible, wise»), an adjective that we find in the parable so-called "of the dishonest administrator" (Lk 16:1-9):

A rich man had an administrator, and he was accused before him of squandering his possessions. [...] «You must give account of your administration, because you can no longer administer». [...] «I know what I will do so that, when I will be removed from the administration, there is someone who welcomes me in his house». He called one by one the debtors of his master and said to the first: «What do you owe to my master?». He answered: «A hundred barrels of oil». He said: «Take your receipt, sit down immediately and write fifty». Then he said to another: «How much do you owe?». He answered: «One hundred measures of wheat». He told him: «Take your receipt and write eighty». The master *praised that dishonest administrator*, because he had acted with cunning. For the sons of this world are more

> cunning to their peers than the sons of light. Well, I say to you: *make friends with dishonest wealth,* because, when this will be lacking, they will welcome you in the eternal dwellings (Cei 2008).

Although translations generally contain the adjective "shrewd" and the noun "cunning", the meaning of *frònimos* in Greek is «sensible», «wise». There is, in these words, not the halo of negativity that can have the word "cunning". Jesus defines as unwise the man who earns wealth for himself from his hard work, honestly. Wise, instead, is the dishonest administrator who comes to defraud his master arbitrarily, remitting the debt to his debtors:

- by telling of this character who – going against every good and honest norm – does harm to his master himself, does Jesus refer in particular to someone?
- is "debt forgiveness" a literal remission of a debt of money or, in the usual parable's language, does these words refer to remission of something else?

What we can say with certainty is that the parable ends with a paroxysm: the master praises the administrator who has done him harm. The literal translation of the verse we are referring to is as follows:

> The master praised the administrator *of the unrighteousness,* because he had acted with wisdom. The sons of this world, in fact, towards their peers are wiser than the sons of light.

It follows this equation:

$$\text{wisdom} = \textit{unrighteousness}$$

He who practices unrighteousness acts with wisdom. He who practices righteousness (respect for the norms) acts foolishly:

$$\text{wisdom} : \textit{unrighteousness} = \text{foolishness} : \textit{righteousness}$$

Wisdom is related to unrighteousness as foolishness is related to righteousness. If we match the meanings of righteousness and unrighteousness with the meaning that these words had in Jewish society (observance and transgression of norms), we will have that the transgressor is wise; the observant is foolish. Using the neologisms of Jesus, we will have that who is "small-least" is wise, who is "great" is foolish. The "least" Jesus is sensible. The "great" John is a mindless.

Moreover, in the Greek text the noun "world" ("the sons of this *world*"), in the common sense that this term has today, does not appear. Instead, the word *aiòn* [αἰών] is present: «Time, duration, life, age, present century». Reading the translation «the sons of this *world*», the reader will think that the text is referring to a world that is only earthly and not "spiritual"; while the expression "sons of light" would instead identify the members of a higher reality, not tangible.

However, the Greek text simply says that the generation contemporary to Jesus, "the sons of this age, of this time, of the present century" are wiser than the "sons of light". It is enough to consult part of the bibliography about the Qumran Scrolls, or even just some works by Robert Eisenman, to learn that the expression "sons of light" refers to the Essenes and Essenism: areas not unknown to John the Baptist.

Jesus here affirms that the men of the present age (the "*younger*-little ones"), thanks to the practice of unrighteousness (transgression of the precepts) are *wiser*: because they achieve goals that the "great ones" who preceded them had not succeeded in achieving. They manage to make many more friends, thanks to the unrighteousness or the "remission of the debt": which, however, paradoxically makes the very master of the parable happy. It makes him happy because, even if by illicit means, the servant achieves the established aims.

According to this singular conception that we could define "of healthy unrighteousness", the verse that follows is better clarified:

> How could one penetrate the house of the strong man and kidnap his things, if he does not bind him first?

This is a statement that, put in the mouths of the protagonist of the Gospels, which tradition has always painted as a man who abhorred violence, it might seem inexplicable. Instead, if you let the text speak, it only confirms the usual monochord philosophy: the strong man must be immobilized by a man "stronger" than him. He must be wisely immobilized, before being plundered. He is unjustly robbed; but *wisely* robbed in the perspective of those who rob him. The strong man has accumulated riches: he is a fool, in direct proportion to the wisdom of those who ruin him.

The protagonist of the parable is asked to give his life (Lk 12:20):

Foolish, this same night your life will be required to you.

However, in the Greek text there is neither passive form of the verb nor person singular, but active form and plural person: *apaitòusin* [ἀπαιτοῦσιν], «they require» life. The use of the present tense ("they require") harmonizes well with the indication of time ("*this* same night"): the action of demanding the life of a rich man is evidently decisive and completed in a very short time. Jesus here affirms not that life of the fool will be required, but that *just tonight*, shortly, plural subjects not better identified require his life:

- to whom does the messiah refer?
- is he referring to a group of people who break into the rich man's house, and have the power to claim the life of a man guilty of having accumulated property?
- if the reference were to the arrival of a general sudden death that takes the rich by surprise, why is the verb in the plural form?
- does this plural form, the subject of which is not clearly expressed, imply someone not specified? Someone who?
- last but not least: how is it that, in the Cei translation, a verb in the active plural form is translated in exactly the opposite way, that is, in a passive singular form?

What certainly emerges from the Lucan parable, is that the one who accumulates treasures for himself (something that the God of Deuteronomy did not condemn at all) is asked life in no uncertain terms; while the goods and riches left by him ("And what you have prepared, of whom will be?") will become property of others.

We ask ourselves:

- was the unfortunate rich man in the parable immobilized because he foolishly resisted rather than wisely turning the other cheek?

- did he not give the cloak to those who entered his house, while he should have given the cloak and also the tunic?

- to whom should the "other cheek" be turned?

- should it be turned to unlikely Roman soldiers who entered the homes of wealthy Jews to plunder them, or to organized groups of Jewish criminals who became the enemies of their own countrymen? Enemies that paradoxically needed to be loved and to whom it was necessary to hold out the other cheek?

- were these the persecutors for whom Jesus said it was necessary to pray?

If in all this discourse there were nothing transcendent and "spiritual", but the text were simply talking about a human life that is violently ceased and of riches that end up in the hands of those to whom they were not entitled, this would not be different from what happened to Ananias and Sapphira:

A man named Ananias, with his wife Sapphira, sold a piece of land and, having kept it for himself, in agreement with his wife, a part of the proceeds, handed over the other part to the apostles. But Peter said: «Ananias, why [...] did you lie to the Holy Spirit and withhold a portion of the proceeds of the field? Before selling it, was it not your property and the amount of the sale was not perhaps at your disposal? [...] You did not lie to men, but to God». Hearing these words, Ananias fell to the ground and died.

Ananias was undoubtedly asked for life. What Peter affirms before his death is nothing more or less than what is written in the parable of Luke:

> So is he who accumulates treasures for himself and does not get rich before God.

Again, this translation risks not conveying to the reader the message contained in the Greek text. In fact, it does not speak of a person who does not enrich "inwardly, spiritually" in the presence of God, but of a man who does not become rich «*towards* God», «*for* God» (the Greek preposition "*èis*" is used to express to whom the action is directed). The riches must be given *to* "God". To those who dedicate their wealth to themselves, instead, some X subjects require life.

Ascertained this, will give us reason to reflect other maxims and evangelical sentences always transmitted as detached from any context, while they seem to fit in context very appropriately:

> To him who has, will be given and will be in abundance; to him who has not, what he has will be taken away.

In the case of the Lucan parable as well as in the episode of Ananias, the one who has not accumulated goods for God is undoubtedly taken away what he has: life.

The violence and the violent, to which the evangelist Matthew refers by placing them in connection with the kingdom of heaven, emerge from the text in a very decisive way. In extrabiblical sources, rather than finding resounding denials, we find analogies that give us food for thought: for example in Josephus Flavius (*Jewish War* 2, 265), when he describes the working methods of the zealots towards their own countrymen (not dissimilar contents are also found in some works written by Philo of Alexandria):

> Distributed in teams, they plundered the houses of the lords, then killed them,
> and set the villages on fire so that all of Judea was full of their heinous deeds.

The chronicle lends itself to a comparison, already proposed by various scholars, with an evangelical passage in which two disciples of Jesus, since the inhabitants of a Samaritan village refused to receive him, address their master in this way (Lk 9:54):

> Lord, do you want perhaps that we make to come down a fire from the sky
> and that it consumes them?

These words are spoken in the Gospel of Luke (9:51) by James and John, nicknamed by Jesus himself "sons of thunder": is there a link between this nickname and the request for consent in order to burn down a village?

Other parables have the function of veiling the power of a message that can have recipients as illustrious as strongly opposed, as scribes and Pharisees (Lk 20:17):

> «What is it, then, that is written: "The stone that the builders have discarded has become a cornerstone"? Anyone who falls on that stone will be shattered and whoever falls on it will be crushed». Then the scribes and the chief priests tried to put their hands on him, but they were afraid of the people. They had understood that he *had said the parable for them.*

It is yet another confirmation that the parables alluded to known things that were to be hidden, and not to unknown things that were to be revealed. The kingdom will be taken away from those who do not establish it or do not want to establish it (the Pharisees), and will be entrusted to those who can succeed (Mt 21:43):

> The kingdom of God will be taken away from you and given to a people
> that will make it bear fruit.

It will be given to men who have no other occupation but to look after the realization of the kingdom. They do not work. They have no family. Or they have abandoned it (Mt 19:27):

> Peter, taking the word, said: «Behold, we have left everything and have followed you; *what then will we get?*».

In this regard it is useful to compare Matthew and Deteuronomy:

Dt 24, 5	Mt
When a man is newly married, *he shall not go to war*, and no charge shall be imposed upon him; he shall be free for a year to look after his house, and he shall delight the wife whom he has married.	A man prepared a great dinner and invited many [...] All together they began to apologize [...] Another said: *"I have taken a wife, and therefore I cannot come"*.

Getting married is definitely an obstacle to something that keeps husbands away from wives: war. The Law prevented new husbands from fighting. It would be desirable, for the one who has set up the "banquet", that this article of the Law should fall, so that obstacles to the establishment of the kingdom should not be placed and multiplied.

It seems clear by now that behind the expressions "Law and prophets" and "Kingdom of heaven" there are nothing but the two charismatic personalities who fully represent them: namely, John and Jesus. Summarizing:

- Yahweh gives Moses a Law that his people must keep;
- Jesus (the son of that Father?) calls his "brothers" those who transgress and teach to transgress that same Law.

In Matthew (12:50) the messiah states:

> Who does the wish of my Father is my brother, sister, mother and father.

In the kingdom, no relationship is important. It is important to obey orders. We know that the Father has revealed his mysteries to "small ones" and "least": therefore, in the now clear logic of Jesus, who wants to do the will of the Father *transgresses his Law*: just like the dishonest administrator. He defrauds the master. But the master praises him for his unrighteous wisdom. All this is no wonder and brings us back to the parable of Matthew (21:28-31) that speaks of the son who at the beginning does not do the will of his father; yet then does it, going to work in the vineyard:

> A man had two sons; turned to the first he said: "Son, go today to work in the vineyard". And he answered: "Yes, Lord"; but he did not go. He turned to the second, and said the same to him. And he answered, "I have no desire for it". But then, *having changed his mind*, he went there. Which of the two has fulfilled the will of the father?». They say: "The last".

Those who "change mind" are those who do the will of the Father; not the "first" son, but the "last".

In order to realize the Father's will for his people – that is, to finally have a kingdom free from enemies and oppressors – it was necessary to be in a very precise category of people (the violent) that any norm were used to violate it, rather than to observe it. This is the profound and simple reason why Jesus in the synoptic Gospels is addressed exclusively to sinners. The statement "none more than John is observant of the Law" (Mt 11:11) corresponds, in the fullness of its meaning, to the statement "not even an iota or a sign of the Law shall pass" (Mt 5). As long as there is the Baptist, the Law does not collapse. For this reason he must step back.

"Little" disciples and adults "sons of the precept"

To square the circle about the argument we started from (the semantic area of "smallness"), we need to ask ourselves:

- can the use of "small" and "least" neologisms – and therefore what concerns *the text* – be explained by a precise *context*?
- is the link between "small-least" neologisms and the transgression of precepts a completely arbitrary association, or does it have a concrete reference in the history, society, religion and culture of the Jewish people in general?

In deepening the investigation, we will discover that a direct and motivated bond not only exists, but is closely linked to the conduct of life of the Israelites and the observance of the norms. In the culture of that people, in fact, one becomes responsible in Law before the beginning of adolescence, when the age of childhood is ending and from "small-little" one officially becomes "great" in front of the community: whose life is founded on total and unconditional respect for the precepts.

The "call to the Law" identifies the moment when the pre-teen accepts the burden of "rising to the Torah": the so-called "Aliah" ("rising to the Torah") is accomplished, for the first time, when the male child turns thirteen, thus becoming "Bar-Mitzvah" ("son of the commandment"); "Bat-Mitzvah" in the case of a female (at the age of twelve and one day).

Trace of this age seems to have remained – we would say not coincidentally if this information is kept in mind – in some episodes of the synoptic Gospels, in which synagogues and daughters of synagogue's leader appear: it was (and still is) the place where this very important initiation of the Jew to the Mosaic precepts is solemnly celebrated. From that moment, the "no longer child" (or no longer "small-little one") has the inescapable duty, like the adult individuals of the community, to observe all the precepts. He reads on this occasion, for the first time publicly, a chosen passage of the Biblical Law.

The former child, now an adult, becomes personally responsible for the application of the Mitzvot ("norms"). He is a full member of the religious community, becoming completely responsible for his own actions. In other words: he is obliged to follow the precepts. While, as a "child", he is not yet.

Of the fact that children, before the Bar-Mitzvah, are in a condition of *non-responsibility* with respect to the Law, there is also evidence in Talmudic literature (where reference is made to the one-year-old child who has not yet felt "the taste of sin"). But he who has become a "Bar-Mitzvah" is now subject to the Law, having become able to control his instincts. And he's responsible for the legal implications of his actions.

In Jewish culture the concepts of responsibility or non responsibility before the Law are rendered very effectively by the expressions related to being or not being "under the yoke" of precepts. The Law given to Israel was a yoke. It imposed obligations and responsibilities in relation to Yahweh.

The words "kingdom of God" and "kingdom of heaven" meant the close bond with the Lord in the observance of the precepts; the acceptance of his will; the fidelity to his covenant. Man must take upon himself the "yoke of the kingdom" and the "yoke of precepts": as Gunter Stemberger writes, the basis of the Jewish religion is the revelation on Sinai and the consequent covenant between God and his people. At that moment, Israel assumed upon itself the "yoke of the kingdom of God" (more literally, "of the kingdom of heaven") and the yoke of the commandments: in the future, every Jew must renew this commitment.

In the light of all this, one can have a more precise idea, together with all its devastating implications, of Jesus' statement:

> The kingdom of heaven is raped and the violent take possession of it.

The precepts constituted a yoke because they were numerous and very heavy; a burden that could be carried from the thirteen years of life onwards, at the beginning of what was and is considered to be the adult age by the Jews. This means that, if adults are asked to be accountable for the transgression of norms, the "little ones" are not asked to be accountable.

The established knowledge of these elements of the Gospel cultural context undoubtedly marks a turning point in the understanding of the text; and in the understanding of why Jesus uses "small" and "least" neologisms to identify the violators of the Law. This is because in the Jewish religion the "small-least" *were not held responsible* for the violation of precepts. They were not under the yoke of the Law. Therefore, the association between the semantic area of "smallness" and that of transgression is not arbitrary, but in all respects shaped on (and anchored to) the essential foundation of the life of the observing Jew.

Jesus calls the transgressors of the Law "least" or "small-little" because they, acting *as if they were not responsible* for the precepts and therefore violating them, behave *like children* with respect the norms. Although they are adults and well aware of what they do, they do so "like children". That is, as if they were not to give account of their voluntary transgressions; which for them become, being "similar to children", as if were involuntary. So, they can be forgiven.

A textual indicator of this is the famous passage we dealt with when these conclusions could only be seen in a blurred light:

> He called to himself a child, he placed him in the midst of them and said: «Truly I say to you: if you will not convert and become like children, you will not enter the kingdom of heaven».

By setting in motion an exemplary gesture, teaching the disciples to understand his communicative code, the messiah takes a child (in Greek language *pàis* [παῖς] designates precisely the pre-teen) and puts him among his followers. This is what anyone would do, wishing to explain that the "little ones" represent something that the disciples must grasp with their intellect.

Then, the Messiah sets as an unavoidable condition on entering the kingdom the "turning back" (from the Greek verb *strèfo*, of which we have already spoken). This is very clear in its meaning, if we let ourselves be enlightened by the cultural context of which we have said: if the disciples do not "turn back" and become "like children", they will not enter the kingdom. Its doors will remain closed if they do not commit transgressions to take possession of it; knowing full well, however, that they will most likely be held accountable for these sins (Mt 10:17-22):

> Beware of men, because they will deliver you to the courts and scourge you in their synagogues; and you will be brought before governors and kings for my sake [...] The brother will make his brother die and his father his son, and sons will stand up and accuse the parents and kill them. *You will be hated by all because of my name.*

A verse, the latter, incomprehensible if we rely exclusively on tradition, or rather on theological-cultural hypnosis in the broad sense, which has always proposed an image of Jesus and the disciples as champions of non-violence. While, if we are faithful to the Gospel text in which the disciples are defined by Jesus as "least" (that is, transgressors), we can formulate some more hypotheses:

- as to why they should be hated by all;
- and why, precisely, because of the name of their leader.

A leader sought and hunted by the authorities and, finally, executed by cross-fission: capital punishment inflicted by the Romans exclusively on those guilty of sedition against the imperial power (Lk 14:25-33):

> Who does not carry his own cross and does not come behind me, cannot be my disciple.

A Jewish adult who behaves "like a child", remains subject to the Law. But he becomes a transgressor. Then, if he teaches transgression, he becomes a transgressor raised to power. The yoke of precepts consists of 613 norms: it is too "heavy" and "great". The vilified Pharisees impose it. John imposes it. Well before them, Moses imposed it, by the will of Yahweh.

The messiah is a candidate to be their antagonist: he sets himself up as a point of reference for those sections of the population for whom the yoke of the commandments had always been too heavy (Mt 11:28-29):

> Come to me, all of you, who are weary and oppressed, and I will restore you.
> Take my yoke upon you and learn from me, for I'm meek and humble in
> heart [...] For my yoke is sweet and my burden light.

To think that, in this passage, Jesus uses the word "yoke" by chance, without wanting it for a specific reason, would in our opinion amount to believing that, in a book with religious contents, the author uses the word "altar" by chance.

To all those who are oppressed by the yoke of the "great" ones, Jesus proposes the *metànoia*: change your mind, and from the yoke of the "great" ones you will now move to that of the "small" and "least" ones. The "lightness" of the load is, yet, another redefinition of the semantic area of "smallness": the "little ones" must not observe the entire Law, but only what the messiah imparts. They are "meek" (like Jesus himself) because they accept the possible consequences of the "lightness-smallness" of the yoke, to the exact extent that Jesus accepted them.

Conscious use of the code

Keeping in mind what has been said so far, there would seem to be good reasons to believe that the authors make use of the same communication code used by the protagonist, and with the same purposes he pursues: veiling (and thus transmitting), under the cover of the neologism, things and events that cannot and must not be fully revealed (Lk 18:15-17; same contents in Mt 19 and Mk 10):

> People were also bringing babies to Jesus for him to place his hands on them.
> When the disciples saw this, they rebuked them. But Jesus called the children to him and said, «Let the little children come to me, and do not hinder
> them, for the kingdom of God belongs to such as these».

The followers of Jesus here scold and rebuke those who bring children to him. Luke even speaks of "newborns" (*brèfe*): therefore, undoubtedly they are "small" and "least".

Only Mark makes known that Jesus, in this situation, is indignant with his own disciples:

- but why do they reproach, and even prohibit children being taken to the master?
- those who carry them in all probability must be persons already close to the followers, or willing to become followers; just as the children they brought could be destined to follow Jesus. So, for what purpose and according to what bizarre and counterproductive logic do the disciples act like this?
- even if they are in close contact with the messiah, have they not yet understood that one enters the kingdom only if one becomes "like children"? That is, belonging to the same category to which they are preventing rapprochement?

Evidently, the "children" were too many; just as in other passages it happens to many "blind, crippled, lame". According to the disciples, it is not possible to "heal" everyone. But the messiah thinks differently. He knows that the more "children" arrive, the better for him. There are many "dinner guests". There's still plenty of room in the banquet hall.

The word "child", unsuspected in its common use, in the slang code comes to assume, in substance, the opposite meaning: from "innocent" to "guilty". The transmission of the message *outside the code* has the effect of being reassuring ("you must do like children") and of not raising suspicion in those who do not know the jargon. Only those who are like "children" enter the kingdom:

Mark 10 (coded message)	Mark 10 (decoded message)
People introduced him *children* so that he touched them, but the disciples sent them back. Jesus, seeing this, was indignant and said to them: «Let the *children* come to me, do not hinder them: for to him who is like them belongs the kingdom of God. In truth I say to you: who does not accept the kingdom of God as a *child* welcomes him, he will not enter it».	People introduced him *transgressors* so that he touched them, but the disciples sent them back. Jesus, seeing this, was indignant and said to them: «Let *transgressors* come to me, do not hinder them: for to him who is like them belongs the kingdom of God. In truth I say to you: who does not accept the kingdom of God as a *transgressor* welcomes him, he will not enter it».

The "children" or "little ones" are the lost sheep of Israel. They will be to the right of the messiah. The goats will not. The goats have not "strayed" because of him. The "good news" is addressed to the "least" (sinners). These are very numerous, compared to the "first" recipients (righteous). With the "small-least-last" ones you could finally fill the room of the "banquet".

In Matthew (21:14-15), the blind, the crippled and the children appear together:

They approached him in the temple blind and crippled, and he healed them. But the chief priests and the scribes, seeing the wonders he had done and the children who cheered in the temple "Hosanna to the son of David", they were indignant, and said to him: «Don't you hear what they say?».

Chief priests and scribes have the same reaction of the crowd that wanted to silence the blind (category of individuals that regularly appears here):

- do the "learned and wise" scribes and priests want to silence helpless children, who literally «shout» Hosanna (messianic hymns for the intronation of a king) to the son of David?

In a single sequence we have *blind, crippled* and *children*, united by being for some reason envy to scribes and Pharisees. They (paradoxically) do not like the "healings" of blind and crippled, nor the cries of "children". We wonder whether it is likely that Jesus, in the temple of Jerusalem, heals the blind and the crippled (those categories of physical impairments that Yahweh did not like in that place); or that the blind and the crippled, who are presumed to have major difficulties in walking, «they come (and not "are brought") to» Jesus. This is what happens to the blindman Bartimaeus, who «jumps up» in front of him.

We ask ourselves:

- what were many blind and crippled people doing in the temple, where they could not even bring offerings?
- did they know that Jesus, from distant Galilee, was a healer?
- why should the chief priests and the scribes, even though they dislike the messiah, be indignant at the instantaneous "healings" he has made?
- did they not rejoice at the miraculous healings that would have freed so many "sons of Abraham" from such great plagues?

If Matthew 21 had reported genuine miraculous healings, he would certainly have referred to the absolute amazement of scribes and priests; and not only to indignation. Instead, he just writes that what makes the scribes indignant are the blind and crippled healed, along with the screams of "children":

- but what are *children* doing in the temple, if they have not even yet become "sons of the commandment"?
- why are wise and learned men so concerned about what comes out of the mouths of innocent children, not yet able to distinguish between good and evil?

We will then still have to consider the hypothesis that the "blind and crippled" are not blind and crippled. And that the children in the temple are not "children" but all, in different ways, belonging to the usual semantic area preferred by Jesus: "smallness".

In the case of "blind and crippled", these are violators who are not yet part of the followers of Jesus: this will happen when they are "healed". In the case of the "children", it is a question of those who had already become his disciples and who accompanied him from Galilee (in fact, they sing the Hosanna that "blind and crippled" do not sing). Scribes and priests, knowing perfectly who they are and what they do, have much to be indignant about.

In the Gospel of Luke (chapter 19), Jesus is close to the descent of the Mount of Olives and is about to enter Jerusalem: «All the crowd of the disciples» (this clearly indicates that it was made up largely of his followers) exults loudly for the "wonders" seen, which the evangelist does not directly mention. They can be inferred from the corresponding passage of Matthew in which the messiah, just entered the temple, "heals" blind and crippled: a "wonder" for which scribes and chief priests are indignant.

The fact that Matthew calls "children" people who do the same things that in Luke the disciples do, clearly shows that in this passage Matthew uses the slang code, while Luke does not. The terms "children" (*in code*) and "disciples" (*out of code*) are always interchangeable and because of this interchangeability consciously used by the evangelists.

In Matthew, the slang code is almost always alive and working. It is up to him the primacy in having revealed to us, more clearly than the other synoptic authors, how it works. In this specific case, it is appropriate to conceal the evidence, disruptive by its implications, that Jesus in the temple of Jerusalem is surrounded by individuals who should not even enter that place (Mt 21:12):

> Jesus then entered the temple and drove out all those he found as they were buying and selling; he overthrew the tables of the money changers and the chairs of the sellers of doves.

An action that would seem to be violent and that, given the pressing vigilance of many well-armed Roman soldiers in the temple, could hardly be accomplished by a single person who did not have a large number of loyal supporters around him, accustomed to this type of raids. The disciples, numerous, shout words that identify and elevate their leader to king of Israel. This greatly concerns the Pharisees: because of the kind of proclamations and, above all, the kind of individuals who are making such proclamations. The ears of the guardians of the Law could not bear to hear hymns to the anointed of Yahweh on the lips of the transgressors of his Law.

However, in Luke we read (19:40):

> I tell you that, if these will be silent, the stones will cry.

The messiah had great interest in his supporters shouting those words in those precise, decisive moments. While Matthew, to the question of the scribes «do you not hear what they say?», prefers that Jesus answer in turn with a question (21:16):

> Have you never read "From the mouth of children and infants did you get a praise?"

Here the messiah would be saying that, if children and infants are daring him, it is because this was largely provided, centuries and centuries before, by Psalm 8 of David: a text being part of "the Law and the prophets" (that is, the Bible: even if, according to Jesus, the Law and the prophets prophesied *until John*). The psalmist praises Yahweh for reasons that would seem, however, to be outside the hymns sung for the enthronement of a king:

> O Lord, our Lord, how glorious is your name in all the earth. You have exalted your majesty above the heavens. *Out of the mouths of newborn babes and infants* you have brought forth praise as a bulwark against your foes, to silence the enemy and the avenger. When I look up at your heavens that have been formed by your fingers, the moon and the stars that you set in place, what is man that you are mindful of him, the son of man that you care for him?

Here the praise is attributed to Yahweh by a specific person, in an equally precise context. The Jesus of Matthew, instead, would be attributing it to himself. In a completely different context. The manner in which the evangelist, having used the noun "infants", sews a fragment of the Old Testament verse containing the same word, having forcefully removed it from a completely different context, is an operation that could be successfully conducted by any author. Any excerpt from any source, precisely because of its fragmentation, could be adapted with some success in a new context.

All this probably did not create any problem, neither for Matthew nor for the future recipients of the work. At the time when the evangelist was writing, it would hardly have been possible to ascertain what the Old Testament passage quoted was. Today, it is enough a single click to ascertain that Psalm 8 has no affinity with what is narrated by Matthew 21.

Keeping in mind the slang code he intends to use, he seeks a connection in the Old Testament. Possibly, with a passage where we talk about children, even infants. But in Psalm 8 we speak of real infants, and not of infants *in the code* we know. Matthew uses, as he pleases, a fragment from a textuality (moreover in another language) light years away, to sweeten an objective contradiction: the future king of Israel is not acclaimed by those "great" ones who observe and make observe the Law, but by the "small-little" ones, transgressors. With the approval («if these will be silent, the stones will cry») of Jesus himself. It will be easier for the stones to scream, than for a "great" one to support the aspiring king of Israel.

Speech on the text, speech of the text

From the point of view of the drafting of the synoptic Gospels, one cannot have absolute certainty about the genesis of the text, namely:
- we can't be sure that the authors did nothing other than transcribe, more or less faithfully from previous sources (in

languages other than Greek), a story whose architecture was already standing;

- we can't be sure that the parables and speeches, by which Jesus coined his language, were already present in the sources at their disposal, ready to be translated.

Therefore:

- did the messiah actually speak in parables and express himself in jargon aimed at veiling the contents of his action?
- or did he not speak at all in parables, but did the evangelists (or one of them, and the others have followed suit) coin the cryptic code, to reshape and veil the unusual harshness and ferocity of proclamations with a clear subversive matrix? Subversive not only towards the laws of the Roman rulers, but also towards that Mosaic Law which, if observed and transmitted in its 613 norms, taught submission since adolescence? And therefore necessarily prevented the birth of the seed of every rebellion, even violent if necessary, including that against the foreign ruler?
- finally: if the slang code is created by the evangelists, why in several passages (beginning with Matthew) do they provide all the elements to trace the meaning veiled by the code?

That said, we could formulate the following hypotheses (the first seems to us the most probable):

1. The sources and news available to the evangelists recount, in a very clear way and outside of any metaphor, events of subversive matrix, occurred in precise places in a given historical epoch, which had as protagonist a claimant to the throne of Israel who imposed himself, with his willpower and above all with his methods, on another leader (John): he too hateful to the Roman ruler but not entirely to the political-priestly class from which he came and was linked by lineage.
   Since these texts, imbued with messianism, it was necessary to be purged precisely by messianism, to make them usable

to a non-Jewish audience that needed to be educated about the foundations of a nascent religion, the evangelists coin the slang language to put under code the most compromising parts (or almost all).

In this perspective, the universally known "preacher" Jesus would not exist, as parables and discourses would be constructed by the authors to make the reader understand that the protagonist could be anything but a preacher: as he is exclusively engaged in procuring transgressors of the Law, even willing to die on the cross for his cause as an aspirant to the throne of Israel.

The relentless activity of intense recruitment in the villages, beaten palm to palm, needed tight times that could have given very little to parabolic narratives. The way to reach the kingdom had to be indicated very quickly, and not waiting for some ear to be able to hear. Recruitment based only on the understanding of the parables could not have allowed to have satisfactory results in numerical terms, and especially with the speed necessary to achieve the goals (then failed); nor would this be in line with the fundamental trait of Jesus' "preaching": violence. Which has little space to leave to the understanding or not of any parables.

2. The synoptic evangelists had sources, or had certain news of events that occurred at that time in Israel, of clear messianic matrix and involving two charismatic leaders, both ended dramatically (the second more than the first).

In particular, the authors were well documented on what the second, in chronological order, of these two leaders did. Since he was acting in a way drastically opposite to the former (which followed a well-established tradition, that of the "*Zaddik*-righteous" ones), his work could only stand out. His methods, not being in the wake of the Law, were kept hidden from most people through a message management system he governed. On the one hand, he relied on secret cooperation based on cryptic word-of-mouth, and on coercion (violence). The slang code that Jesus used is then used by the evangelists themselves, who well understand it and reuse it to achieve the twofold goal that was intended by the same protagonist of their writings: veiling the truth on the one hand, suggesting it on the other.

Whatever the hypothesis for which we are leaning more, certainly the inexhaustible activity of supernatural miracle worker of the messiah collides with what is the dramatic and tragic ending of history: why does a man, who worked miraculous healings, end up dying the most atrocious death awaiting the most ferocious criminals?

The question will never be answered if we attribute to the terms "blind", "crippled" and "lame" the meanings that fall within the semantic area relating to the sick. If, instead, we make operative on those terms the equation imposed by Jesus himself (sick = *sinners*), we can venture some hypothesis on the reason why an undisputed leader, who surrounded himself with transgressors, is finally handed over to the authorities by one of them, as in the most obvious of the scripts of these news events; and why he suffered the death to which, at the time, the foreign occupiers destined only those who were protagonists of sorties against the imperial power, followed by a large number of followers. They, if captured, met no better fate; that is what Peter desperately tries to avoid (Mt 26:69-74):

«You too were with Jesus, the Galilean». «I don't understand what you say» [...] Another servant saw him and said to those present: «He was with Jesus, the Nazarene». But he denied again, swearing, «I do not know that man» [...] «It is true, you too are one of them: in fact your accent betrays you». Then he began to curse and to swear: «I do not know that man».

Since the "good news" is nothing more than the transmission, to the greatest number of people in a sufficiently short time, of a restricted type of content, the sources to which the evangelists could have access had to speak of nothing but the massive recruitment of men (willingly or unwillingly, by good manners or by force), far and wide, from Galilee to Judea. Numerous followers. Like fish in a net.

So that this activity of "fishing" would not be too evident in its substance, the evangelists applied the slang code to news reports (fishing = proselytism), thus creating Jesus "the healer". However, he always heals preferably the same categories of sick: "blind", "crippled", "lame", "lepers". Exactly those for which John, inexplicably, is amazed or "scandalized".

The "thaumaturgy" in the literal sense drastically collides with the very statements of Jesus (Mk 8:11-12):

> Then the Pharisees came and began to argue with him, asking for a sign from heaven to test him. But he, taking a deep sigh, said: «Why does this generation ask for a sign? Verily I say unto you, *no sign shall be given to this generation*».

It is the programmatic declaration of the will *not to operate* prodigies: that nevertheless clashes against the worked wonders. It clashes with them if you understand them as extraordinary wonders and not as proselytism put in code. The messiah does not perform miracles (healings), but does equally great wonders (recruitment). One could cite a good number of passages from the Gospels, in which the profile of the generous healer does not at all match the face of the one who appears to be a violent and despotic character.

From the following verses, it is clear that the evangelists do nothing but make Jesus the protagonist of the parables he himself told:

Mk 11	Mt 21	Lk 13
Having seen a fig tree with leaves from afar, he came to see if he could find anything there, but when he got close to it, *he found nothing but leaves*. It was not the season of figs. He turned to the tree and said: «*No one ever eat your fruit again for ever*».	Seeing a fig on the road, *he approached but found nothing but leaves*, and said: «*Never again shall fruit be born from you*». And immediately *the fig dried up*. Seeing this, the disciples were amazed and said: «Why did the fig dry up immediately?»	***He also said this parable:*** «A man had a fig tree planted in the vineyard and *came to look for fruit there, but he did not find any*. Then he said to the winemaker: Behold, I have been coming for three years to look for fruit on this fig, but I cannot find any. *Cut it.*

The story of Mark and Matthew has always seemed bizarre, unlikely, in need of a symbolic reading not better specified. The superhuman goodness of the son of God, who praises creation and the lilies of the field dressed better than Solomon, cannot be questioned. However, he is given to curse and dry an innocent fig, that does not bear fruit because it is not the season of fruits.

It suffices a comparison between the synoptic authors to understand that Mark and Matthew do nothing but make Jesus the protagonist of the parable that he himself made: that parable of which Luke has left inexorable trace, according to the usual scheme relating to any passage of information, so it may happen that what some strive to conceal, someone else makes it clear (Lk 13, 6-9):

> *He also said this parable*: "A man had a fig tree planted in the vineyard and came to look for fruits, but he did not find any. Then he said to the winemaker: behold, I have been coming for three years to look for fruits on this fig, but I don't find any. *Cut it*».

Or "dry it out". Matthew and Mark have knowledge of the parabolic repertoire, and do not give up transforming this episode told by Jesus into a miraculous fact that involves him in the first person: yet another metaphorical declination of those followers who do not provide new followers; and are therefore to be considered useless servants. Servants to be cursed. Servants to be dried.

Jesus is going to Jerusalem, where he knows that no "fig tree" planted by him can take root. No proselyte of the kingdom can ever be earned in the capital of the scribes and Pharisees (Mt 23:37-38):

> Jerusalem, Jerusalem [...] how many times have I wanted to gather your children, like a hen gathers her chicks under her wings, and you did not want it.

"Blessed is he who comes in the name of the Lord", cried out the crowds of disciples that the messiah had brought from Galilee: the blind, the crippled, the lame, the lepers who were also found out of the bushes, willingly or unwillingly. And not the inhabitants of Jerusalem: a city that, according to Matthew 21, at the entrance of Jesus surrounded by his crowd was literally «upset, taken by upheaval, agitated, shaken» [ἐσείσθη]: but why should the entry into Jerusalem of a peaceful non-violent preacher even upset, agitate and shake the whole city?

Probably because the population feared precisely the occurrence of episodes such as the one the evangelist recounts in the following verses (Mt 21:10-12):

> «Who is this man?». And the crowd answered: «This is the prophet Jesus, from Nazareth of Galilee». Jesus entered the temple and drove out all those who in the temple sold and bought; he overturned the tables of the changers and the chairs of the sellers of doves.

It is a chronicle about which no veil has been placed. In the same way, the miraculous facts of which the authors make the messiah the protagonist, do not mean what the words transmit (healings), but what the words transmit *in the slang code* used by Jesus (enlisting of transgressors).

On this peculiar mode of operation of the synoptic authors, many other observations could be made; as well as many discourses on the

Gospel language; many considerations on infinite hermeneutic hypotheses, more or less literary fascinating.

But this is not the purpose of our analysis. Which wants to be a speech *on the text*, starting from the speech *of the text*. The goal is not to talk about the text endlessly, but to let the text speak and tell its truth. Not an absolute truth. Not a truth with a capital letter. Simply, the truth according to Matthew: in the kingdom of heaven will enter the transgressors of the Law and those who supported them. Everyone else will burn in Gehenna.

BASIC BIBLIOGRAPHY

Biblical texts, dictionaries and lexicons

AA. VV. 2008 *Vangelo e Atti degli apostoli. Nuova versione ufficiale della Conferenza Episcopale Italiana*, San Paolo Edizioni, Milan.

AA. VV. 2014 *Nuovo Testamento. Versione interlineare in italiano*, edited by M. Zappella, San Paolo Edizioni, Milan.

AA. VV. 2015 *La sacra Bibbia. Testo bilingue latino-italiano Nova Vulgata e Cei*, edited by F. Frezza, Libreria Editrice Vaticana, Rome.

Dufour, Xavier L. 1978 *Dizionario del Nuovo Testamento*, edited by A. Bonora, Brescia, Queriniana.

Georges, Karl E. - Calonghi, Ferruccio 1989 *Dizionario latino italiano*, Rosenberg & Sellier, Turin.

Nestle, Erwin - Aland, Kurt (edited by) 2015 *Novum Testamentum Graece et Latine*, German Bible Society, Stuttgart.

Rocci, Lorenzo 1990 *Vocabolario greco-italiano*, Dante Alighieri, Rome.

Thayer, Joseph 1995 *Thayer's Greek-English Lexicon of the New Testament*, Hendrickson Academic, North Shore.

Studies on Christianity and the Jewish context of reference

AA. VV. 2002 *Indagine su Gesù. Bilancio storico e prospettive fenomenologiche* (edited by N. Ciola, A. Pitta, G. Pulcinelli), Glossa, Milan.

AA.VV. 2010 *Il processo di Gesù*, edited by A. D'Orsi, Aragno, Turin.

Aguirre Rafael, Bernabé Carmen, Gil Carlos 2010 *Cosa sappiamo di Gesù di Nazaret? Il punto sulla ricerca attuale*, San Paolo, Cinisello Balsamo.

Barbaglio, Giuseppe 2003 *Gesù ebreo di Galilea. Indagine storica*, EDB, Bologna.

Bornkamm, Günther 1968 *Gesù di Nazaret*, Claudiana, Brescia.

Boyarin, Daniel 2004 *Border Lines. The Partition of Judaeo-Christianity*, University of Pennsylvania Press, Philadelphia.

Boyarin, Daniel 2012 *The Jewish Gospels. The Story of the Jewish Christ*, New Press, New York.

Brandon, Samuel 1967 *Jesus and the Zealots: a Study of the Political Factor in Primitive Christianity*, Charles Scribner's Sons, New York.

Bultmann, Rudolf 2003 *Gesù*, Queriniana, Brescia.

Calimani, Riccardo 2017 *Paolo. L'ebreo che fondò il cristianesimo*, Mondadori, Milan.

Crossan, John D. 1991 *The Historical Jesus. The Life of a Mediterranean, Jewish Peasant*, T&T Clark, Edinburgh.

Del Verme, Marcello 1977 *Comunione e condivisione dei beni. Chiesa primitiva e giudaismo esseno-qumranico a confronto*, Morcelliana, Brescia.

Den Heyer, Cees J. 2000 *La storicità di Gesù*, Claudiana, Brescia.

Destro, Adriana - Pesce, Mauro 2014 *Il racconto e la Scrittura. Introduzione alla lettura dei vangeli*, Carocci, Rome.

Dodd, Charles H. 2007 *Il fondatore del cristianesimo*, Elledici, Turin.

Donnini, David 2015 *Gesù messia di Israele. La mistificazione storica della passione*, Uno Editori, Orbassano.

Dunn, James 2006 *Gli albori del cristianesimo. Fede e Gesù storico* (vol. 1), Claudiana, Brescia.

Durante Mangoni Maria B., Garribba Dario, Vitelli Marco (edited by) 2015 *Gesù e la storia. Percorsi sulle origini del cristianesimo. Studi in onore di Giorgio Jossa*, Il Pozzo di Giacobbe, Trapani.

Eisenman, Robert 1998 *James the Brother of Jesus: The Key to Unlocking the Secrets of early Christianity and the Dead Sea Scrolls*, Penguin Publishing Group, US.

Fabris, Rinaldo 1983 *Gesù di Nazareth. Storia e interpretazione*, Cittadella, Assisi.

Fitzmyer, Joseph A. 1995 *Qumran. Le domande e le risposte essenziali sui Manoscrittti del Mar Morto*, Queriniana, Brescia.

Flavio, Giuseppe 1998 *Antichità giudaiche*, edited by L. Moraldi, Utet, Milan.

Flavio, Giuseppe 1992 *Guerra Giudaica*, edited by G. Vitucci, Mondadori, Milan.

Flusser, David 1997 *Jesus*, Morcelliana, Brescia.

Focant Camille, Schlosser Jacques, Marguerat Daniel, Sevrin Jean-Marie 1997 *Le Jésus de l'histoire*, Lumen Vitae, Bruxelles.

García Martínez, Florentino 1996 *Testi di Qumran*, Paideia, Brescia.

García Martínez, Florentino - Trebolle Barrera, Julio 1996 *Gli uomini di Qumran. Letteratura, struttura sociale e concezioni religiose*, edited by A. Catastini, Claudiana, Brescia.

García, Martínez - Tigchelaar, Eibert J. C 2000 *The Dead Sea Scrolls Study Edition,* Brill, LeidenBoston-Köln e Michigan/Cambridge, U.K.

Gianotto Claudio, Norelli Enrico, Pesce Mauro 2008 *L'enigma Gesù. Fonti e metodi della ricerca storica*, edited by E. Prinzivalli, Carocci, Rome.

Gibert, Pierre - Theobald, Christoph 2002 *Le cas Jésus Christ. Exégètes, historiens et théologiens en confrontation*, Bayard, Paris.

Hanson, Kenneth - Oakman, Douglas 2003 *La Palestina ai tempi di Gesù. La società, le sue istituzioni, i suoi conflitti*, San Paolo, Cinisello Balsamo.

Horsley, Richard A. 2006 *Galilea. Storia, politica, popolazione*, Paideia, Brescia.

Ibba, Giovanni 2014 *Il Vangelo di Marco e l'impuro*, Morcelliana, Brescia.

Joachim, Jeremias 1972 *Teologia del Nuovo Testamento. La predicazione di Gesù*, Paideia, Brescia.

Johnson, Luke T. 1996 *The Real Jesus. The Misguided Quest for the Historical Jesus and the Truth of the Traditional Gospels*, Harper-Collins, San Francisco.

Jossa, Giorgio 2001 *Gesù Messia? Un dilemma storico*, Carocci, Rome.

Jossa, Giorgio 2008 *Il cristianesimo ha tradito Gesù?*, Carocci, Rome.

Jossa, Giorgio 2014, *Tu sei il re dei Giudei? Storia di un profeta ebreo di nome Gesù*, Carocci, Rome.

Jossa, Giorgio 1998 *La verità dei vangeli. Gesù di Nazaret fra storia e fede*, Carocci, Rome.

Kähler, Martin 1964 *The so-called historical Jesus and the historic Biblical Christ*, Fortress Press, Philadelphia.

Käseman, Ernst 1985 *Il problema del Gesù storico (Saggi esegetici)*, Marietti, Casale Monferrato.

Kümmel, Werner G. 2010 *Il Nuovo Testamento: storia dell'indagine scientifica sul problema neotestamentario*, EDB, Bologna.

Lambiasi, Francesco 1978 *L'autenticità storica dei Vangeli*, EDB, Bologna.

Latourelle, René 1989 *A Gesù attraverso I Vangeli. Storia ed ermeneutica*, Cittadella, Assisi.

Malina, Bruce J. 1993 *Windows on the World of Jesus. Some Scenarios for Considerate Reading*, Westminster John Knox Press, Louisville.

Malina, Bruce J. - Neyrey, Jerome H. 1988 *Calling Jesus Names. The Social Value of Labels in Matthew*, Polebridge Press, Sonoma (Ca).

Manns, Frédéric 1994 *Il Giudaismo. Ambiente e memoria del Nuovo Testamento*, EDB, Bologna.

Manns, Frédéric 2013 *Il giudaismo e l'Israele di Dio. L'ambiente del Nuovo Testamento e le origini cristiane*, EDB, Bologna.

Marguerat Daniel, Norelli Enrico, Poffet Jean Michel 1998 *Jésus de Nazareth. Nouvelles approches d'une énigme*, Labor et Fides, Genève.

Meier, John P. 2001 *Un ebreo marginale. Ripensare il Gesù storico. Le radici del problema e della persona*, edited by F. Dalla Vecchia, Queriniana, Brescia.

Monti, Ludwig 2006 *Una comunità alla fine della storia. Messia e messianismo a Qumran*, Paideia, Brescia.

Moraldi, Luigi 1996 *I manoscritti di Qumran*, Utet, Turin.

Moxnes, Halvor 1988 *Social Conflict and Economic Relations in Luke's Gospel*, Fortress Press, Philadelphia.

Moxnes, Halvor 2003 *Putting Jesus in His Place. A Radical Vision of Household and Kingdom*, Westminster John Knox Press, Louisville.

Muscolino, Giuseppe 2015 Οὐκ ἔστ᾽ ἔτυμος λόγος οὗτος: *"Non è vero questo discorso". L'attacco storico-filologico di Porfirio alle Sacre Scritture*, «Mediaeval Sophia», 17.

Perrot, Charles 1981 *Gesù e la storia*, Borla, Rome.

Porfirio 2009 *Contro i cristiani. Nella raccolta di Adolf Von Harnack con tutti i nuovi frammenti in appendice*, edited by G. Muscolino, Bompiani, Milan.

Powell, Mark A. 1998 *Jesus as a Figure in History. How Modern Historians View the Man from Galilee*, Westminster J.K. Press, Louisville.

Robinson, James 1977 *Kerygma e Gesù storico*, Claudiana, Brescia.

Sanders, Ed P. 1992 *Gesù e il giudaismo*, edited by P. Stefani, Marietti, Casale Monferrato.

Schäfer, Peter 2012 *The Jewish Jesus. How Judaism and Christianity Shaped Each Other*, Princeton University Press, Princeton.

Schürer, Emil 1998 *Storia del popolo giudaico al tempo di Gesù Cristo (175 a. C.-135 d. C.)*, III, edited by C. Gianotto, Claudiana, Brescia.

Schweitzer, Albert 2019 *Storia della ricerca sulla vita di Gesù*, edited by F. Coppellotti, Claudiana, Brescia.

Schweitzer, Albert 1996 *Gesù la parabola di Dio. Il punto sulla vita di Gesù*, Queriniana, Brescia.

Segalla, Giuseppe 2010 *La ricerca sul Gesù storico*, Queriniana, Brescia.

Stegemann Wolfgang, Malina Bruce J., Theissen Gerd 2006 *Il nuovo Gesù storico*, Claudiana, Brescia.

Stegemann, Ekkehard W. - Stegemann, Wolfgang 2015, *Storia sociale del cristianesimo primitivo. Gli inizi nel giudaismo e le comunità cristiane nel mondo mediterraneo*, EDB, Bologna.

Stemberger, Günter 1991 *Il giudaismo classico: cultura e storia del tempo rabbinico (dal 70 al 1040)*, edited by D. e L. Cattani, Città Nuova, Rome.

Testaferri, Francesco 2011 *Gesù e il suo ambiente. Una rilettura del contesto storico, economico, politico, sociale e religioso in cui visse Gesù*, Cittadella, Assisi.

Theissen, Gerd 2007 *Gesù e il suo movimento. Storia sociale di una rivoluzione di valori dell'opera*, Claudiana, Brescia.

Theissen, Gerd - Merz, Annette 1999, *Il Gesù storico. Un manuale*, edited by F. Dalla Vecchia, Queriniana, Brescia.

Trocmé, Étienne 1975 *Gesù di Nazaret visto dai testimoni della sua vita*, Claudiana, Brescia.

Unterbrink, Daniel T. 2008 *Gesù e Gesù. Un ribelle ebreo, sfidò Roma, morì su una croce e la Chiesa lo trasformò in un Dio*, AlterEgo, Viterbo.

Unterbrink, Daniel T. 2010 *The Three Messiahs: The Historical Judas the Galilean, the Revelatory Christ Jesus, and the Mythical Jesus of Nazareth*, iUniverse.

Unterbrink, Daniel T. - Wilson, Barrie 2014 *Judas of Nazareth: How the Greatest Teacher of First-Century Israel Was Replaced by a Literary Creation*, Bear & Company, Rochester.

Vermès, Geza 1981 *Jesus the Jew. A Historian's Reading of the Gospels*, FortRess Press, Minneapolis.

Vermès, Geza 1981 *The Gospel of Jesus the Jew,* University of New Castle Upon Tyne.

Vermès, Geza 2002 *La religione di Gesù l'ebreo. Una grande sfida al cristianesimo*, edited by A. Lova, Cittadella, Assisi.

Weiss, Johannes 1993 *La predicazione di Gesù sul regno di Dio*, edited by F. Coppellotti, D'Auria, Naples.

Witherington III, Ben 1997 *The Jesus Quest. The third Search for the Jew of Nazareth*, InterVarsity Press, Downers Grove.

Studies on the "historical Jesus"

Akenson, Donald Harman, *Saint Saul: A Skeleton Key to the Historical Jesus*, New York, Oxford University Press, 2000

Allen, Charlotte, *The Human Christ: The Search for the Historical Jesus*, New York, Free Press, 1998

Allison, Dale C., *The Historical Jesus and the Theological Jesus,* Grand Rapids, Eerdmans, 2009

Allison, Dale C., *Jesus of Nazareth: Millenarian Prophet*, Minneapolis, Fortress, 1998

Anderson, Paul N., *The Fourth Gospel and the Quest for Jesus*, Modern Foundations Reconsidered, New York: T&T Clark, 2006

Anderson, Paul N., Felix Just, Tom Thatcher, eds. *Jesus, John, and History: Critical Appraisals of Critical Views*, Atlanta, Society of Biblical Literature, 2007

Aulen, Gustaf, *Jesus in Contemporary Historical Research*, Philadelphia: Fortress, 1976

Bermejo Rubio, Fernando *La invención de Jesús de Nazaret. Historia, ficción, historiografía*, Siglo XXI de España Editores, Madrid 2018

Blomberg, Craig, *The Historical Reliability of the Gospels*, Downers Grove, IL: InterVarsity Press, 1987

Bock, Darrell L, *Jesus According to Scripture: Restoring the Portrait from the Gospels*, Grand Rapids: Baker Academic, 2002

Bornkamm, Günther, *Jesus of Nazareth*, New York: Harper & Row, 1960

Carver, Stephen, *The UnGospel: The Life and Teaching of the Historical Jesus*. Eugene, OR: Wipf & Stock, 2004

Charlesworth, James H., *The Historical Jesus: An Essential Guide*, Nashville: Abingdon, 2008

Crossan, John Dominic, *The Historical Jesus: The Life of a Mediterranean Jewish Peasant*, San Francisco: HarperSanFrancisco, 1991

Dunn, James D. G., *Jesus Remembered: Christianity in the Making,* Grand Rapids: Eerdmans, 2003

Dunn, James D. G., *A New Perspective on Jesus: What the Quest for the Historical Jesus Missed*, Grand Rapids: Baker Academic, 2005

Ehrman, Bart D., *Jesus: Apocalyptic Prophet of the New Millennium*, Oxford: Oxford University Press, 2001

Ehrman, Bart D., *The Text of the New Testament in Contemporary Research: Essays on the Status Quaestionis*, Wm. B. Eerdmans Publishing Company, 1995.

Ehrman, Bart D., *The New Testament: A Historical Introduction to the Early Christian Writings*, Oxford University Press, US, 1997

Ehrman, Bart D., *A Brief Introduction to the New Testament*, Oxford University Press, US, 2004

Metzger, Bruce M. - Ehrman, Bart D., *The Text of the New Testament: Its Transmission, Corruption, and Restoration*, Oxford University Press, 2005

Ehrman, Bart D., *Misquoting Jesus: The Story Behind Who Changed the Bible and Why*, HarperSanFrancisco, 2005

Ehrman, Bart D., *Studies in the Textual Criticism of the New Testament*, Brill Publishers, US, 2006

Ehrman, Bart D., *Jesus, Interrupted: Revealing the Hidden Contradictions in the Bible (And Why We Don't Know About Them)*, HarperCollins, US, 2009

Ehrman, Bart D., *Did Jesus Exist? The Historical Argument for Jesus of Nazareth*, HarperCollins, US, 2012

Ehrman, Bart D., *The Other Gospels: Accounts of Jesus from Outside the New Testament*, Oxford University Press, US, 2013

Ehrman, Bart D., *How Jesus Became God: The Exaltation of a Jewish Preacher from Galilee*, HarperOne, US, 2014

Ehrman, Bart D., *Jesus Before the Gospels: How the Earliest Christians Remembered, Changed, and Invented Their Stories of the Savior*, HarperOne, US, 2016

Ehrman, Bart D., *The Triumph of Christianity: How a Forbidden Religion Swept the World*, Simon & Schuster, US, 2018

Evans, Craig A., - Paul Copan, eds., *Who Was Jesus? A Jewish-Christian Dialogue*, Louisville: Westminster John Knox, 2001

Hoffman, Matthew, *From Rebel to Rabbi: Reclaiming Jesus and the Making of Modern Jewish Culture*, Stanford, CA: Stanford University Press, 2007

Loader, William, *Jesus's Attitude towards the Law: A Study of the Gospels*, Grand Rapids: Eerdmans, 2002

Meier, John P., *A Marginal Jew: Rethinking the Historical Jesus*, 4 vols. ABRL, New York: Doubleday, 1991–2009

Oakman, Douglas E., *Jesus and the Peasants*, Eugene, OR: Cascade, 2008

Sanders, E. P., *The Historical Figure of Jesus*, New York: Viking, 1994

Schweitzer, Albert, *The Quest of the Historical Jesus: A Critical Study of the Progress from Reimarus to Wrede*, Translated by W. B. D. Montgomery, 1906. Reprint, New York: Macmillan, 1968

Theissen, Gerd - Mertz, Annette *The Historical Jesus: A Comprehensive Guide*, translated by John Bowden, Minneapolis: Fortress, 1998.

Vermes, Geza, *The Changing Faces of Jesus*, New York: Penguin, 2002

Studies on literary communication, semantics and semiotics

Barthes, Roland 1968 *L'analisi del racconto*, Bompiani, Milan.

Barthes, Roland 1991 *L'avventura semiologica*, Einaudi, Turin.

Barthes, Roland 1998 *Scritti. Società, testo, comunicazione*, edited by G. Marrone, Einaudi, Turin.

Bertrand, Denis 2002 *Basi per la semiotica letteraria*, Meltemi, Rome.

Corti, Maria 1976 *Principi della comunicazione letteraria*, Bompiani, Milan.

Corti, Maria 1978 *Il viaggio testuale. Le ideologie e le strutture semiotiche*, Einaudi, Turin.

Eco, Umberto 1975 *Trattato di semiotica generale*, Bompiani, Milan.

Eco, Umberto 1995 *Sulla traduzione*, in AA. VV., *Teorie contemporanee della traduzione*, edited by S. Nergaard, Bompiani, Milan.

Fabbri, Paolo - Marrone, Gianfranco 2000 *Semiotica in nuce. I. I fondamenti e l'epistemologia strutturale*, Meltemi, Sesto San Giovanni.

Fabbri, Paolo - Marrone, Gianfranco 2001 *Semiotica in nuce. II: Teoria del discorso*, Meltemi, Sesto San Giovanni.

Genette, Gerard 1972 *Figure II. La parola letteraria*, Einaudi, Turin.

Geninasca, Jacques 2002 *La parola letteraria*, Bompiani, Milan.

Greimas, Algirdas J. 2000 *Semantica strutturale*, Meltemi, Rome.

Greimas, Algirdas J. 1985 *Del senso 2*, edited by P. Magli e M. P. Pozzato, Bompiani, Milan.

Greimas, Algirdas J. - Courtes, Joseph 1986 *Semiotica. Dizionario ragionato della teoria del linguaggio*, edited by P. Fabbri, La casa Usher, Florence.

Halliday, Mica A.K. 1983 *Il linguaggio come semiotica sociale. Un'interpretazione sociale del linguaggio e del significato*, Zanichelli, Bologna.

Jakobson, Roman 1960 *Linguistics and Poetics*, in T. Sebeok, ed., *Style in Language*, Cambridge, MA: M.I.T. Press, pp. 350-377.

Jakobson, Roman 1966 *Saggi di linguistica generale*, Feltrinelli, Milan.

Lotman, Jurij 1980 *Testo e contesto. Semiotica dell'arte e della cultura*, edited by S. Salvestroni, Laterza, Bari.

Lotman, Jurij 1995 *Il problema del testo*, in A.A.V.V., *Teorie contemporanee della traduzione*, edited by S. Nergaard, Bompiani, Milan.

Meschonic, Henri 2000 *Il traduttore e l'odio della poetica*, edited by N. Mataldi e M. Sopranzetti, "Testo a fronte", n. 23.

Miceli, Silvana 1982 *In nome del segno. Introduzione alla semiotica della cultura*, Sellerio, Palermo.

Pagnini, Marcello 1967 *Struttura letteraria e metodo critico*, D'Anna, Messina-Florence.

Pagnini, Marcello 1988 *Semiosi. Teoria ed ermeneutica del testo letterario*, Il Mulino, Bologna.

Panosetti, Daniela 2015 *Semiotica del testo letterario. Teoria e analisi*, Carocci, Rome.

Pezzini, Isabella 2005 *Lezioni di semiotica*, Meltemi, Rome.

Pozzato, Maria Pia 2001 *Semiotica del testo*, Carocci, Rome.

Propp, Vladimir 1966 *Morfologia della fiaba*, Einaudi, Turin.

Pugliatti, Paola 1985 *Lo sguardo nel racconto*, Zanichelli, Turin.

Ricoeur, Paul - Greimas, Algirdas J. 2000 *Tra semiotica ed ermeneutica*, edited by F. Marsciani, Meltemi, Rome.

Segre, Cesare 1985 *Avviamento all'analisi del testo letterario*, Einaudi, Turin.

THANKSGIVING

No finished work can be without thanks. The author is not the only author. There is always something or someone, outside the work and the author, who acts as a muse. A word is enough. A verse. A meeting of gazes. The doubt, the questions that follow.

So I sincerely thank (but no word can ever be enough) the friend to whom the book is dedicated, Claudio Carente (fraternal friend now), who several years ago brought to my attention a word. A verse. I thank the meeting with his intelligent gaze that followed. Then the doubt. The question that generated all the other questions. With years of work, they found their answers in the text. I thank him for always being present, for wanting to open eyes and have ears, for the courage to have listened to the Greek translations of the Gospels and almost every paragraph of this book before it was written and during its writing. Without that eye contact, these pages would probably never have seen the light.

Thanks to the fraternal friend Gian Mario Salis, who had the patience (and courage) to be informed by the author of all the ongoing research, and to want to discuss passionately, always honoring the free thought.

Thanks to Alessandro Marongiu, who has read the text several times with meticulous precision, never missing his valuable critical advice, even at the level of content.

The greatest gratitude, for the volume as such, goes to the Publisher who wanted to have the courage to publish a book not easy; to all the editorial staff, who will have worked hard on not simple content. In their case, besides professionalism, they needed a surplus of courage in reading: if they have finished the reading, it means that the courage has not been missed.

In written works like this, thanks cannot be many. In the work you proceed, to 90 percent, alone. So finally I thank the author: for not throwing away the study of the Greek language and an interest (the canonical Gospels) cultivated since 1994; for having learned and not forgotten how to translate; for doubting unreliable translations; for biting the tail of the dragon (that is, the Greek text). In short, for not having closed eyes and having had ears.

INDEX